Acknowledgements

This publication would have been impossible without the generosity of the Merseyside and Wirral Former Boxers' Association, who have had the foresight to preserve a diverse range of boxing memorabilia including photographs, programmes and tickets. Also, the extensive *Liverpool Echo* archive has been vital to making this book a visual success. Thanks also go to Stephen Done of the Liverpool FC Museum for the photographs of Cyril Done in the Anfield section of the book.

The unstinting behind the scenes work of various *Liverpool Echo* staff has been vital to the success of the book. The author would specifically like to thank Brian Johnston and Les Rawlinson from the *Echo* library who met every request for material with enthusiasm. The layout and design work of Barry Parker, along with Jamie Dunmore has greatly enhanced the written and visual material. It was Barry's idea to give the book a 'scrapbook' feel, and it works brilliantly in my view. The seemingly more mundane tasks of proof reading are essential to any such book and thanks go to Michael Haydock for his diligent work.

Not forgetting the administrative staff including Amelia MacDonald, who ensured that all necessary paperwork and meetings associated with the book were done efficiently and with the minimum of fuss. Making contact with large organisations can often be difficult but the man on the frontline desk Ray Thorburn always got me to the right person and the right place without too much distress. His courteous manner and concern is most appreciated.

The idea for this book came from a discussion I had with Ken Rogers about doing a book about boxing at Anfield. It was his idea to expand this into a wider look at Liverpool boxing venues. He is not responsible, however, for any inaccuracies that may occur in the text! Ken's colleague Paul Dove also deserves credit for the way he facilitated the production of the book, for consulting with me at each stage about how the book would look in its final form.

I would also like to pay a heartfelt thanks to James Cleary who has in effect pulled things together. He organised the team that has done such a brilliant job on the proofing and the layout. At each stage he ensured I was kept informed and that I was happy at the progress of the book. He has played a first class editorial role. His passion for boxing is clearly evident, a passion that has been matched by all the staff I have worked with at the paper.

A special thank you also needs to be made to John Conteh, who has kindly written the foreword to the book. In my view John is not only one of the greatest British boxers, but one of our finest sportsmen.

Lastly, clichéd though it may sound, I would like to thank all the boxers that have enriched the sport on Merseyside. Only a fraction of their story has been told here but they are the sportsmen who have climbed into the ring and thrilled Liverpool fight fans for over 200 years. I only hope their courage and commitment has been adequately reflected in these pages.

Ray Physick, September 2008

About the author

Unsurprisingly, being born in Norris Green and raised in Kirkby Ray Physick, like so many people from Liverpool, has been mad about sport since childhood. Ray is a passionate Liverpool supporter and saw his first match at Anfield against Leyton Orient when Liverpool were in the old Second Division. In addition to football Ray is a keen cricket fan and remembers being awoken by his father in the early hours of the morning to watch Muhammad Ali win the world heavyweight title.

In more recent times he has written widely about various sports and has had articles published in the Encyclopaedias of British Sport and British Football. Articles, co-written with his friend and colleague Dick, about professional golfers and sport on Tyneside were published in 'Contemporary British History' in 2000 and in 'Newcastle: A Modern History' in 2001 respectively.

In 2007 Ray wrote 'Played in Liverpool', which is part of the 'Played in Britain' series, a book that chronicled Liverpool's sporting heritage. Working in a freelance capacity with the Merseyside and Wirral Former Boxers' Associations, Ray helped to record the lives of 60 former Mersey boxers and is assisting the associations in their aim to establish a Mersey Boxing Hall of Fame.

Ray also hopes that this book, and a forthcoming exhibition in the new Museum of Liverpool in 2010, will make people aware of the cultural significance of sport in general and boxing in particular. With the exception of the museum located at Liverpool Football Club there is no sports museum with open public access on Merseyside. Considering what Liverpool has contributed to sport this is an area that needs to be addressed; failure to do so will result in undervaluing a significant part of our cultural heritage. Ray also lectures at John Moores University on sport for the American Studies degree and is always ready to talk to sports clubs and other institutions about the historical significance of Liverpool sport.

Recently, Ray was awarded a research post at the University of Central Lancashire, in conjunction with the National Football Museum at Preston, to undertake a three-year study into the 'Representation of Football Art'. The university established the International Football Institute in 2003 to enhance research into the role and impact of football in society. Ray's research will create a body of work that should help to extend this understanding.

Produced by Sport Media, Trinity Mirror North West.

Executive Editor: Ken Rogers. Editor: Steve Hanrahan.
Production Editor: Paul Dove. Art Editor: Rick Cooke.
Sub Editors: Roy Gilfoyle, James Cleary, Michael Haydock.
Designers: Colin Sumpter, Barry Parker, Lee Ashun, Glen Hind,
Alison Gilliland, Jamie Dunmore, James Kenyon, Lisa Critchley, Charles Hearnshaw.
Writers: Chris McLoughlin, David Randles,
Gavin Kirk, John Hynes, Simon Hughes.
Sales and Marketing Manager: Elizabeth Morgan.

Published in Great Britain in 2008 by: Trinity Mirror Sport Media,
PO Box 48, Old Hall Street, Liverpool L69 3EB.

ISBN: 978-1-905266-71-5

Photographs: Trinity Mirror, Ray Physick.
Front cover image of Peter Kane.

Printed by Scotprint.

PRESENT

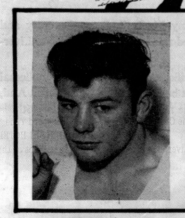

Chic Calderwood

Stan Cullis

Harry Scott

Jimmy McCrail

TUESDAY, 24th OCTOBER, 1961
LIVERPOOL STADIUM

Programme 1/-

Contents

Liverpool and Boxing
– A Perfect Match

Liverpool and boxing somehow go together. In a city that has endured its fair share of deprivation, a place where life has been a daily struggle, sport has often provided a way out of the daily grind of life. In local communities where space was limited and leisure facilities almost non-existent, local people got together to establish amateur boxing clubs in places such as church and community halls. It was these clubs with their basic facilities that provided the place for young boys to get away from the street to find warmth, companionship and a place where they could hone what for many were natural boxing skills.

The boxing clubs were places for the committed, run by men who were dedicated and determined to give young boys a good start in life. They instilled discipline and a sense of loyalty in young men many of whom came from backgrounds that were often hard and sometimes cruel. Moreover, many of these boys developed into young men capable of becoming stalwarts in their community.

If boxing clubs had just made this contribution to local communities they would have justified their existence but the fact that clubs developed boxers capable of boxing for world and British titles makes them places for serious study for social and sport historians.

Over the years Liverpool has developed some great boxers. In the first decade of the 20th century Ike Bradley thrilled Liverpool fight fans with his boxing skills. Ike went on to fight for the world title at Pudsey Street, only losing on points to Digger Stanley. Like so many boxers Ike did not leave the sport when he retired. He gave his time in a voluntary capacity to train other young boxers in the fine art of the sport. Up to the time of his death in 1951 he was a corner man at the Liverpool Stadium. Yet a glance at Ike's childhood will show a boy who sold newspapers on the streets of Liverpool, whose background was tough to say the least. When Ike found his way to Harry Thorne's gymnasium he very quickly demonstrated that he had the skill to become a boxer.

Bradley's tale is not untypical. No two life stories are the same but boxers such as Dom Volante, Nel Tarleton, Ernie Roderick and Peter Kane, in the inter-war years; and Pat McAteer, Johnny Cooke and John Conteh in the post-war period demonstrate that boxers are overwhelmingly from working-class backgrounds.

However, boxing is not just about boxers. A crucial player in the sport is the boxing promoter. The promoter is in effect the matchmaker, the person who tries to ensure a good contest takes place between two well-matched fighters. Among the finest of promoters was Liverpool's Johnny Best. Best was perhaps unique among promoters in that he had the total trust of his boxers many of whom boxed for him without a contract.

However, Best was more than a promoter. He was an entrepreneur who realised that the fight fan wanted to watch boxing in an arena that generated great atmosphere, an atmosphere that would engender good boxing contests. Boxing, like other sports, has its good times and bad times and when Best took over Pudsey Street in 1928 boxing in Liverpool was at a low ebb. However, through careful matchmaking he enticed the fans back to Liverpool's first stadium. That he achieved this during a time of economic crisis is remarkable in itself, but his greatest achievement was his foresight to have a new

THROUGH THE AGES: A Breck Park bill from 1932 (top) and Dick Duffy v Gordon McAteer at the Stadium, 1967

'The overarching aim of this book is to celebrate a sport Merseyside has excelled at'

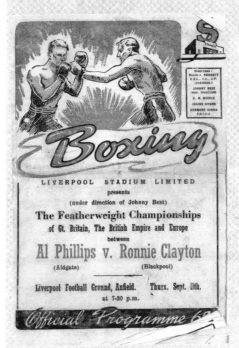

Liverpool Stadium built in 1932 following the demolition of Pudsey Street a year earlier.

In the period between the closure of Pudsey Street and the opening of the Stadium, Best established boxing at Anfield. The move to Anfield was inspired as the first show there in 1931 saw a Liverpool boxer win a Lonsdale Belt for the first time. Boxing at Anfield is significant. It was not the first open-air venue to host boxing, but it was the first British venue that brought mass crowds to boxing over a prolonged period of time.

The overarching aim of this book is to celebrate a sport that Merseyside has excelled at for over 100 years. The chosen method was to look at the venues that held boxing shows over this period. The boxing hall is a place where the intimacy of the boxing fan merges with the boxer. There is no greater interaction in sport. The fight fan is at one with the boxer while boxers feed off the atmosphere generated in the boxing stadium. The many boxers I have interviewed over the years bear testimony to the great atmosphere of the Liverpool Stadium. Indeed, all who boxed there regret its passing, and wonder if there will ever be a boxing arena of its like ever again.

Arenas certainly create their own atmospheres, but what is also clear is that they can only create an atmosphere if there is the talent out there to generate a sporting spectacle. Over the last 20 years, since the demolition of the Stadium, Merseyside has produced great boxing champions – Paul Hodkinson, Andy Holligan and Shea Neary are just three examples. However, on too many occasions they have had to box outside of the city, as there has not been a venue capable of accommodating big crowds. The Echo Arena is an opportunity to bring back big time boxing to the city. Given the right promotions it is a venue capable of bringing large crowds back to watch the sport. Who knows, it might even develop an atmosphere comparable to that of the great Liverpool boxing venues described in this book.

COVER SHOTS: Programme from Liverpool Stadium, 1947 (left); Liverpool's Johnny Cooke at the Free Trade Hall, Manchester, 1963 (right)

OLD AND NEW: Boxing show at The Grafton Rooms, 1970 (above); former world featherweight champion Derry Mathews (right) – a possible Echo Arena competitor in the future?

Foreword
by John Conteh

Liverpool is a great sporting city. Football of course dominates our passions – whether you are a Red or a Blue is of great importance. However, in the midst of this it is often forgotten that the second sport for many working-class Liverpudlians is boxing. Indeed, football and boxing fans are often the same people. This is why I welcome this book that explores the major boxing venues of Liverpool. It demonstrates the passions that boxing generates among boxers and boxing fans alike, and shows why the sport has penetrated into the pores of the city. When great contests have taken place in the city, the expectation and excitement generated among the public is as great as any high-profile football match. I personally experienced this both as an amateur and a professional boxer at the finest of all British boxing halls, the Liverpool Stadium.

My boxing career began in the modest surroundings of Kirkby Amateur Boxing Club at the age of 11. Our modest surroundings, however, belied a commitment on behalf of our trainers Charlie Atkinson and Tucker Hetherington. Their patience, commitment and, above all, skill resulted in Kirkby ABC becoming one of the finest boxing clubs in the land. I was one fortunate beneficiary of Kirkby ABC, but Kirkby should also be remembered for other great boxers – most notably Joey Singleton and Paul Hodkinson.

Like Joey and Paul I grew up in Kirkby – a planner's dream but in reality a place that offered little in way of top-class sports facilities for young people. One could argue that such a situation has always been the case for working-class youths growing up in Liverpool, and this is very true. To me, however, this underlines the greatness of Liverpool boxing. People who have struggled in the midst of acute social deprivation have often found a way out, and sport has often been a chosen field.

But let us not kid ourselves. Boxing is not an easy route out of the 'ghetto'. It requires dedication, determination and years of hard work – not only for young and up-and-coming boxers, but also for the unsung trainers as well. Naturally, the media follow success – champions in any sport bring an audience for them – but for every appearance on TV or at a venue such as the Stadium there are 20 or more shows at small, often draughty halls just a few miles from your home.

My career had many highlights both as an amateur and a professional. As an amateur I appeared at the Stadium on many occasions – what a venue it was. The size of the ring suited my style: it enabled me to express the skills I had learnt at my boxing club. Boxing rings do not make an arena, however. A boxing arena is both a product of its design and of the type of boxing fan that goes there on a regular basis. Yes, it is the contest that is the most important aspect of any boxing show, but an audience can inspire a boxer and help him to lift his performance. I have to say that in my time I found the crowd at the

EARLY DEFENCE: An early shot of John Conteh in fighting pose

'...an audience can inspire a boxer and help him to lift his performance. I have to say that in my time I found the crowd at the Liverpool Stadium the most exciting and uplifting crowd in the country'

Liverpool Stadium the most exciting and uplifting crowd in the country.

At the time of writing, David Price has won the bronze medal at the Beijing Games, a fantastic achievement for any boxer – I still treasure the gold medal I won at the Commonwealth Games in 1970. David's success demonstrates that boxing in the Liverpool city region is resurgent; he reflects a very healthy amateur scene in Liverpool. We have been here before, and each time our talented amateurs have gone on to win British and world titles at professional level. Currently, we have the likes of Derry Matthews, Stephen and Paul Smith, who are all capable of bringing titles home to the city. Derry, of course, has already brought us the world featherweight title.

However, for a long time we have not really had an arena big enough to host the really big title fights. The Olympia, St George's Hall, Everton Park Sports Centre and Kirkby Sports Centre have all hosted British and world title fights. We also had the one-off night in Stanley Park when Shea Neary won the world title in front of 5,000 fight fans. But as boxing is booming once more, the top promoters are looking for large venues that can accommodate the demand for tickets. At last we have a Liverpool venue, the Echo Arena, that is capable of hosting the most prestigious title fights. We have the boxers; the question is: do we have a promoter with Johnny Best's vision to bring British and world championship boxing back to the city on a regular basis?

There is nothing like your home crowd. Retaining the world title against Len Hutchins in 1977 at the Stadium is undoubtedly the highlight of my career. The excitement and the atmosphere of that night is still with me. I only hope that our present generation of boxers have a similar experience in front of a passionate Liverpool crowd. Meanwhile, you can re-live some of Liverpool's finest boxing nights that are featured throughout the book.

OLYMPIC HERO: 2008 bronze medallist David Price is welcomed home from Beijing by daughter Katie

ARENA VISIT: John making an appearance at the Echo Arena, 2008

★

INTRODUCTION

★

Where It All Began – and the City's Influence on Modern-Day Boxing

The beginnings of modern boxing can be traced to 18th century London, when Jack Broughton, following the opening of his amphitheatre, drew up the London Prize Ring Rules in 1743; hitherto there were no written rules laid down to govern bare-knuckle boxing. Broughton's Rules prohibited both hitting an opponent whilst down on the floor and grasping an opponent around the waist. A floored boxer had 30 seconds to come up to the 'scratch' – the marker in the middle of the ring. Broughton also introduced padded gloves, called 'mufflers', but these were only to be used in training or sparring sessions – the sport was otherwise unregulated. There were no defined rounds: a round only ended with a knock-down. Moreover, time lapses between rounds were not determined. Broughton reigned as champion of England from 1734 until 1750, when he was defeated by Jack Slack at his amphitheatre. This contest resulted in the influential Duke of Cumberland losing his £10,000 bet on Broughton to retain his championship. Cumberland accused Broughton of a fix, a situation that resulted in Broughton's amphitheatre being closed

down. From this point onwards, bare-knuckle boxing became increasingly illegal in London, a situation soon copied by authorities throughout Britain, thereby extending the de facto ban to the rest of the country. Henceforth, pugilism increasingly became an underground sport, albeit one with a big following and could only be held at secret locations, often on county boundaries to enable prize-fight contests to be moved from one county to the next should the organisers be troubled by the law. This situation was reinforced in December 1824 following a court ruling over the Jem Burns v Ned Neale contest, organised by the Pugilistic Club, that declared boxing with bare knuckles was outside the law.

Technically, though illegal, boxing without gloves was impossible to suppress. Moreover, as urban centres expanded in the 19th century a growing audience for all sports became increasingly evident. Expanding crowds watching regular sporting events provided the base for dedicated sports venues such as football grounds and boxing arenas. But before these were established, sports ▶

BOXNG GRANDFATHER: Jack Broughton, printed in the *Liverpool Sporting Register*, 7 October 1826

'Broughton's Rules prohibited both hitting an opponent whilst on the floor and grasping an opponent around the waist. A floored boxer had 30 seconds to come up to the "scratch" – the marker in the middle of the ring'

FIGHT SCENE: The *Liverpool Sporting Register* carried detailed reports of many bare-knuckle fights that took place around Merseyside. Many of the articles were illustrated by the boxing ring as shown above; below, reports of the Liverpool Fancy

LIFE IN LONDON.

No. 15.   Saturday, March 5, 1825.   Price Two-pence.
In the Country, Two-pence Halfpenny.

LIVERPOOL FANCY.

GREAT FIGHT,
BETWEEN KNOWLES AND KNOWLAN,
IN CHESHIRE,
For Six Pounds a-side, March 1, 1825.

This fight, which has excited great interest in the

time, till at length Knowlan made an attempt to strike but drew up again ; in a second or two he made the first blow, and hit the butcher on the side of the head ; a close, and both fell, Knowlan under.

2. Knowlan came to the scratch laughing, his clear skin now exhibiting a reddish hue. After sparring some time, Knowles hit his opponent a heavy blow on the neck, and in a close, they both fell.

3. The ground had now become so slippery, that the men could scarcely keep on their legs, and was much in the same state as the ring at Stony-Stratford, when

FIRST: Jem Mace with the first black man to win a British title, Andrew Jeptha

'*The Liverpool Sporting Register*, 14 May 1825, tell us that a fight between John Jones and Pat Toney, following intervention by the beakies, had to be moved...the contest lasted three hours and 25 minutes'

took place on makeshift ground. Like many other cities in Britain, Liverpool has a fine tradition of producing top-quality boxers, a tradition that pre-dates the Queensberry Rules. Indeed, on Merseyside pugilism under Broughton's Rules was an extremely popular sporting attraction. During holiday periods, Liverpool's well-to-do classes would take flight to the Wallasey Pool, where fights took place on the sandbanks that form today's East and West Floats. *The Liverpool Sporting Register*, 14 May 1825, tell us that a fight between John Jones and Pat Toney, following intervention by the beakies (see page 19), had to be moved from Woodside to Wallasey Pool. Despite being further troubled by the law, the contest progressed and lasted three hours and 25 minutes. The report reveals that there was a festival atmosphere for the day: crowds came in their thousands from Liverpool and the 'river was thronged with boats to a late hour', with the local public houses doing great business.

Other places for watching milling bouts for the Liverpool elite included Welch Leys near Chester. An account of one such fight at Welch Leys, as recorded in *The Liverpool Sporting Register* of 15 October 1825 between Ralph Boscow and Pat M'Gee, lasted an incredible 35 rounds. The paper reports that on Monday evening 'great numbers of people left Liverpool for Chester and other places adjacent to the field of action' to be

ready for the fight, which was to be held the following day. On the day of the fight, there 'was a dense multitude in the road as far as the eye could reach, intermixed with stage coaches...gigs, cars and other vehicles, with a great number of horsemen'.

Preparations for the fight arena were clearly meticulous: the ring was described as being formed on a 'beautiful green-sward', while the outer ring was larger than usual because of the great crowds.

The following week, the paper produced a 16-verse poem about the Boscow-M'Gee fight (see page 29). Described as the 'Fight in Doggerel Verse', it began with the lines:

'It was in Liverpool's sea-port town,
Where lots o' fancy dwell'

The verse tells us that 5,000 attended the mill and that many a pound was bet on the ground. The great British traditions of the sport and associated gambling were quite clearly evident at this event.

We also learn from the verse that the fight was illegal because in 'Hawarden town the beakies met' to stop the fight, but they were out-manoeuvred by the fight organisers. The fight produced great excitement with shouts from the crowd being heard as far away as Chester. The purse was for £100 a side, with

Boscow emerging as the winner.

In addition to these festivals of pugilism, boxing also took place in Liverpool where there were several popular milling cribs. These included Houghton's Assembly Room, where crowds in excess of 300 were quite common; the Globe Tavern in Thomas Street; the Golden Lion in Dale Street; and Sewell's large room. Entry to the milling cribs was usually two shillings, indicating that they were the preserve of the middle class. The York Hotel in Williamson Square held a fight for 100 sovereigns a side in 1826 between 'well known pupils of the London ring'. Presumably, boxing in the milling cribs was undertaken with gloves, as it was tolerated by the Liverpool authorities.

These milling cribs continued well into the century, but by the mid-1800s many had left the salubrious places established by the merchant classes, finding homes in bars that surrounded the Liverpool docks. Much of our knowledge of these cribs, or coves, comes from the 19th-century journalist Hugh Shimmin, who recorded many elements of Liverpool's low life. Unlike the milling cribs of the middle-classes, the public houses that hosted these pugilistic contests were 'noted for all the sports of the fancy – fighting, running, ratting, dog racing, badger baiting', all of which were illegal because betting took place. Entrance to these cribs was one ▶

The last bare-knuckle champ

TROPHY LIFE: Picture of Jem Mace from *Cheshire Life*, February 2003

Jem Mace was the last bare-knuckle boxing champion of the world. His Merseyside grave has finally been recognised with a permanent memorial
Tribute: David Charters

▶ shilling for front seats and sixpence for seats at the back. Shimmin reveals a telling quote from the landlord of one such crib, who told him that 'the poor coves (the fighters) were out of feather' and 'nearly on the stones', indicating that these boxers were from destitute backgrounds. Boxing at the cribs was unregulated, but this did not mean that it did not have wide support within the town. Indeed, all sports at such bars were popular, and the bars usually displayed portraits of celebrated pugilists, champion dogs and other associated sports images around the walls.

However, boxing was beginning to move out of the milling cribs into private clubs, a movement accelerated in 1867 with the adoption of the Queensberry Rules. The rules, which had been written two years earlier by John Graham Chambers, replaced the revised London Prize Ring Rules of 1853. The Queensberry Rules introduced three-minute rounds and stipulated that a one-minute break should be taken between them; wrestling and hugging were outlawed, and a fallen boxer had 10 seconds to get up on his feet unassisted. Significantly, all contests were to be conducted with fair-sized gloves that were new and of good quality. At the milling cribs described by Shimmin, the gloves that were provided by landlords were well-worn and filthy. Likewise, the boxers had inadequate shoes and sometimes boxed in their bare feet. While such places did not disappear overnight, the Queensberry Rules do mark a significant departure in that they began the process whereby the boxer would box under rules that offered him a degree of protection.

Liverpool's association with the Queensberry Rules have largely gone unnoticed, but Jem Mace, the last British champion of the world under London Prize Ring Rules, had long put into practice key elements of the Queensberry Rules. During his role as a boxing instructor, at both the Liverpool Olympics in the early 1860s and the Liverpool Gymnasium, Mace had insisted

upon the use of gloves. Moreover, during his sparring exhibitions at his own boxing booth and circus, Mace introduced three-minute rounds and also implemented the 10-second knock-down rule. Mace, of course, has a long association with Liverpool and is buried in Anfield Cemetery.

Clearly, bare-knuckle boxing did not disappear following the introduction of the Queensberry Rules but as society became more urbanised, the desire to have more rational forms of sport grew. Prize-fighting, however, still took place as reports in the Liverpool press in the 1870s and 1880s indicate. One such contest at Aintree Racecourse in 1875 ended in tragedy. At 4.30am on 1 August, 300-400 men gathered at the canal locks near Love Lane to watch a bare-knuckle fight for £5 a side between two dockers, Simon Looney and John Mahoney. The police, receiving prior warning, moved the crowd on. After several more attempts at staging the event at various locations between Vauxhall and Aintree, the fight finally got under way at 4.30pm at the racecourse. The police were too few in number to stop the men fighting, and had to wait for reinforcements. Meanwhile, a dozen men were staggered around the ring armed with slings and sticks to stop the crowd from getting too close. The fight was a pretty brutal affair, with Looney taking a severe battering from Mahoney. When the police eventually forced their way into the ring to stop the fight, they found that Looney was unconscious and in need of attention. Five of the ringleaders, plus Looney, were arrested ▶

PAYING RESPECTS: Members of the Merseyside and Wirral Former Boxers' Associations lay a wreath at Jem Mace's grave in 2003. The association were largely responsible for placing the headstone upon his resting place

'The police were too few in number to stop the men fighting, and had to wait for reinforcements. A dozen men were staggered around the ring armed with slings and sticks to stop the crowd from getting too close'

and taken to the local police station. Mahoney fled. Following a medical examination, Looney was transferred to Bootle Hospital where he died the following day. Mahoney was arrested soon after his opponent had passed away and, along with the five other men, was charged with manslaughter. The whole squalid affair mirrored the decline of boxing under the London Prize Rings Rules. It also demonstrated the vital need for strong regulation in boxing contests and medical supervision at ringside.

Despite this tragic series of events, bare-knuckle boxing still continued in Liverpool. During the late 1880s there were reports of George Vaughan having several bare-knuckle contests close to Liverpool – the reports do not reveal the location or the opponents he boxed. Another report from January 1912 in the *Liverpool Echo* showed there were still bare-knuckle fighters in the city. John Harvey of Liverpool travelled to Nottingham to take on Leicester fighter Dick Collier for £25 a side. Once again the police were forced to intervene to halt proceedings.

Although bare-knuckle fighting had largely become discredited, the introduction of the Queensberry Rules was gradual, although its acceptance in an urbanised society was inevitable. Once established, the rules took boxing in two distinctive directions – amateur and professional. Both had unique codes, but were also dependent upon each other. The former began as a sport for the middle classes, the latter was rooted in the working class. With regard to professional boxing, it was increasingly being organised in the private clubs run by promoters. Boxing clubs grew rapidly in Liverpool from 1880. Although the Liverpool clubs were not as exclusive as the National Sporting Club, they were usually only open to private members or bona-fide guests. They also indicate that the sport was becoming more organised and better regulated. The city was at the forefront of this new era for boxing.

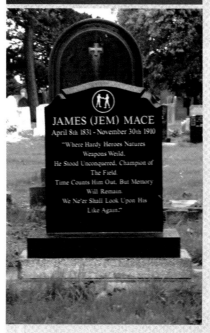

JEM'S GRAVES: Mace is remembered in his home town of Beeston, Norfolk (above), and in Anfield Cemetery (below)

Language of the Day – A Glossary

Boxing second – Another term for 'corner man', they would often be the trainer although not always the case (as with Ike Bradley).

The Liverpool Fancy – People who followed the sport in the 19th century were known as 'the Fancy', when there were no enclosed grounds. Incidentally, the term 'fan' derives from this.

The Liverpool Olympics – Held in the city between 1862-1867, although the 1865 event was held in Llandudno. They led to the establishment of the National Olympic Association in Liverpool in 1865. A key figure within the organization was John Hulley, the man who co-founded the Olympics in Liverpool.
Hulley also founded the Liverpool Gymnasium. There were two further Liverpool Olympics in 1892 and 1894. It is known that Pierre de Coubertin consulted with Herbert Gladstone (son of Prime Minister William Gladstone) about the first world Olympics in 1896.

Quoits – A popular game in the 19th century, often played in the grounds of a pub. It involves throwing a circular piece of metal over a set distance over a pin. Liverpool's oldest existing sports club is Childwall Quoits Club, and still survives to this day.

Pedestrianism – A term used for running in the 19th century. It was a professional sport, and also very popular.

Beakies – A term used for the policing authorities, although there was no national police force in 1825. However, there was local enforcement.

Boxing in Liverpool Becomes Unified, Regulated and Popular

In the 20-year period prior to the opening of the Pudsey Street Stadium in 1911, boxing was hosted at various locations throughout the city. Among the most significant venues were the Lyceum Theatre in Pembroke Place; the Liverpool Boxing Club, 16, Pitt Street; the Malakoff, Cleveland Square; the Adelphi Theatre, Christian Street; the International Athletic Club, Midgehall Street; the Haymarket Theatre, Beare Street; and the Gymnastic Club, 140 Dale Street, later known as Harry Thorn's New Gymnastic Club. As the legality of boxing was not completely secure in this period, most of these venues functioned as private gentlemen's clubs. In addition to membership fees, the cost of watching an evening of boxing at these venues was beyond the means of most working-class people. For example, in February 1896 the Malakoff Club hosted three professional contests at reduced prices to give 'the poor class a chance' to see competitive boxing. The admission charges were 5s, 2s 6d, 1s and 6d. Despite these reductions, many of the 'poor class' would have found it difficult to afford the entrance fee. The average weekly wage in this period was around £1.30-£1.40 per week. Like any average, it hides what the lowest paid received, but what is clear is that many households in this period could only provide basic necessities from their weekly wage.

However, from about 1890 onwards two distinctive trends – higher wages and shorter hours at work – were producing the conditions for a massive growth in commercial leisure for working-class people. By this time the overwhelming majority of the Liverpool working class had secured Saturday afternoons off work. This had provided a time-slot to enable entrepreneurs such as John Houlding to establish successful and well-supported football clubs. Moreover, growing affluence throughout the 1890s and into the early 20th century provided the opportunities for entrepreneurs to develop successful boxing venues throughout the city.

Boxing at these venues was normally held under Queensberry Rules, but at this stage there was no official governing body for the sport. This meant that championships were at best unofficial. Indeed, such was the unregulated nature of championships that boxers would often issue challenges in the local press inviting other boxers to fight for a particular championship.

In the absence of a board of control, there were no defined contracts for boxers. Usually articles of agreement were drawn up by boxing entrepreneurs with a local sports paper or gentlemen taking control of the stake money. One such agreement from 1896 is reproduced as follows:

'Articles of Agreement between William Keech & Punch Vaughan

'Articles of Agreement made and entered this eighth day of December 1896, between Punch Vaughan, of Liverpool, of the first part; and William KEECH, of Liverpool, of the second part; whereby it is mutually agreed that the said Punch Vaughan and William Keech shall box under the Marquis of Queensberry's Rules for a bet of £25 aside, upon the terms and conditions following:-

'The £25 aside shall be paid to the Editor of the "City Racing Record" (who is empowered to appoint referee and timekeeper) as follows:- £10 aside on the signing hereof, £10 aside on the fourteenth, and £5 aside on the twenty-first instant. In case default be made by either party in payment of any instalment, the money down shall be forfeited to the other. All the purse shall go to the winner.

'The contest shall be at catchweight, for ten rounds of three minutes each (one minute time), and shall take place at a suitable club, in a fourteen-foot ring or thereabouts. The competitors are to be in the ring at eight o'clock in the evening, and each competitor will be allowed three attendants only. The ▶

'Growing affluence throughout the 1890s and into the early 20th century provided the opportunities for boxing entrepreneurs to develop successful boxing venues throughout the city'

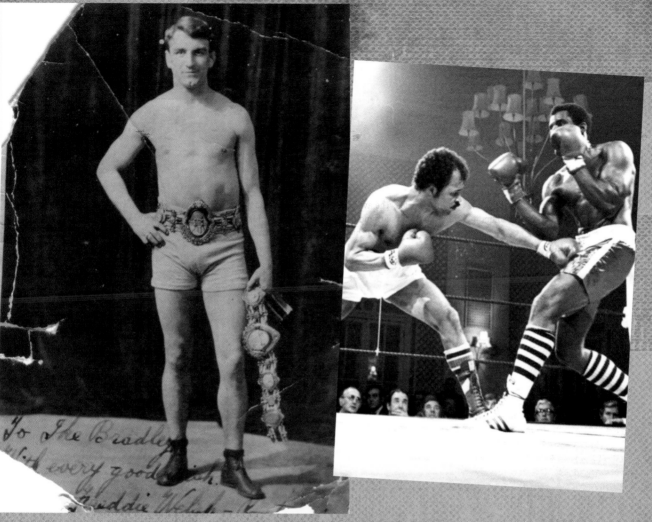

THROUGH THE AGES: Clockwise from top left – Freddie Walsh, the first winner of a NSC belt; John Conteh in action at the Adelphi; (left to right) Stephen Burke, Lee Ramsey, Alan Reynolds and Darren Edwards outside the Adelphi at the launch of the first home international boxing championships

PRE-FIGHT: Kirkby's Joey Singleton waiting for his bout at the Adelphi

gloves shall (be) provided by the stakeholder, and each shall be as nearly four ounces in weight as possible, but no question shall be raised thereto, or to the size of the ring. Either side failing to comply with any of the above conditions, to forfeit all money down. The referee's decision shall be final, and subject to no appeal at law or otherwise.

'Signed by the said William Keech in the presence of Jack Brown; and by the said Punch Vaughan, in the presence of G. Adamson.'

These articles reveal some interesting insights into early boxing contests. The contest was catchweight, a contest in which the boxers meet at an agreed weight rather than a defined weight category such as bantamweight or heavyweight. Equipment was not standardised: weight of gloves was to be as near as possible to four ounces. Moreover, the gloves, although an improvement upon the skin-tight two-ounce gloves still in use at this time,

would be unacceptable today – the standard glove used today varies between eight and 10 ounces.

Although there was no board of control at this time, championship boxing was gradually coming under the direction of the National Sporting Club. The problem with the NSC was that only contests held at the club could be considered as national championships. This situation was reinforced in 1909 when, to enhance its reputation, the club began to issue engraved belts for the national champions. The costs for the first belt, won by Freddie Welsh after he beat Johnny Summers at the NSC, was met by Lord Lonsdale, whose name the belts have subsequently taken. Henceforth the Lonsdale Belt has become one of the greatest trophies in sport. Initially, these belts could only be competed for at the club but as it ran into financial trouble in the 1920s, contests outside the club began to be held in areas other than London.

Boxing venues in Liverpool before Pudsey Street ranged from holding several dozen spectators to several thousand. However, with greater disposable income and more leisure time to spend this money, boxing venues were finding that they were putting up the 'house full' signs with greater regularity. Moreover, the quality and quantity of boxers Liverpool was able to attract helped to draw large crowds. Many of these boxers, such as Andrew Jeptha and Bobby Dobbs came from overseas, but every sport needs a local hero and the emergence of Ike Bradley in the early 1900s provided Liverpool with a boxer who had genuine championship qualities. It was Bradley who became the first Liverpool boxer to fight for a world title. It was boxers of his calibre that provided the platform for boxing entrepreneur Arnold Bennett, along with a group of local businessmen, to take over the Albert Hall roller-skating rink in Pudsey Street and re-open it as a venue fitted out for boxing. With a capacity of nearly 4,000, it was amongst the largest boxing venues in Britain. It was to develop into one of the most important venues for boxing in Britain, and establish Liverpool as a centre for national and international boxing.

March 16, 1861.   THE PORCUPINE.   291

lery, and seemed to be engaged in a mental calculation as to the length of time it would require the two bruisers to regain their "wind." Having settled this to his own satisfaction, he called out "time," and the men again faced each other, and pummelled away until they were told by "Jem," at the suggestion of some lovers of art in the pit, to "rattle it off and wind up," a direction which was readily and heartily complied with, and the men were loudly applauded.

The band, which seemed to have been considerably strengthened for the occasion, then struck up a lively air; ginger beer and oranges were carried round amongst the audience, and several stiff-built men with square cut coats and closely cropped heads, amused themselves by throwing the rind of oranges at any head which presented a good mark. It was clearly apparent very soon that the great bulk of the people did not care for music. Shrill whistles were given, and calls "give us summat to lok at," "Where's Mace?" &c., proclaimed dissatisfaction. After a lapse of ten minutes "Jem" came on again with his towel, followed by two young men, one with a florid complexion, round plump pleasant face and merry twinkling eye. He had nothing on him but his trousers and the boxing-gloves. His muscular development was good, and he seemed proud of it. The other was a short spare man, with a "hatchet face and his nose like a scimitar." He had on a very dirty flannel shirt, ragged trowsers, and "the gloves." At the command of "Jem," these two young fellows pretended to shake hands, and then went to work at each other with great vivacity. They leaped about, ducked, danced, dodged, and fenced, evidently to their own enjoyment. This was not relished on the part of the audience; besides several professors at "the wings" were calling out, that they must "go in," Whereupon the little half-naked red man "let go his left" heavily upon his opponent's nose, and the blood flowed freely. This was said to be the way to "turn on the tap." And now "Old Jem's" towel was brought into use. Again and again the little fellow turned round to Jem to receive a friendly wipe, then, nothing daunted, he faced his man and acquitted himself so well, by hitting hard and fiercely, as to call forth loud applause.

There was, after this round, more music. Then "two blacks," were introduced—one called Mace's Black, a young tawny man, broad chest and shoulders, long arms, "standing well on his pins," and with an expression of coolness and determination; the Big Black was a genuine nigger, with dark trowsers and red shirt, curly head, powerfully made about the shoulders, but "loose on his pins." Mace's Black was termed "The Wolf," and there was interest felt in his performance, as he is matched to fight "The

Gypsey" in three weeks. The Big Black soon shewed symptoms of distress. His leg was bad, and he limped across the stage. The audience hissed. He was stung by this and went to work with renewed vigour; but "The Wolf" was wary and cool, and there was some terrific hitting between these two; eventually, the Big Black was tired of it and got away. "Mace's Black" then came on with "Young Collins," and, from the excitement of the audience, a scientific treat was expected. Collins seemed to rely more upon his legs than his arms for getting him out of mischief, and he was reminded several times of this by the gentle remark, "Keep still, do you think it's a dancing lesson?" or, "He really thinks he's running a foot race." These rebukes had the effect of keeping him to "his work," and, eventually, there were loud cries, that the men should "rally it off and no flies," when they made a violent onslaught on each other, hitting as hard, and fighting as fiercely, as it was possible for men to do—greatly to the delight of the audience.

There were now loud cries for Mace and Langham —the professors who were said to be "giving the benefit." Langham came forward and said that "Mace has been busy getting his license to-day and could not get down in time, but he will be here directly and then we will set-to." (Applause.) The master of the ceremonies then introduced "two jolly Jack tars," and lively little fellows they were. They did not lose a moment, but with the greatest rapidity hit away right and left at each other, and the audience laughed vociferously. Indeed their set-to might be said to be one continued rally, performed to the tune of "Jack's the Lad." Then two cousins were introduced, youths about seventeen years of age, nothing on their spare, ill-formed bodies, but trowsers and "the gloves." There was no attempt at "sparring"—it was a fight. There was neither science nor skill, but plenty of "longeous hitting." Yet the laughter with which it was received, and the "friendly way" in which the cousins bruised each other, was a suggestive spectacle. "Tom King," (Jem Ward's big un,) and Frank Donnelly, a well-known Liverpool professor, were next introduced. King was a tall, well-proportioned, powerful man. Donnelly having devoted himself for some years to less scientific pursuits, was full of flesh, and seemed "finished." They both were on their metal—King to show what he could do, and Donnelly to maintain his reputation amongst his friends. There was caution exercised by both; but Frank "got home neatly" once or twice, which stirred the bl of King, who let fly his left, caught Frank o'of lower jaw and floored him, amidst the enthus' his the audience. Donnelly was laid hold He was friends, but was found to have "gone off" therefore drawn between the wings, and restoratives were applied to him, which in a quar' of an hour

290   **THE PORCUPINE.**   March 16, 1861.

TO THE TRADE.

Mr. JOSEPH SHEPHERD, 99, Scotland Road; 8, Exchange Street East; and 105, Brownlow Hill, *is our Agent for the Northern district,* and Mr. JOHN VAUGHAN, 64, Brownlow Hill, *is also Agent for the Eastern district. The Trade in these localities can, at all times, receive from them an ample supply of the Porcupine.*

Parties subscribing to the *Porcupine* will have their copies delivered by eight o'clock on the morning of publication. Subscribers' names received at 19, South John Street. Subscriptions payable in advance.

No. 1 *of the Porcupine is now ready, price* 2*d.*

The Porcupine.

LIVERPOOL, MARCH 16, 1861.

PORCUPINE PAPERS.—No. XXII.

THE BOXERS' BENEFIT.

HEARING what a wide field Liverpool presented for the cultivation of Science and Art; and having been in communication with some humble yet devoted brethren who reside amongst us, and, naturally feeling interested in the spread of their principles, several distinguished and justly celebrated metropolitan professors—men who have taken high honours—who have won glory and renown, have been induced to visit us. They were anxious to afford the public an opportunity of witnessing the application of their Science and Art, to what really are, just now, the affairs of every-day life. The announcement created considerable excitement; and as the gatherings at our Social Science meetings prove that a laudable curiosity is felt to see the men (if nothing more), who, by their genius, bravery, science, or skill, are said to have conferred such great and lasting benefits upon the human family; so in this case, the inaugural meeting at which these distinguished professors would appear, in which they were announced to take a part, called forth in the breast of the humblest mechanic feelings somewhat akin to reverence and awe.

The Adelphi Theatre was the place of meeting; the time—last Monday evening. There was no sipping of tea as a prelude to this great scientific meeting. There was none of the languid air of our overworked philanthropists about those who turned in.

There was not even the simper of amiability or brotherly love. No pump-handle shake of recognition. No: men—yes, and women too—came with an evident desire to learn all they could, and carry away what would be useful to them.

The audience, although not large, was highly appreciative. The gallery contained about one hundred persons, the boxes about the same number, but the pit was densely crammed. The names of Nat Langham (the only man who ever defeated Tom Sayers), and Jem Mace, the Wonder, the best boxer in Britain—the champion of the middle weights, together with "Blacks," "Pets," "Chickens," and "Sailor-boys," all of whom were to give practical illustrations in Science and Art, had formed the attraction for this assembly, and at eight o'clock, amidst loud applause, the curtain rose.

The scene represented a drawing-room. There was a small table, on which were displayed the trophies won by the distinguished scientific men who were to appear, consisting of massive silver cups, a tankard, and the champion's belt. The stage was covered with sawdust, and ropes were placed across the front, over the footlights—perhaps to prevent any of the learned *savans* from tumbling into the orchestra during the excitement consequent upon the illustrations of "applied science."

Consistent with that humility which is the attribute of true greatness, and quite in opposition to preconceived notions of scientific gatherings, there was a total absence of "stiff formality" in the introduction of the business of the evening. A man with a contorted visage and pale dinged face, without coat, hat in hand, and a *towel* under his arm, came forward with a nasal twang, announced that "two gentlemen will set to for the fost." This was met by cries of "good lad Jem," "Keep 'em to it, old un." Two broad-set muscular men, in "sparring costume," were then introduced to the audience, and they began to fight. There were some neat exchanges made, but seemed to be part of the performance that when one or the other received a rattling good hit, he was bound to smile. This was done very often in a gracious manner, but yet it was done, and the audience seemed to like the effect. These two men battered at each other until they were out of breath, and they rested against the wings to recover it. One professor with the twisted face, who was master of the ceremonies, took a pinch of snuff as soon as a round was finished, and this was done with a screw motion of the hand that displayed no ordinary skill. Perhaps the fact of his face being as said, "all cocked hats," had something to do with the mode of snuff-taking. Thus refreshed, he, standing in the middle of the stage, looked steadily at the

292   **THE PORCUPINE.**   March 16, 1861.

brought him round. The appearance of a policeman on the stage at this moment added to the excitement of the audience. The old feeling of the abuse which "the bobbies" receive in a pantomime seemed to have been awakened, and the representative of law and order was met with a universal howl of indignation. Donnelly had to show himself to the audience when he had recovered, and was greeted with rounds of applause, mingled with the cry of "Frank, you soon got your gruel."

Sprinkled amongst the audience, but more particularly behind the scenes, in the wings and "green-room" were many of "the Fancy"—men who take a lively interest in fighting—who back a man now and then—read *Bell's Life* regularly—do a little private sparring to oblige friends and keep their hands in, and yet do not care to be seen publicly associated with those who "fight for their living." It did not seem to surprise these "gentlemen" to find that few of the great professors who had been advertised to appear never "showed." It did not seem to excite their disgust when they saw "Mace's Black" stripped and having his tawny hide rubbed down by some youths who evidently took great delight in their work. These "gentlemen" saw nothing to remark upon in the fact that this poor young Black was being made a tool of, was taken on to the stage again and again to be "lunged at" and battered. No: what they saw in it was thus expressed by one of them, "Oh! the work will do him good, he is in training and has to fight in three weeks, and this will help to get him in condition." It is quite true that the Black seemed to like all he got—he seemed to court the inspection of strangers and patrons—and such an impression did the form and performance of this "Wolf" make upon the mind of one young man, that he slipped half-a-crown into the hand of the sable bruiser!

Behind the scenes, at a boxer's benefit, is altogether a disgraceful sight! What takes place on the stage is bad enough, but the characters,—their language, habits, manners, and doings behind the scenes are most repulsive. "Those who lie with dogs may expect to rise with fleas," and gentlemen who mix in such gatherings are fully prepared, indeed have made up their minds, what to expect. Some of them seemed on very familiar terms with all the boxers, and discussed, in the wings, the various points made and hits given, with a gusto that indicated real, full, hearty appreciation of the exhibition. Some people say, that this is the class of men that supports boxers. Not at all. When one saw in the pit at 2s., in the pit stalls at 2s. 6d, hundreds of men who, taken individually, you would not suppose worth a penny in the world, it was very clear no one need care to ask after that, "tell me where is *Fancy* bred?"

The "wind-up" of the evening was between Jem Mace and Nat Langham. The men were neatly attired, and before they began a young man came forward to exhibit the cups and belt. There was no satisfying the audience unless Mace put the belt on, and this he submitted to turning round to show how neatly it fit. There were science, skill, good temper, consideration and manly bearing exhibited in this set-to. It formed a strong contrast to all that had gone before. The men felt that they were not fighting and put on no appearance of it, and the grace and rapidity of their movements were something to admire.

It may be that there is no chance of severing the connection between a knowledge of the "manly art of self-defence" and downright ruffianism. It may be that when men make a profession of boxing or fighting that thereby they degrade themselves and the profession also. But there can be little doubt that there is some good, yes, much good, in a man developing his muscular power, and being able skilfully to apply it in his own defence. The great ground for sorrow lies in the fact that, according to our present usages, no one can associate with the professors of the "manly art" and not be morally contaminated. There is such a display of animal passion; such a love for "drawing the ruby;" such brutality exhibited in the so-called scientific "tourneys" that no one who has retained any feeling of true manhood or self-respect can be associated or mixed up with them. This is to be regretted every way.

Ex Fumo Dare Lucem.

While public attention is being called to the last wise act of our local legislature, viz.: the placing of a large lamp to endeavour to block up the road at the top of Bold-street, *Porcupine* thinks it might be well to ask, if it has ever entered into the wise understandings of those gentlemen to place anything of the kind on the long crossing, between The Landing Stage and the south end of the George's Dock, where it would be not only useful but ornamental.

A Literary "Shave."

A New York paper says, that Messrs. Harper Brothers, the well-known Printers, Publishers, and Bookbinders, save upwards of 7000 dollars per annum by their "shavings," yet, odd enough, they are very liberal employers, and there is not a razor on their premises.

By a rabid Press Guardman.—Which of the hands in a printing office suggests one of the Crimean battles? The Inker-man.

THE MOST VINOUS OF PLANTS.—Rum shrub.

Bradley – The First Liverpool Boxer to Fight for a World Title

Ike Bradley stands at the crossroads of Liverpool boxing. His philosophy on boxing was quite simple:

"My job has been to give and take hard knocks. That is a boxer's life and it often depends upon how hard you can punch how well you get on. There is no sense in losing your temper in the ring. Give and take as much as you can, but be good pals afterwards."

It was a philosophy that Bradley attempted to adhere to throughout his career, a career littered with famous fights and great stories, none more so than that Bradley was the first Liverpool boxer to fight for a world title.

When his professional career began in 1902, Liverpool had several established boxing clubs based largely upon private membership. Although many local boxers had established themselves within the city and were popular within the clubs, Liverpool had yet to find a boxer that had the ability to challenge for national or world titles. By the mid-point of

his career Bradley had won the English bantamweight title, boxed world bantamweight champion Digger Stanley three times and had developed a national reputation as one of Britain's finest boxers. He had a fearsome presence in the ring and was regarded by many as the hardest man in the world to knock out. The latter part of his career saw the opening of the Pudsey Street Stadium, the venue that was to make Liverpool into a boxing city with an international reputation. Bradley's biggest fight at the stadium was his fourth and final contest, just a few weeks after Pudsey Street opened, for Stanley's world bantamweight crown.

Like so many boxers of the day Bradley came from a poor family, a background he was able to escape from because of his sporting prowess. As a nine-year-old he attempted to escape his poverty by running away from home. He took the midnight ferry to Birkenhead from where he walked barefoot through the night to Chester. He attended the Chester Races and tried to make a living ▶

DEFEATED IKE: Digger Stanley: successfully defended his world title against Bradley at Pudsey Street

'My job has been to give and take hard knocks. That is a boxer's life and it often depends upon how hard you can punch how well you get on. There is no sense in losing your temper in the ring. Give and take as much as you can, but be good pals afterwards'

ONE OF BRITAIN'S BEST: Bradley, right, built up a fearsome reputation selling racecards. Failure to earn a living in this way forced him to return home after three days and go back to selling newspapers on the street.

Ike's first two fights were bare-fisted affairs that took place at Lock-Fields on the corner of Lightbody Street against another local boy named Jack O'Brien. The second of these fights lasted more than two hours, with both boys battering each other to a stop. Onlookers at the scrap urged Bradley to take up boxing at a local gymnasium as he seemed to have natural boxing talent.

Soon after his bare-knuckle fights, Ike went to Harry Thorne's gymnasium on Dale Street where he met Willie Gill, son of the boxing promoter Paddy Gill. Willie Gill agreed to spar with Ike for 10 rounds as part of his training schedule. For a severe battering that left him bruised and bloodied, Ike received five shillings – still, it was better than selling newspapers. The significance of the session is that Ike went back and served his apprenticeship at the Thorne's gymnasium. While there, he was often required to box exhibition bouts in front of crowds of 500. For his pains, the spectators would often throw coins into the ring signifying their support for the contest they had witnessed.

Alongside these bouts, Ike began to compete in the boxing booths. On Bank Holidays he would sometimes be expected to take on up to 20 opponents at 1s 6d a time. The boxing

booth was a hard school, but like so many boxers at this time Ike learned the skills of his trade the hard way. This was an age when boxers could not afford to engage trainers or to have long gaps between fights to recover full fitness. To keep in shape boxers would often fight weekly, as it was the only means that they could maintain their income and stay in the game. Such a schedule helps to explain why boxers would have hundreds of fights; in Ike's case it is thought he had more than 400 gloved contests during his boxing career.

One of the greatest honours a boxer could receive in the early years of the 20th century was to be invited to box at the National Sporting Club, an honour Ike performed on 10 April 1905. Such invites usually came after a trial bout, but in Bradley's case he received a straight invitation to take on Jim Kenrick for the English bantamweight title. His invitation came soon after he had beaten Willie Gill at New Brighton to become bantamweight champion of Liverpool. Although he lost on points over 15 rounds to Kenrick, he was not disgraced – a creditable performance against a very experienced boxer who fought at the NSC on many previous occasions. Remarkably, although stiff and sore from the fight, he was back in the ring three nights later in Liverpool to take on, and knock out, Johnny Hughes of London.

Bradley's next major milestone came a year later when he travelled up to Newcastle ▶

BACK IN THE RING: After retirement, Bradley (far right) became a second – he is pictured in 1937 with Maurice Huguenin

▶ to take on Harry Slough at Ginnett's Circus for the English bantamweight title. Slough was hot favourite, but Bradley knocked him out in the fourth round. A disgruntled Slough demanded a rematch, which he got three weeks later. Ike knocked him out again, this time in the first round but Slough claimed a foul and after some discussion it was agreed that the fight should start again. After a 15-minute break the two squared up once more – this time it took Bradley 18 rounds to find a knock-out punch to Slough's jaw.

Soon after beating Slough for the second time Ike met his nemesis, Digger Stanley, for the first time. The 20-round contest took place at Ginnett's Circus on 20 January 1906, and in some circles this fight was billed as for the world bantamweight title. Stanley was regarded as the best boxer in Britain, and had just defeated Jimmy Walsh of Boston for the eight-stone championship of the world. During the fight Bradley had Stanley on the canvas several times, but the champion prevailed to take the contest on points. A return was arranged in Liverpool for 13 December 1906, with Bradley having an incredible nine fights in between these contests. Three were in America; another was for the north of England bantamweight title against Harry Brodigan, who Bradley knocked out in the ninth round.

In America Ike was due to meet Jimmy Walsh for the eight-stone championship of the world. When this fell through he was matched with Tommy O'Toole, followed by three other contests, all of which he lost. Joe Walcott, who was Bradley's second in his fight against Freddie O'Brien, asked Bradley to stay in America and train with him. Bradley refused the offer and returned to face Stanley for a second time.

Like the first contest with Stanley, Ike had his opponent on the canvas. In the last two rounds the champion was hanging onto the ropes when each time he was saved by the

bell and won on points. Their third contest took place at Mile End, London in 1908, with the result being the same as the previous two, a defeat for Bradley on points.

Following his fourth and final defeat to Stanley, Bradley's career went into terminal decline. From February 1912 he was barred from fighting at Pudsey Street for not trying. However, following the intervention of Freddie Welsh, Bradley was given another chance to fight at the now famous stadium. When Welsh beat Eddie Beatty on points in March 1913, the Stadium directors asked him would he fight Beatty again. Welsh replied: "Yes I will do you a favour, if you will do me another." "What is that?" came the reply, to which Welsh said: "Give Bradley another fight." Bradley got his fight against Robert Dastillon in July 1913 and a return the following month. He lost both – the first on points; in the second fight the referee stopped the fight in the 11th round. Bradley's last professional fight was at Pudsey Street on 18 February 1915 against Fred Anderson, losing the 10-round contest on points. A career of more than 400 gloved fights was clearly taking its toll.

Upon retirement, Bradley became a taxi driver and for many years he was a second at both stadiums. He died in 1951, leaving behind a wonderful legacy from which Liverpool boxing has greatly benefited.

TATTOOS: Ike Bradley's body art was almost as well-renowned as his prowess in the boxing ring

'Following his fourth and final defeat to Stanley, Bradley's career went into terminal decline. From February 1912 he was barred from fighting at Pudsey Street for not trying'

Boscow And M'Gee; Or, The Fight In Doggeral Verse

(Tune – Chevy Chace)

It was in Liverpool's sea-port town,
Were lots o' the Fancy dwell,
It will be shown, two Lads of renown,
Were determined to have a mill.

Ralph Boscow, big, weighed thirteen stone,
With arms as strong as an Ox;
And M'Gee was all bone, and as hard as
stone,
And both were the Lads that could box.

The Jemmy, with his hairy chops'
And stakes and ropes likewise,
Set off at his ease, to the famous Leach-Hays,
And pitch'd then without any noise.

Head-quarters they were at Ha-war-den,-
All met with right good will;
Bold horsemen were then, mix'd with toddling
men,
And assembled to see the mill.

Five thousand Lads stood all around,
And there was many a drag;
And many a pound, was bet on the ground,
And the prigs they div'd for the swag.

Ralph, he enter'd the ring with glee;
Dick Davis and Cheetham too;
And merry-men three, Reynolds, Neale and
M'Gee'
Form'd a jolly, and milling crew.

The Lads then peel'd upon the heath,
And they stood up to spar;
A blow that was good , and which drew the
first blood,
M'Gee gave, - that son of war.

'Twas blow for blow, with horrid force,
They struggled with all their might;
There were betting and shouts, but great
were the doubts,
Which Hero would win the fight.

And so for many a round they fought,
And dealt out thund'ring blows;
Paddy's head and neck was a perfect wreck,
And shocking he look'd, God knows.

And Boscow he had got the gasps,
And often lost his pin;
He was tott'ring and weak, and great odds
were at stake,
That Paddy the Battle would win.

At length in round the thirty-fifth,
Although quite out of breath,
Ralph Boscow again, struck the jugular vein,
'Twas like a blow of Death!

The vic'try crown'd the butcher-boy,
Pat was lifeless as the tomb;
But his conduct was right, in this
slaught'ring fight,
So ev'ry cove he scamper'd home!

REMARKS

Or when he was out of breath,
M'Gee with a push, had made a good rush,
He'd have won as sure as death!

In Hawarden town the Beakies met,
And thought to have stopt the fight;
But good Master Beak, made a sorry mistake,
And so it was "al right!"

'Twas honest Pat he thought to grab,
but he nabb'd good Mr. Rutter,
and Pat if you please, was popt in a chaise,
And left the Beak in a sputter.

So now ye milling coves attend,
With courage bold and free,
Your glasses all fill, drink to the next mill,
And to Boscow and M'GEE!

(Life in London and the Liverpool Sporting
Register October 1825)

ABOUT THE POEM: Such was the passion of the Liverpool Fancy for boxing they often set the events of the day to poetry. The poem reveals more than a boxing contest, however. It tells us about the legal obstacles to the sport, that boxing had a huge fan base and that it evoked great passions both for boxers and spectators alike. Sport has long been associated with the wider leisure pursuits of ordinary people and here the verse does not disappoint as it reveals that people liked a side bet and a drink to enhance their enjoyment of the sporting spectacle. Traditions kept going by many sports fans today.

Boxing Before Pudsey – Liverpool's Growing Club Scene

In the two decades prior to the opening of Pudsey Street in 1911, boxing was hosted at various venues around the city. Some were in small gymnastic clubs, others in large halls such as theatres. The most important venues were the boxing clubs, as these put on promotions regularly throughout the period. It was the boxing clubs that nurtured and developed boxing in Liverpool. By 1911 the demand to see top tournaments was so great that a hall able to hold weekly tournaments, offering good facilities and with a large capacity, was needed to satisfy demand. To date, more than 20 venues have been identified – some of the most important are identified below:

School of Arms, Devon Street: Boxing was held there from 1888, if not earlier. *The Liverpool Review*, 29 September 1888 described it as a venue that rarely failed to attract 'a large and select audience'. The *Review* also revealed that over the previous six years 'the noble art has gradually got a firm hold on certain sections...of young Liverpool'. Promoter Paddy Gill told the reporter that Liverpool had some fine boxers, and 'at their respective weights are as good as anybody in the world'.

Liverpool Boxing Club: Established circa 1889, pre-dating the National Sporting Club in London. Located at 16, Pitt Street (off Paradise Street), the proprietor was Tom Meadows. The venue attracted top regional contests, with Punch Vaughan appearing there on many occasions. Two sides of the auditorium had fixed seating that cost five shillings for members. Cheaper seats costing 2s 6d were located by the entrance to the arena. The usual audience was made up of neatly dressed commercial men. The club also provided full gymnasium facilities during the day; members could pay three pence to watch the sparring and the training. There was also a shop at the entrance that was decked out with sporting prints.

Malakoff Boxing Club: Established 1889. Proprietors were George and William 'Punch' Vaughan. Located in Cleveland Square, boxing was held twice weekly, usually Saturday and Monday. The club was described by the *Sporting Chronicle* (30 April 1895) as a 'commodious and well-conducted' club. You needed to be a member or a bona-fide guest to gain entry. Was sometimes referred to as the Provincial Sporting Club.

Lyceum Theatre: Certainly in existence in 1888, was also known as the Continental Club, the Continental Chequered Club and the Grand Continental Club. Located at 3A Pembroke Place, the proprietor was Jem Butler, one of the earliest black boxing promoters. Attracted top local boxers such as Punch Vaughan, who signed articles of agreement to box Jack McKay (champion of Yorkshire) at the club on 26 November 1896. At one of the earliest promotions at the Lyceum, on 31 December 1888, Jem Mace appeared on a bill that included Alf Mitchell (champion of Wales), Teddy O'Neil, John Smith, Lachie Thompson, Punch Vaughan, George Vaughan, Sol Burns, Albert Pierce and Pooley Mace.

Adelphi Theatre: Although the Adelphi opened as a boxing venue in 1902, it had hosted boxing as far back as 1861 when Jem Mace and Nat Langham put on an exhibition of boxing. The programme also included a contest between two black boxers, one of whom was being trained by Mace. Mace at this time had strong associations with Liverpool, refereeing boxing bouts at the Liverpool Olympics as well as becoming an instructor at the Liverpool Gymnasium in 1865. The Adelphi, known locally as the 'Delly', changed its name to the Arena prior to its closure in 1911. It developed a strong reputation for hosting top-class contests. Among the most famous was a 20-round catchweight contest between Freddie Welsh, the British and European lightweight champion, and Joe Heathcote of Wigan. Welsh gave away 20lbs to Heathcote. The fight lasted for six fiercely-contested rounds ▶

'By 1911 the demand to see top tournaments was so great that a hall able to hold weekly tournaments, offering good facilities and a large capacity, was needed to satisfy demand'

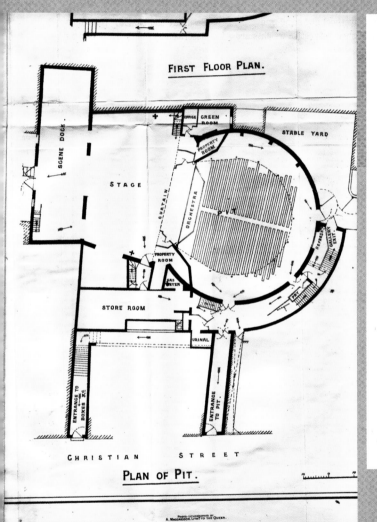

FIRST FLOOR PLAN.

PLAN OF PIT.

THE MALAKOFF MUSIC HALL.

HALLS FOR ALL: Floor-plan of the Adelphi and the Malakoff Music Hall

▶ before Welsh opened up with a left and right to the body followed by two telling left-handers to the head, forcing the referee, Dan Whelligan, to stop the fight. Fittingly, one of the last boxers to appear at the Arena was Ike Bradley, who took on Harry Thomas on 26 January 1911, in a 20-round contest that Thomas won on points.

International Athletic Club: The International was probably the largest of all the Liverpool boxing venues prior to the opening of Pudsey Street, holding in the region of 2,000 spectators. It continued to function following the opening of Pudsey Street, but suffered as the new stadium, with its greater capacity and better facilities, was able to attract national and international champion boxers. Ike Bradley, Dom Vario and Johnny Best were among the crowd favourites, while the club usually held top-class boxing twice a week.

Some Liverpool boxers and proprietors pre-1911

Liverpool had a thriving boxing scene from the 1880s onwards. How many actual Liverpool boxers there were is impossible to determine. For the years 1888-1902, more than 140 boxers have been identified. Below are listed a few of the more significant ones prior to the emergence of Ike Bradley.

Tom Meadows: Proprietor of the Liverpool Boxing Club, was described in the *Liverpool Review* of 1 August 1891 as a teacher of boxing. Although he was born in Liverpool, he was a former champion of Australia and

California. He was taught boxing by Peter Jackson, who was a former heavyweight champion of Australia. Jackson boxed bare-knuckle and gloved contests. J.L. Sullivan refused to fight Jackson on the grounds of his colour.

George Vaughan: *Sporting Life*, 11 January 1888 describes Vaughan as the 9st 4lbs champion of Liverpool. One report from 1890 indicates that he had boxed several times bare-knuckle, twice within the vicinity of Liverpool. Was also proprietor at the Malakoff Boxing Club along with his brother William 'Punch' Vaughan. The present-day George Vaughan, trainer of Derry Matthews, is related to the Vaughan family of the 19th century.

William 'Punch' Vaughan: Often described as the champion of Liverpool and the lightweight champion of the north. One report from 13 February 1897 describes him as the welterweight champion of Lancashire. Another report from 1888 indicates that he had boxed in America, where he had three contests. Several reports refer to him as a boxing entrepreneur. Along with George Vaughan he was a key boxing promoter in the city and did much to promote Liverpool boxing.

Paddy Gill: *Sporting Life*, 14 February 1888 refers to him as a boxing entrepreneur and a

proprietor of the School of Arms, Devon Street. He put on events at all Liverpool boxing clubs, a notable one being at the Lyceum when he offered two silver belts, made by Elkington's of Church Street, as prizes. His son Willie Gill also developed into a fine boxer and fought Ike Bradley on at least two occasions for the championship of Liverpool.

Jim (Jem) Butler: One of several Liverpool black boxers around in the 19th century, he was regarded as one of Liverpool's finest boxers at 9st 6lbs. What makes Butler interesting is that he was also a boxing entrepreneur and promoter. His various boxing clubs at the Lyceum also seem to have been a nursery for other black boxers. Was a close associate of the Vaughans and Paddy Gill.

Harry Brown: Won the coloured championship of the north in 1896. In this period, black boxers were generally barred from competing for national honours – a bar that was only removed in 1948 by the British Boxing Board of Control. There were several other important Liverpool-born black boxers competing in the period, most notably Joe Taylor, who was the coloured champion of Liverpool.

Harry Thorne: Was boxing champion of the north in the 1890s. Played a key role in ▶

NSC SHOT: The National Sporting Club in Covent Garden, Britain's most prestigious boxing club. Liverpool had several private boxing clubs in the late 19th century that adopted the rules of the NSC

THE VAUGHANS: Punch (inset and main picture right) and George (left)

'In 1866 Mace defeated Joe Goss for the heavyweight championship of England. Upon returning to Liverpool, more than 10,000 fans greeted Mace at Lime Street Station and carried him shoulder-high through the streets'

FINAL CHAMPION: Jem Mace, the last British boxing world champion under London Prize Ring Rules

promoting boxing in Liverpool. His Gymnastic Club on Dale Street hosted many top-class boxing tournaments, including Ike Bradley's second fight with Digger Stanley in December 1906. It also attracted top American boxers such as Bobby Dobbs, known as the Kentucky Rosebud, who was the coloured lightweight champion of America.

Did You Know?

The great American J.L. Sullivan, the first gloved heavyweight champion of the world, came to Liverpool on 6 November 1877. After staying overnight in the Grand Hotel he left for London, where he made his first public appearance in Britain. Upon arrival and departure he was met with a great ovation by large crowds from the Liverpool Fancy. Indeed, his reception was so great, the *Daily Post* commented 'that while it lasted this was one of the most prodigious demonstrations, and the police say it quite eclipsed the furore of a Royal visit'. Of real significance, perhaps, is that the reception for Sullivan was organised by members of the Liverpool Fancy, which would indicate that boxing in Liverpool was both organised and had a large following in this period. Sullivan came to Liverpool on two other occasions, giving demonstrations of his boxing skills on these visits. His first appearance was at Hengler's Circus at West Derby, 22 March 1888, where he treated the audience to a 'four-round scientific passage at arms' with Jack Ashton. The *Daily Post* reported that the champion did not put on such a good show, being outshone by the local boxer. Sullivan's second appearance came the following year, 11

September 1889, at the Haymarket Music Hall. The welcoming party that met Sullivan at Exchange Station included the boxing promoter Jem Butler. On this occasion he treated two separate, packed shows to sparring sessions under Queensberry Rules against Jack Dunkhurst.

Jem Mace: The last British champion of the world under London Prize Ring Rules, Jem is buried in Anfield Cemetery. Mace had a long association with Liverpool dating back to the mid-19th century. Mace had been an instructor and a judge at the Liverpool Olympics in the 1860s. He must have impressed John Hulley and Charles Melly, the key organisers behind the Games, because when they opened the Liverpool Gymnasium on Myrtle Street in 1865 they invited Mace to become the boxing instructor. Mace at this time also bought the Strawberry Tavern on West Derby Road from where he promoted sports such quoits, pedestrianism and boxing with gloves. In 1866 Mace defeated Joe Goss at Purfleet for the heavyweight championship of England. Upon returning to Liverpool, more than 10,000 boxing fans greeted Mace at Lime Street Station and carried him shoulder-high through the streets. Mace maintained his links with the city, returning on many occasions to box exhibition matches. He died in 1910 at Jarrow, but his body was brought back to Liverpool where he was buried in a pauper's grave at Anfield. His grave remained in this state until 2003 when the Merseyside and Wirral Former Boxers' Association arranged for a headstone to be placed at Jem's place of rest.

ONE OF THE FIRST: How the Adelphi Theatre looked in 1863

THE ADELPHI THEATRE (1863).

★

CHAPTER 2

PUDSEY STREET

Liverpool's **BOXING** Venues

★

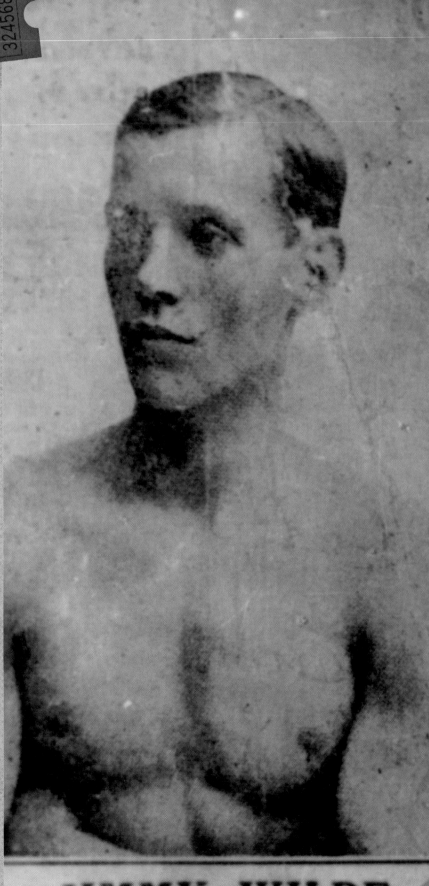

JIMMY WILDE.

STADIUM
LIVERPOOL

Easter Monday
(April 24, 1916)

JIMMY
WILDE
(WALES)

v

JOHNNY
(YOUNG)
ROSNER
(U.S.A.)

REFEREE:
Eugene Corri, Esq.

Box Plan now open.
SEE OVER

WILDE V ROSNER: At Pudsey Street,
11 July 1916

JOHNNY ROSNER

The Opening Night of Pudsey Street

The opening of the new stadium aroused great interest in the city, with more than 1,000 boxing fans being turned away from the doors, unable to obtain admission.

Before the evening's entertainment commenced, the stadium's forthcoming attractions were paraded around the ring. These included Johnny Summers, a future British welterweight champion and George Rodel, the South African heavyweight champion. Thus, from the outset, the management of the stadium were making it clear that Liverpool's premier boxing venue would attract top-class fighters.

The opening bantamweight contest was between two local boxers, Young Baker and Billy Gill. They served up 10 close but exciting rounds that had the crowd on the edge of their seats. The verdict was hanging in the balance up to the final round, but Baker was given the decision following his efforts in the final two rounds.

The following 15-round contest between Harry Jones of Cardiff and Fred Sidney of Boston had the crowd on their feet as both boxers fought a spirited contest that ebbed and flowed. Sidney seemed to be getting the upper hand during the middle rounds of the contest, but from the 12th round onwards Jones took the initiative and nearly secured a KO in round 12. To loud cheers from the crowd, the popular Jones received the verdict.

Top of the bill was a heavyweight contest between Bandsman Dick Rice and Alf Langford. Their 20-round fight failed to live up to expectations as Rice struggled to perform up to his reputation. Despite his lacklustre performance, Rice got a points verdict.

But it was the Liverpool public that got the overall verdict. Their enthusiasm for boxing had been clearly demonstrated – an enthusiasm that was to be rewarded over the coming decades.

EARLY DAYS: A former roller-skating rink was converted into the stadium

'From the outset, the management of the (Pudsey Street) stadium were making it clear that Liverpool's premier boxing venue would attract top-class fighters'

BANDSMAN DICK RICE

Boxed Bombadier Billy Wells here on two occasions, lost on points after having Wells down for a count in the 1st in a 20rd contest and in second contest Wells k.o. him inside 5 rounds.

JOHNNY BASHAM   V.   BADOUD

Boxed on two occasions, Basham winner on points and Badoud by k.o. return contest.

PUDSEY STREET: Pages from the final-night programme

A photo taken before the opening of the Stadium, of Major Arnold Wilson, Nat Williams and Johnny Best. When Arnold Wilson founded the Stadium, boxing was at its lowest ebb in Liverpool.

The advent of the Stadium had a wonderful effect on the game and in a few years Liverpool had a reputation all over the world.

Major Wilson repeated the process when he opened out in London and his shows at Albert Hall and Olympia attracted many notable Society people and H.R.H. the Prince of Wales saw most of the big contests there. There is not the slightest doubt that Arnold Wilsons' entry into the boxing game marked a new era in the history of the noble art.

Nat Williams is probably one of the cleverest Featherweights Liverpool has produced. During a period when there were a number of exceptionally clever boxers Nat held his own. He boxed a draw with Kid Lewis, Johnny Basham, Jerry Delaney who was killed during the war and was undefeated.

Nat took a trip to Australia and his first contest was with Herb McCoy, the Lightweight Champion of Australia. Nat created a sensation by outpointing him over 20 rounds. He is now on the Stadium Staff as Chief Second.

Pudsey Street Stadium – Liverpool's Original Graveyard of Champions

The opening of Pudsey on 13 July 1911 marked a new departure for boxing stadia in Britain. It was regarded as the finest all-purpose boxing stadium in the country, with only St James Hall in Newcastle being the other large venue outside London. However, St James Hall's capacity was smaller than Pudsey Street – 2,500-3,000, compared to 4,000 at the Liverpool arena. Prior to its opening, Liverpool had a vibrant and developing boxing scene, but to attract top international and championship contests on a more regular basis, a larger stadium was required. The inspiration behind the new stadium was Arnold Wilson, who became involved in boxing following visits to a dingy cellar where a young Johnny Best and Nat Williams used to spar together. Seeing the full-up signs night after night at the Arena and the International Athletic Club, Wilson recognised the great potential for a new and enlarged boxing stadium in the city. When the former roller-skating rink in Pudsey Street became available in 1910, Wilson had the idea of getting a syndicate together to lease the hall.

The business syndicate established the Liverpool Sporting Association to provide the capital for his ambitious project. The Association began with capital of £3,000, the leading shareholders being Jas Fairrie (200 shares), Mr Jas Wilson of Aintree (125 shares), Mr A.L. Percival of New Brighton and J.A. Sloane of Waterloo (125 shares each), Mr William and E. Backhouse (100 shares each), and Mr Albert Taylor of Clubmoor and Mr Tom Taylor-Stanley (50 shares each). Interestingly, Arnold Wilson does not appear in the list of shareholders. The building remained under the ownership of the Albert Hall Company, who leased the hall to the Liverpool Sporting Association, the holding body that ran Pudsey Street until 1928. That year, the stadium came under the control of Johnny Best, who promoted shows until its final closure and demolition in 1931.

Upon its opening, *Boxing* described the stadium as 'palatial...the equal of which will not be found outside the metropolis'. The article continues, stating 'that each patron will have his own tip-up chair, while a perfect view will be obtainable from all parts of the big building. The management are after top-notchers, the first pair being Bandsman Rice and Alf Langford'. It was indeed the finest hall in the country; extra comfort was offered for spectators on summer evenings as the Liverpool Stadium (as it was called) had a sliding roof to facilitate the circulation of air.

Mr Harrison, who had been in charge of the Arena, was made matchmaker. Within a few months, however, Harrison was forced to retire, paving the way for Arnold Wilson to take over the role. It was under his direction that Pudsey Street developed a reputation as a world-class venue that hosted some of the world's outstanding boxers. Wilson would later promote many shows in London, most notably the Carpentier–Beckett contest at the London Olympia that drew a 26,000 crowd – a huge gate in those times.

From the opening night right up to the First World War, weekly, sometimes twice-weekly shows of top quality drew crowds in their thousands. More often than not, the full-up sign was posted on the entrance doors. The programme often included leading American boxers on the bill such as Dixie Kid and Joe Jeanette. Boxing continued at Pudsey Street during the war, one of the few centres in Britain to put on regular shows. In the post-war period, management of the stadium passed to Pa Taylor, who remained in control until 1928 when Pudsey Street was forced to close for a short period.

In contrast to the pre-war years, which were ones of economic boom and increasing leisure time, the post-war situation was marked by severe economic fluctuations resulting in high levels of unemployment in Liverpool. This had a severe impact upon attendances at Pudsey Street, a situation that was compounded by the lack of top-class bills at the stadium. Another factor affecting attendances was the opening of several greyhound tracks in the city. These offered ▶

BOXING THURSDAY EVENING
STADIUM, PUDSEY STREET, LIVERPOOL.

One Minute from Lime Street Station and Three Minutes from Central Station.

Under the direction of Johnny Best.

THURSDAY OCT. 3rd. 1929 at 7-45 p.m.

15 Three Min. Rounds Contest. Weigh in 9st. 12lb. at 2 p.m.

HARRY FENN
London

Contender for lightweight title. Fenn fought a close decision with Fred Webster last July.

V.

HAYDN WILLIAMS
Official Lightweight Champion of Wales

Williams has won his last 34 contests, and has defeated Fred Green, Frank Carberry, Kid Brooks, Sonny Bird, Franz Kruppel and others.

15 Three Min. Rounds Middleweight Contest.

KID MOOSE
Southport

V.

SANDY McKENZIE
Scotland

10 Three Min. Rounds Contest.

Lew. Sullivan v. Alf. Grisdale
Liverpool   Liverpool

10 Three Min. Rounds Special Return Contest.

Dave Craig v. Bert Mills
Liverpool   Rock Ferry

A grand slam, like the previous one.

ALSO OTHER CONTESTS   LADIES INVITED

HARRY FENN

PRICES (Including Tax)

5/9, 2/4, & 1/2

Henry Hughes & Co., Printers, 37 & 39. Vauxhall Road, Liverpool.

KID MOOSE

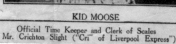

Official Time Keeper and Clerk of Scales
Mr. Crichton Slight ("Cri" of Liverpool Express")

STADIUM
PUDSEY STREET, LIVERPOOL.

...day, Nov. 10th, 1921, at 7-30 p.m.

...en 3-Min. Rounds Contest

ANDRE
...SIMETH
...ght-weight Champion Switzerland, V.

FRANCIS
...ROSSI
Pontypridd

Weigh in 9 st. 9 lb. at 2 o'clock under forfeit.

Three 10-Rounds Contests

..RY HILL v HYMAN GORDON
...verpool   Newcastle

...PERRY v. JACK LAVIN
...rpool   Wigan

Hughie   Young
...PATTERSON v. DOWD
Liverpool   Wigan

...ES: 1/-, 2/- & 5/- (Ringside Reserved)
PLUS TAX
...7 Royal.   Booking Office 10 to 5.
All Booked Seats must be claimed before 7-45 p.m.

TOMMY ROSE   Liverpool

This hard hitting local is improving with every contest may yet win honours in the Bantamweight Division

---

LIVERPOOL STADIUM PUDSEY St.
PROGRAMME.

THURSDAY, DEC. 17th, 1912.

1. 10 Round Contest:—
GINGER JAMES v. YOUNG GRAINGER
(Birkenhead)   (Birkenhead)

2. 10 Round Contest:—
DOM VARIO v. WILL ESCOTT
(Liverpool)   (Bolton)

3. 10 Round Contest:—
ALF. LANGFORD v. CYCLONE WARREN
(America)   (Australia)

4. 15 Round Contest:—
GEORGE BECKETT (Southampton)
V.
CURLY DAVIES (Birkenhead).
Both men weigh-in at 11st. 6lbs. 2 o'clock day of contest

5. 10 Round Contest:—
YOUNG BENYON v. CHARLIE FOX
(Merthyr)   (Somers Town)
Both men weigh-in at 8st. 6lbs. 2 o'clock day of contest.

WEEKLY BATTLES: In the early 20th century Thursday nights became the established night for boxing at Liverpool venues

▶ nightly sporting entertainment at more competitive admission prices. Indeed, to attract custom, admission at some tracks was often free, with revenue being based upon profits from betting. Moreover, in this period the main event was often devalued as Taylor frequently had to find substitutes. This combination of factors led to the temporary closure of Pudsey Street in December 1928.

The announcement to close Pudsey Street came as a shock to the boxing public on 22 November 1928. That night's show was to be the last, with the exception of two special promotions scheduled for 4 and 18 December. The headliners for these shows demonstrated that with a suitable promoter the venue could be viable – the headliners were, of course, Dom Volante and Nel Tarleton.

Only five days passed and an announcement was made that Johnny Best was to take over the stadium, and that after a short closure it would reopen on 10 January 1929, and weekly thereon. Best's intervention was to have a dramatic effect upon the future of Liverpool boxing – an act that was to put Liverpool on the international boxing map once more.

Best had realised that while the stadium had developed a reputation for being the graveyard of champions, it was also a nursery for future champions. Outstanding local talent was emerging, talent that would ensure that the 'house full' sign could be dusted off and hung out each Thursday night. Apart from Volante and Tarleton, boxers of the calibre of Alf Howard, Harold Higginson and Dick Burke also helped build up a loyal spectator base and restore Pudsey Street as the venue with the highest boxing attendances in the country.

Other factors were going Best's way as well. For example, the National Sporting Club had come to accept that British title fights should be staged outside the capital. Indeed, the Johnny Cuthbert/Nel Tarleton British featherweight title fight, held at Pudsey Street on 6 November 1930, was only the second such contest for a Lonsdale Belt to be held outside London. It was billed as a joint promotion between the NSC and Johnny Best of the Liverpool Stadium. The first NSC title fight to be staged outside London was the Al Foreman/George Rose fight held at Belle Vue, Manchester on 20 October 1930. Another factor was the establishment of the British Boxing Board of Control in 1929, which brought greater regulation to the sport and improved conditions for boxers.

However, it was tough going to begin with. Best's first promotion brought a profit of just £39. Indeed, for the first six months the viability of the venue was in the balance and Best was urged by many to cut his losses. But in the words of Johnny Best Jnr, his father "may have lost cash, (but) he never lost faith", and eventually the crowds returned. However, having re-established itself, the whole site – bounded by London Road, Lord Nelson Street, Pudsey Street and Hotham Street – was bought by a property developer in February 1929.

There was no immediate threat to the stadium as some of the properties on the site had short leases to be considered. However, within a year it was clear that the whole site was to be re-developed, with a cinema being at the centre of the development. It was ▶

SHAKE ON IT: Paddy Carroll (left), with Ike Bradley. Carroll was a contemporary of Bradley who boxed at the Stadium

'Best realised that the stadium was a nursery for future champions. Outstanding local talent was emerging, talent that would ensure that the "house full" sign could be dusted off and hung out each Thursday night'

PUDSEY SCENE, 1927: (L to R) unknown, Jaffa Owens (trainer), Jim Boyd, Pat Taylor (promoter), Freddie Tilston, Charlie Tonner, others unknown

JOHNNY BEST JR: On the phone, and presenting the Fletcher Cup to F. Seery at Clubmoor (above left)

eventually demolished in March 1931, with the last night for boxing at the original Liverpool Stadium being 5 March 1931. Today the Odeon cinema on London Road stands on the site of the Pudsey Street Stadium.

The problem for Johnny Best was how to maintain the fan base for boxing he had developed over the course of the previous two years. He was involved in negotiations for the building of a new stadium, but despite his promises on the last night at Pudsey Street, that a new venue for boxing could be open by the turn of the year, these plans were no nearer fruition.

Best's initial solution was to hold his regular Thursday night promotions at New Brighton Tower. He had anticipated the closure of Pudsey Street and had been staging promotions at 'the Tower' for three weeks prior to 5 March. However, the Tower was no 'stadium', having a capacity of just 2,000. Its location was also a problem, with the ferry and the train the only way of getting there from Liverpool. In order to keep in touch with his Liverpool patrons, Best opened a ticket office at his offices in Camden Street. Moreover, to promote the shows at the Tower, the weigh-ins were also held on the Liverpool side of the water at Camden Street.

Best's problems were well chronicled in the local press, particularly prior to a promotion on 19 March that featured a contest between Alf Howard and Harry Corbett of London. The *Liverpool Echo* stated that the programme on offer could fill the hall twice over. There was also talk of a Tarleton/Cuthbert rematch, but there was no way such a contest could be held in Liverpool, as there was no suitable venue to stage such a large promotion.

Towards the end of March, Best revealed that his promotions were losing money. He still had to pay top rates to the likes of Tarleton and Howard, but the limitations on numbers meant he could not generate sufficient income from the box office. In the first five weeks at the Tower he lost £291; the only promotion that paid was the Alf Howard one, but this only realised a profit of £11. Other venues such as Southport were tried but these had similar problems to New Brighton.

Best was keen to continue with quality boxing shows, and he wanted to ensure that championship boxing still came to Liverpool. He found the answer to his problem, not in a boxing arena, but at Liverpool's oldest football ground.

'Towards the end of March 1931, Best revealed that his promotions were losing money. In the first five weeks at the Tower he lost £291; the only promotion that paid was the Alf Howard one, but this only realised a profit of £11'

THE STADIUM,

PUDSEY STREET, LIVERPOOL.

Proprietors:—THE LIVERPOOL SPORTING ASSOCIATION LIMITED.

Telephone:—ROYAL 647.   Telegrams: "STADIUM," LIVERPOOL.

Articles of Agreement

entered into this _17_ day of _Dec_ 191_7_

Between The Liverpool Sporting Association Limited
(hereinafter called "The Management") of the one part and _Curley Davis_
of _Birkenhead_
(hereinafter called "the Contestant") of the other part wherein the Contestant
subject to the conditions hereinafter set out agrees to appear on the _10_
day of _Jan_ 191_8_ at the STADIUM,
PUDSEY STREET, LIVERPOOL, and box _Liscombe Moreland_
of _Nottingham_
at _Three_ stone — lbs. with 6 oz. gloves _Fifteen_ rounds of
Three minutes each with an interval of one minute between each
round fairly and to the best of his ability under the National Sporting Club Rules
(a copy of which are printed hereunder) for the sum of £_30_
to be paid to the Contestant if he wins, £_20_ if he loses the said
contest and £_25_ if the said contest is drawn and no sum to be
paid in the event of the said contest not taking place.

Copy

CONDITIONS.

1. The Contestant to weigh in at   p.m. at the Stadium on day of contest, and if overweight to forfeit the sum of £

2. The Contestant not ready to enter the ring at time specified by the Management shall be liable to forfeit £1 at the discretion of the Management.

3. The Contestant not trying, or guilty of a deliberate foul, to be disqualified, and if he be disqualified for that or any other cause to receive no sum under this Agreement.

4. No Kidney Punches allowed.

5. The Referee and Timekeeper, whose decisions respectively shall be final and binding, to be appointed by the Management.

6. In the event of any question arising which may not be provided for in these Articles, the Referee to have full power and authority to decide such question, his decision to be final, conclusive, and subject to no appeal in any Court of Law.

7. The Contestant undertaking not to box publicly ten days before the date of the contest without the consent in writing of the Management.

8. The Contestant to be certified by the Medical Officer of the Management to be in a fit condition to box.

9. The Management not to be liable for any injury or accident whatsoever to the Contestant and whether caused by the negligence of the Management, or their servants or not.

10. The sum of £   to be deposited with the Management by the Contestant at the time of signing these Articles as a guarantee of his appearance and weight.

NATIONAL SPORTING CLUB BOXING RULES.

1. All contests to be decided in a roped ring not less than 14ft. or more than 20ft. square.

2. Contestants to box in light boots or shoes (without spikes) or in socks. The gloves to be of a minimum weight of 6 oz. each. Contestants to be medically examined before entering the ring, and to weigh on the day of contest.
Should Bandages be agreed to, the length and material of same to be approved and deposited with the Management of the Club at the time of signing Articles. The length of Bandage for each or either hand not to exceed six feet, and width not to exceed one inch.

3. In all contests the number of rounds shall be specified. No contest shall exceed 15 rounds, except Championships, which shall be limited to 20 rounds. No round shall exceed three minutes in duration. The interval between the rounds shall be one minute.

4. A Contestant shall be entitled to the assistance of two seconds, whose names shall be submitted to the Committee for approval. The seconds shall leave the ring when time is called, and shall give no advice or assistance to the contestants during the progress of any round.

5. In all contests a Referee and a Timekeeper shall be appointed by the Committee. The Referee shall award a maximum number of five marks at the end of each round to the better man, and a proportionate number to the other contestant, or, when equal the maximum number to each.
If a Contestant is down, he must get up unassisted within ten seconds, his opponent meanwhile shall retire out of striking distance, and shall not resume boxing until ordered to do so by the Referee. A man is to be considered down even when he is on one or both feet, if at the same time any other part of his body is touching the ground, or when in the act of rising. A Contestant failing to continue the contest at the expiration of ten seconds shall not be awarded any marks for that round, and the contest shall then terminate.

The Referee shall decide all contests in favour of the contestant who obtains the greatest number of marks.

If at the conclusion of any round during the contest one of the contestants should attain such a lead on points as to render it an impossibility for his opponent to win or tie, he must then be declared the winner.

Marks shall be awarded for "attack," direct clean hits with the knuckle part of the glove of either hand on any part of the front or sides of the head, or body above the belt; "defence," guarding, slipping, ducking, or getting away. Where contestants are otherwise equal the majority of marks shall be given to the one who does most of the leading off or who displays the better style.

6. The Referee shall have power to disqualify a contestant for any of the following acts. For hitting below the belt, for using the pivot blow, for using the kidney punch, for hitting with the open glove, the inside or butt of the hand, or with the wrist or elbow. For holding, butting, shouldering, intentionally falling without receiving a blow, wrestling or roughing, or for any other act which he may deem foul. The Referee shall also have power to stop the contest if in his opinion a contestant is outclassed or accidentally disabled.

7. If in the opinion of the Referee a deliberate foul is committed by a contestant, such contestant shall not be entitled to any prize.

8. The breaking of any of these rules by a contestant or his seconds shall render such Contestant liable to disqualification.

9. The Referee shall decide (1) any question not provided for in these rules; (2) the interpretation of any of these rules.

Signed by the said

in the presence of

Name

Address

Description

PUDSEY CONTRACT 1918: Prior to 1929 there was Boxing Board of Control but most boxing clubs and promoters came to accept the rules of the National Sporting Club as standard

Pudsey Street's First Major Championship Fight

Although the old Pudsey Street Stadium developed a reputation as a 'graveyard of champions', its first major championship followed the formbook. The contest was between local favourite Ike Bradley and Digger Stanley for Stanley's world bantamweight title. Such was the clamour to see the fight, the Stadium Syndicate was able to double admission prices and still turn people away at the door. General opinion before the fight was that Bradley would have to knock out Stanley to win the title, as over 20 rounds Stanley's greater boxing skill would be decisive.

The first two rounds went easily in favour of the champion. Bradley was keen to force the pace but he was being out-boxed by the superior skills of Stanley. However, between the third and sixth rounds it seemed that Bradley's tactics were going to land him the title. Towards the end of the third round, Bradley got Stanley on the ropes, his efforts had the crowd cheering as he closed in. Such was the noise from the crowd that both boxers did not hear the bell to end the round, and the referee had to separate the pair. The fourth continued as the third ended – this time Bradley had Stanley on the canvas. Bradley was later to claim that the champion was down for 14 seconds, but to no avail as

Stanley was back on his feet before the referee had reached the knock-out point. Bradley continued his attacks in the fifth round, and Stanley was clearly struggling as he went down on one knee, to great boos from the crowd, to seek a breather. He was holding on, and in the clinches he was using his head in an unsporting manner. Bradley's corner were calling foul but the referee ignored their claims. It seemed only a matter of time before Stanley would fall to Bradley's famed KO punch. In the sixth round he was in further trouble from Bradley's powerful punching, with the referee cautioning the champion for holding and using his head.

However, Stanley weathered the storm. During Bradley's onslaughts he had landed quite a few telling punches of his own and these began to force Bradley back. By the halfway stage the champion was ahead on points, an advantage he increased as the contest progressed to its conclusion. Bradley still tried to force the pace but he was out-boxed, with Stanley landing telling left jabs to the head and mouth of the challenger.

At the end of the contest, many well-seasoned fight followers asserted that they had never seen a man take so much punishment as Bradley without taking a count. Although the

decision went to the champion, the crowd sportingly gave Bradley a tremendous ovation. When the boxers retired to the dressing rooms Bradley begged Stanley's manager to give him another chance at the 'Digger'. Alas, this was to be Bradley's last chance at the world title.

Fight details: Bradley weighed in at 8st 4lbs, Stanley at 8st 3lbs. Bradley had Bob Wilkinson, Fred Spike and Mr Benson in his corner. Stanley was seconded by Alf Mack, Jim Lloyd and Jim Campbell. Prices for the Bradley/Stanley title fight were more than doubled. The Saturday preceding the contest, admission charges for a top-draw bill involving Geo Rodel and Seaman Pascal were 1/- and 2/-, the balcony was 3/-, ringside cost 5/- with boxes priced at three guineas.

By 1931, prices had barely increased. For the Howard/Thake bill, February 1931, admission prices were as follows: 1/2, 2/4, 5/9 (ringside). There were no prices quoted for boxes. Unlike 1911, the bill specifically states that women would be admitted. Following the closure of Pudsey Street, big-time boxing moved to Anfield. Prices there were 2/4, 3/6, 5/9, 11/6 and 22/6. These remained fairly constant throughout the 1930s, although ringside seats for the Kane/Jurich world-title fight in 1938 were 42/-.

'Stanley was clearly struggling as he went down on one knee, to great boos from the crowd, to seek a breather. He was holding on, and in the clinches he was using his head in an unsporting manner'

DIGGER STANLEY
Digger Stanley defeated Ike Bradley on points in this hall (20 rds contest) after a great struggle.

IKE BRADLEY: The local favourite fought hard against Digger Stanley at the graveyard of champions

They Boxed at Pudsey Street

Pudsey Street Stadium attracted some of the world's best boxers. To list them all is impossible, but below is a small selection of the best local, national and international fighters that appeared there:

Alf Howard:

Howard could win a fight with a single punch, and he was a great favourite of local fight fans. One particular contest in 1929 saw Howard out-boxed by the Londoner Harry Fenn for 12 rounds in a 15-round contest. As the bell sounded for the 13th, Howard shot from his corner and landed a stinging right to the chin, followed by a flurry of blows that finished Fenn off. Howard could also box an opponent off his feet, as witnessed when he out-pointed Harry Mason of Leeds in 1930. Howard's lasting legacy to Liverpool boxing is that he was the first city-born boxer to win a European title, defeating Francois Sybille of Belgium on disqualification at Pudsey Street in January 1930 to win the lightweight crown. This was the first contest in this country to be held under International Boxing Union rules. The referee, Count Volpi, was also controversial – he was a fascist who became one of Mussolini's henchmen. Unfortunately, Howard's spell as champion was short-lived, as he lost the return with Sybille in Belgium just five months later when he failed to make the bell for the ninth round. In a total of 68 fights, Howard won 49 – 34 via knock out – lost 16 and drew three. According to Johnny Best Jnr, Howard was an excellent trainer but was unable to pull a punch, even in the gym. When asked to spar with the heavyweight Larry Gains, who was due to fight Jean Delarge at Pudsey Street, he willingly accepted. Best advised Howard to go easy as Gains was a much heavier man and a bigger hitter. Unable to comply, Howard stung Gains a few times before Gains lost his temper and knocked him out with a blow to the chin. This is one KO that does not appear on Alf's record!

Nat Williams:

Williams will not appear on many lists of Liverpool's most important boxers. However, ▶

HARD-HITTER: Alf Howard built a reputation as a fearsome puncher

ALF HOWARD—Liverpool.

Ex-European Lightweight Champion

The hardest puncher in the Game.

Has knocked-out Ernie Izzard, Geo Rose, (twice), Hadyn Williams.

Contender for Welterweight Championship.

along with Johnny Best, he did make a major contribution to Liverpool boxing. Best regarded him as one of the cleverest featherweights Liverpool has produced. He appeared on the opening night at Pudsey Street, with his son doing likewise at the Liverpool Stadium in 1932. In a period when there was a proliferation of top boxers, he took on the likes of Kid Lewis and Johnny Basham at Pudsey Street, boxing a draw on each occasion. Upon retirement he remained on the stadium staff as a second. A moving tribute was made to him on the last night of boxing at Pudsey Street.

Jimmy Wilde:

Wales has produced some first-class boxers, and in the early days of Pudsey Street several proved to be big draws. Among the best was Wilde, the 'Mighty Atom', who boxed at Pudsey Street at least 15 times, winning on each occasion. Indeed, he made a reputation in Liverpool long before he was known in London. His greatest triumph in Liverpool was when he won the world flyweight title on 24 April 1916 – the first international world flyweight championship bout ever held. To win the title, Wilde knocked out Johnny Rosner of America in the 11th round. He would finally lose this title in 1923 to Pancho Villa in New York.

Freddie Welsh:

Another world and European champion to box at Pudsey Street was the lightweight Welsh. He boxed several times at the stadium, including an outstanding contest against Eddie Beattie of Scotland in March 1913. Beattie had Welsh on the floor in the ninth, only for Welsh to recover sufficiently to win the 20-round contest on points.

Ted 'Kid' Lewis:

One of Britain's greatest boxers, Lewis was the first boxer to win British titles at three different weights – welterweight, middleweight and light-heavyweight. He was also European champion at welterweight. Out of 300 contests, Lewis only boxed three times at Pudsey Street. That he boxed there at all indicates the tremendous pull of the Liverpool stadium. His first contest against Jim Lloyd ▶

WELSH: The lightweight champion beat Eddie Beattie at Pudsey Street in 1913

PAT O'KEEFE

Middleweight Champion and Lonsdale Belt Holder. Appeared here several times.

TANCY LEE

Tancy Lee who often appeared here k.o. Jimmy Wilde at N.S.C. but Wilde reversed the decision in a return by k.o. Lee.

JOE JEANNETTE

Joe Jeannette who k.o. Geo Rodel the South African Heavyweight in the 1st round at Stadium in 1911.

▶ ended in a points victory over 10 rounds. Two weeks later, on 16 January 1913, he returned to face local favourite Nat Williams in a catchweight contest that ended in a draw. His final bout was against Kid Doyle of Manchester, who he knocked out in the 11th round in April 1920. Lewis had won the British welterweight title just three weeks earlier when he had knocked out Johnny Bee in the fourth round at Holborn Stadium, London.

Bombardier Billy Wells:
The first boxer to win the Lonsdale Belt for the heavyweight division boxed Bandsman Dick Rice on two occasions at Pudsey Street. Wells won each contest, the second on a first-round knock out. Wells met the great French boxer Georges Carpentier twice for the European heavyweight title, but was knocked out on each occasion. Incidentally, Carpentier also appeared at Pudsey Street in an exhibition bout before he sailed from Liverpool to America in 1921 to meet Jack Dempsey for the world heavyweight title. In front of a crowd of 80,000, Dempsey knocked Carpentier out in the fourth round.

Johnny Basham:
Basham was another fine Welsh boxer who eventually settled in Liverpool. In a career of 45 contests, more than half were staged at Pudsey Street, his strong punching power making him a great favourite at the stadium. One such fight, however, led to the death of the South African-born Jewish boxer Harry Price. Fighters in those days boxed with much greater regularity; sometimes boxers would be in the ring on a weekly basis. The Basham/Price bout took place on 21 August 1913. It was to be Basham's ninth fight at Pudsey Street in that calendar year. Price, meanwhile, had fought a gruelling 15-round contest with Jules Dubourg just two weeks before the scheduled fight with Basham.

Prior to the contest, a change of referee was required as James Butler, a leading boxing writer and a top-class referee, reported sick – his place being taken by the promoter Arnold Wilson. Wilson was in a difficult position in his dual capacity, so elected to handle the contest from outside the ring. Refereeing boxing contests from outside the ropes had been commonplace at the National Sporting Club and the Liverpool boxing clubs, but the practice had been discarded in favour of an interventionist approach.

From the outset Price took the fight to Basham but this only gave the skilful Welshman the opportunity to pick-off his opponent at will. By the ninth round Price was wobbling but still kept coming forward, taking more punishment in the process. The 11th round proved to be the end. Basham seemed to realise that Price was badly hurt but as Price kept coming forward he was left with little choice but to fend him off. Evading a right swing from Price, Basham countered by hitting the South African in the mouth with a strong left and followed through with a right to the jaw – punches that put Price on the canvas. Even the crowd were telling Price to stay down but at the count of nine he staggered to his feet, only to be met with another stinging right. This time he was counted out.

When Price failed to respond, doctors were called into the ring, and soon afterwards he was taken to hospital. Meanwhile, Basham was escorted from the ring by plainclothes policemen, who had taken his gloves and bandages as specimens for any inquiry that might follow. When he had dressed, Basham was taken to Dale Street police station where he was charged with causing grievous bodily harm. Arnold Wilson and Johnny Best, Basham's second on the night, were also taken to the police station but were released without charge.

After spending the night in the cells, Basham awoke to the news that Price had died. He now faced the possibility of being charged with manslaughter. Throughout the night, Wilson, Best and Liverpool's sugar king, Mr Fairie, worked hard for Basham and engaged a top Liverpool solicitor on his behalf. In the meantime, a large crowd had gathered outside the police station in support of Basham. In light of this difficult situation, the police took the accused out through the back entrance to the courtrooms. After speeches and cross-examinations of all those involved, and close inspection of Basham's gloves and bandages, the case was adjourned ▶

'When Price failed to respond, doctors were called into the ring, and soon afterwards he was taken to hospital. Meanwhile, Basham was escorted from the ring by plainclothes policemen, who had taken his gloves and bandages as specimens for any inquiry that might follow'

FREDDIE WELSH

Freddie Welsh boxed several times at the Stadium and had a narrow escape from defeat in his contest with Eddie Beattie, Scotland, who had Welsh down for a count of 9. Welsh won on points.

JOHNNY SUMMER   V.   DIXIE KID

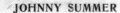

Dixie Kid k.o. Johnny Sumner in 2 rds at 10st. 2lb. weigh in at Ringside. Dixie Kid boxed one of the greatest contest seen at the Stadium against Harry Lewis the American Middleweight who knocked the Dixie Kid out.

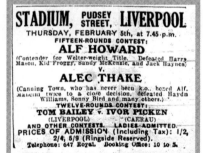

HOWARD V THAKE: Taken from *Boxing, Racing and Football*, 4 February 1931

THE 'MIGHTY ATOM': Jimmy Wilde won at least 15 fights at Pudsey Street

for a week. Meanwhile, Basham, Best, Wilson, Fairie and many Liverpool sportsmen attended the funeral of Price and accompanied his coffin to the Jewish cemetery, where he was buried.

When the case was re-opened, the magistrate cleared Basham, stating that the contest had been fairly conducted and fought in a sporting manner. This was an important verdict, as a guilty one would have jeopardised the future of boxing. However, it did highlight once again that the sport needed strong regulation to ensure the greatest level of safety for boxers.

Basham returned to the ring two months later at Pudsey Street, beating Eddie Beattie on points over 15 rounds. He went on to win British, British Empire and European titles at welterweight. His only title fight at Pudsey Street, for the vacant European welterweight belt in 1915, ended in defeat when the Swiss Albert Badoud won by KO in the ninth round. Basham's worst memory of the stadium, however, was the night he fought Harry Price.

American boxers:
In the first decades of the 20th century, Pudsey Street attracted many top American boxers including Sam McVea, Joe Jeanette, The Dixie Kid, Harry and Willie Lewis, Alf Langford, Bob Scanlon, Harry Stone, Fred Yelle, Noah Brusso, Blink McClosky, Artie Edwards, Young Pierce and Fred Sydney. Many of these boxers were black or Jewish, some of them staying on Merseyside for considerable periods hence their regular appearances at Pudsey Street. Perhaps the finest of them all was 'The Dixie Kid', whose real name was Aaron Brown. A great favourite at Pudsey Street, The Dixie Kid

defended his world welterweight title against Johnny Summers in November 1911. Summers was held in high regard by Arnold Wilson, seeing him as a key crowd puller. The Dixie Kid, however, was too good for Summers, knocking him out in the second round.

The Dixie Kid was involved in one of the greatest contests ever seen on Merseyside against his fellow American Harry Lewis. The Kid was expected to win with ease, but Lewis knocked him out, after seven pulsating rounds, in the eighth round. It was such results that gained Pudsey Street the title as the 'Graveyard of Champions'.

In the days when boxers did not have a dedicated team of trainers, Lewis had Johnny Summers and George Rodel in his corner while Ike Bradley attended to The Kid.

CHURCHMAN'S CIGARETTES

GEORGES CARPENTIER

CHURCHMAN'S CIGARETTES

BILLY WELLS

CHURCHMAN'S CIGARETTES

TED (KID) LEWIS

LEFT TO RIGHT: Georges Carpentier, Bombardier Billy Wells and Ted 'Kid' Lewis

Volante v Tarleton – Four Great Battles

Two of Liverpool's finest boxers from the inter-war years were the Liverpool-born Italian Dom Volante and Anfield-born Nel Tarleton. For a two-year period between 1926 and 1928 they were the greatest of rivals, a rivalry that only served to deepen their friendship for each other. The first three contests between them were held at the Pudsey Street Stadium, the final bout being an open-air fight at Breck Park before a crowd of 17,000 – which was then a record attendance for a boxing show in the north.

Volante won the first contest on points without too much trouble – he was a much more experienced boxer than Tarleton at that time. The second contest took place six months later on 3 March 1927, with Tarleton reversing the decision, securing a points win over 15 rounds. Despite their deepening friendship, boxing fans were clamouring for a 'decider' to determine who was the better of the two boxers. This took place on 1 September 1927, resulting in the ever-improving Tarleton winning on points.

After three contests the rivalry between them died somewhat. Moreover, Volante and Tarleton were often seen together training and had no real desire to batter the hell out of each other once again. However, the two were a big box-office draw, and ideal opponents to fill the vast spaces around the Breck Park Greyhound Track.

The added attraction of another Volante/Tarleton contest was that the vacant Northern Area featherweight title was up for grabs. Consequently, the two met for the fourth time on 26 July 1928, and it was to be the most controversial of their four fights. From the outset, Volante took the fight to Tarleton – by Tarleton's own admission he was on the receiving end of a battering for the first seven rounds.

'When the fight started Dom tore into me in his usual non-stop style, and I was powerless against his relentless punching. I think he used (just) about every punch in the game, and he battered me from the sound of the first bell to the end of each round. I could not keep him out – he was too strong for me...by the end of the sixth round he was well ahead on points'

The seventh round, however, was to be a turning point in the fight. The round began and ended with Volante on top; the crowd were throwing their hats into the air with excitement, such was the power of his performance. When the bell sounded, Tarleton sat down in Volante's corner in an apparent state of disarray. He then went to his own corner where he clung onto the ropes. His second climbed into the ring, asking Nel if he was all right. When the bell sounded for the eighth round, Tarleton came out with his arms all limp. Volante, seeing a chance to end the contest, came tearing at his opponent. But suddenly, Tarleton sprang into life. Volante had taken the bait, leaving himself exposed to a resounding counter attack from the seemingly beaten Tarleton. The pattern of the fight was reversed, with Volante being forced back by his skilful opponent.

At the final bell the verdict was still in the balance but the referee, Bombardier Wells, raised Nel's hand. There was a mixed response from the crowd, with one spectator throwing a chair at Wells as he left the ring. Referring to the verdict, Tarleton said: "I think I caused a surprise when I suddenly sprang into life. I threw more punches in that round than I have done in any round since...If Dom had continued his tearaway tactics he might have won but he did not care to take the chance...I think I deserved the decision."

The only time Dom and Nel would appear on the same bill in future would be at music halls or charity exhibitions. Dom would play the mouth organ and Nel would dance to his tune. ▶

POWER PUNCHING: Dom Volante, a great favourite at Pudsey Street, delivers another knock-out blow (opposite)

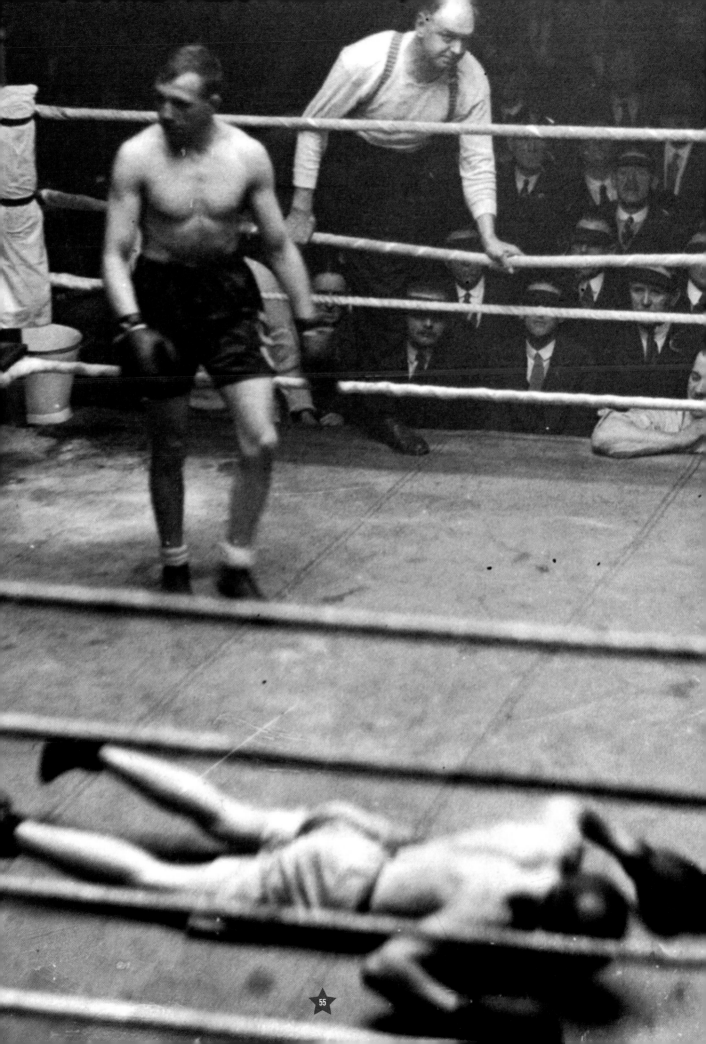

▶ **Dom Volante – A champion in all but name:**

In more than 140 professional contests, Dom Volante took on and beat boxers such as Nel Tarleton, Harry Corbett, Johnny Cuthbert and Seaman Tommy Watson. All these boxers were to go on and win the British featherweight title. Volante, however, only ever had one shot at the title, and that was against Johnny Cuthbert at the London Olympia.

Volante was born in an area which became synonymous with Liverpool boxing – Little Italy. Immigrant Italians had settled in the Gerard Street area of Liverpool from about 1870. In most immigrant areas life was a daily struggle, a situation that formed tightly-knit communities. Out of such places many of Britain's finest boxers emerged. Apart from Volante, first-rate boxers such as Tony Butcher and Joe Curran emerged out of Little Italy, many of whom trained in Dom Vario's gymnasium in Cazneau Street. Volante, however, was the finest of them all.

Johnny Cuthbert was always keen to meet boxers such as Volante and Tarleton as he always fought 'on the gate' and he knew that Liverpool's two finest boxers would always pull a full house. As with Tarleton, Volante fought Cuthbert four times with all the contests going the 15-round distance. Cuthbert beat Volante at their first meeting at Pudsey Street in May 1928 but lost the return bout some 15 months later at the same venue.

Before their next meeting, Cuthbert beat Harry Corbett (whom Volante had beaten at Breck Park Greyhound Track in September 1928) in May 1929 to win the British featherweight title. He had won the title in

1927, beating Johnny Curley at the National Sporting Club. Cuthbert now needed one more successful defence to win the Lonsdale Belt outright. At this stage in British boxing, only contests sanctioned by the National Sporting Club could be regarded as British title fights. Moreover, at this point in time the NSC would not sanction title fights outside London, although this policy was soon to change.

So when Cuthbert came to Liverpool on 1 August 1929 to meet Dom Volante he was British champion, but their fight could not be for the British title. Before a packed Pudsey Street Stadium Volante, in typical style, took the contest to Cuthbert and beat him on points over 15 rounds, which was the recognised championship distance.

Thus Volante's claim for a crack at the title now became unstoppable. However, it took nine months before it could be organised. Between the Pudsey Street fight with Volante and the return at the London Olympia on 22 May 1930, Cuthbert had 12 non-title fights, winning 11 and drawing the other. During the same period Volante also remained unbeaten, scoring a series of wins in America including two victories at the famous Madison Square Gardens in front of 18,000 spectators. The return fight generated great interest on Merseyside, witnessed by the hundreds of fight fans that travelled to London in the hope of seeing a Liverpool boxer win the Lonsdale Belt for the first time.

Press reports from the time indicate that Dom boxed a superb contest, taking the fight to Cuthbert in typical Volante style. Johnny Best, who travelled down with Volante, had him ahead by the 13th round, his feeling being that Cuthbert's only chance was to knock out Dom. As the bell for the final round sounded Volante came out in his tearaway style. He was not content to coast. Cuthbert, however, like a true champion, met the onslaught with a flurry of counter-punches that drew blood from Volante's nose. Such was the power of Cuthbert's punches, many felt Volante would fall but he hung on for what many believed to be a famous victory. However, the referee had other ideas, giving the verdict to Cuthbert who had now won the Lonsdale Belt outright. Sportingly, Dom congratulated Cuthbert, saying: "I have done my best. The winner is one of the best lads in the game." ▶

'First-rate boxers such as Tony Butcher and Joe Curran emerged out of Little Italy, many of whom trained in Dom Vario's gymnasium in Cazneau Street. Volante, however, was the finest of them all'

TARLETON V VOLANTE: At Breck Park.
The referee is Bombardier Billy Wells

▶ Despite his disappointment Volante continued with his boxing career, appearing on the final night at Pudsey Street and on several occasions at the new Liverpool Stadium. He met Cuthbert for a fourth time in 1932, but lost once more on points. By then the peak of his career had passed. He retired in 1936 as one of the finest boxers never to win a title. In retirement, he was a well-respected gymnasium instructor on the luxury Cunard liner Britannic.

In the words of Johnny Best: "Dom Volante had few equals."

Nel Tarleton – The Pudsey Street years

Before taking on Johnny Cuthbert for his British title on 6 November 1930, Tarleton had fought in nearly 70 contests, with at least 45 of these taking place at the Pudsey Street Stadium. Pudsey Street was the place of his apprenticeship as well as being the venue of his first tilt at the British featherweight title. Compare this with modern-day champions who can sometimes be lined up for a national title within their first 10 fights. The significance of Tarleton's fight with Cuthbert was that it was the first time a Lonsdale Belt had been competed for in the city, and only the second time it had been contested for outside of the capital. In 1909 the National Sporting Club, which had established the belt to enhance the status of British championship fights at the NSC, had been forced to sell its headquarters at Covent Garden. During the 1920s it had been staging Lonsdale Belt contests at various venues around London. Dom Volante had taken on Cuthbert in May 1930 for the British featherweight title at the London Olympia, but lost on points over 15 rounds. Now

Tarleton not only had the chance to be the first Liverpool boxer to win a Lonsdale Belt, but the first to do it at the spiritual home of Liverpool boxing.

Tarleton's reputation in the build-up to the fight had been greatly enhanced on the back of a successful tour of America. Moreover, Tarleton had built up a formidable following at Pudsey Street where he had remained unbeaten for more than three years. The fight was billed as the fighter (Cuthbert) v the boxer – the contrasting styles only serving to heighten interest in the title fight. Queues to get into the stadium were formed as early 10am on the day of the fight. Prior to the doors being opened, the queue extended a quarter of a mile up London Road. Inevitably, thousands were turned away but they did not leave the area. Instead, they assembled outside in the hope of soaking up some of the atmosphere. Such was the enthusiasm that many younger fans climbed on the glass roof from where they could look down on the ring. Even in the days before big outdoor screens that today show key sporting events, sports fans would gather in the street to absorb the atmosphere of a live sporting occasion, to hear the roars from an enclosed stadium and await the outcome of a key sporting contest.

The fight itself followed predicated lines, with Cuthbert the fighter taking the contest to Tarleton. However, such was Tarleton's skill that he was able to pick-off Cuthbert at will. The fight reports state that the challenger 'boxed magnificently and he had Cuthbert worried by dazzling footwork and clever defence. Cuthbert could simply not hit him...Cuthbert was given a boxing lesson.' In sport, unfortunately, you do not always get what you deserve. After 10 rounds, Tarleton

was so far ahead on points that it was felt Cuthbert needed a KO to win. He did rally in the last three rounds but at the final bell the stadium thought Liverpool had its first Lonsdale Belt. Referee C.B. Thomas thought otherwise and gave the contest as a draw.

Both Jack 'Kid' Berg and Jimmy Wilde, who were at the ringside, were asked their opinions and both gave the verdict to Tarleton – with Berg stating that "he (Tarleton) outboxed the champion well enough". Some felt that Tarleton had made a mistake in the last round by standing off Cuthbert to avoid a KO. Tarleton explained this later, saying: "I won that fight, I was so far in front that I stalled deliberately in the last round knowing that he had to knock me out to win." Tarleton's manager, Ted Broadribb, described the fight as such: "If both men had been armed with fencing foils Tarleton would have cut Cuthbert to pieces." He did say, however, that Nel should have carried the fight to Cuthbert in the last round to make absolutely certain of the win.

The crowd concurred with the post-fight verdicts and made their displeasure known. Even Lord Lonsdale, making his first visit to the city, could not calm the crowd. When he eventually could be heard he declared that he had never witnessed such a well-organised show and congratulated Johnny Best for his efforts. Lonsdale was to have strong links with the new Liverpool Stadium when it emerged in 1932.

Both Cuthbert and Tarleton declared their willingness for a rematch, a contest that took place in Liverpool but at a venue that was new to boxing – and one that had a more positive outcome for Liverpool.

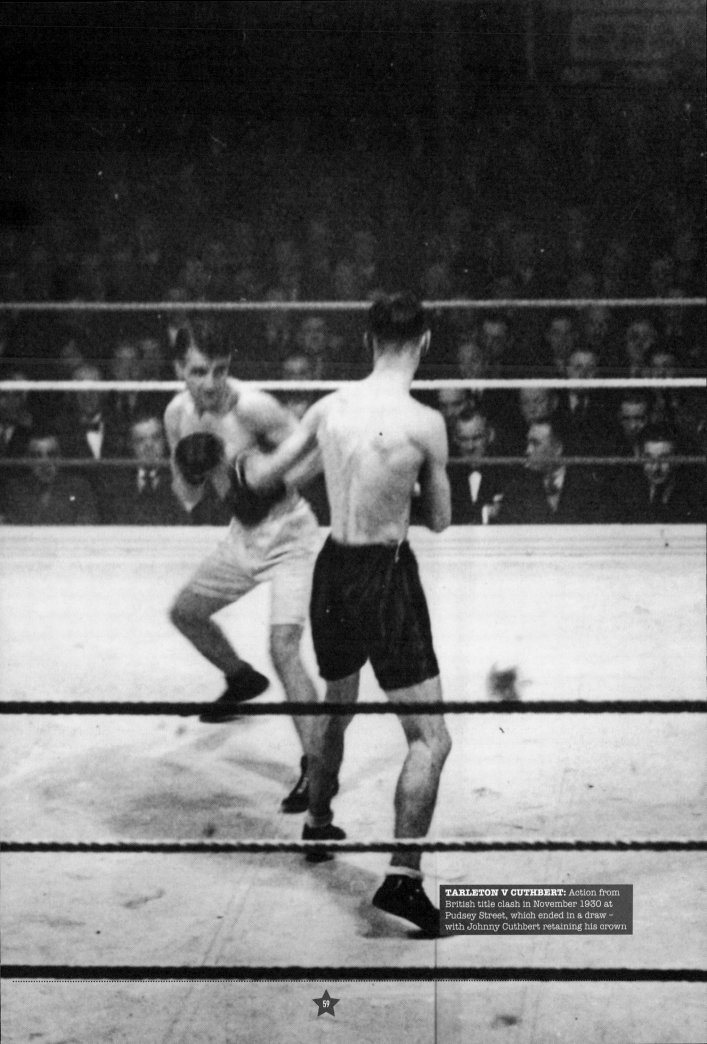

TARLETON V CUTHBERT: Action from British title clash in November 1930 at Pudsey Street, which ended in a draw – with Johnny Cuthbert retaining his crown

Did You Know?

The runners for the Liverpool Marathon would gather at the Pudsey Street Stadium (right) to receive their race briefings. The race would usually begin from St George's Hall and end at Liverpool football ground, another historic venue for boxing in the city.

THEY'RE OFF: In the '40s and '50s, the marathon started on St George's Plateau

Final Night at Pudsey Street – 5 March 1931

The final night at Pudsey Street saw emotion typical of a boxing arena that was rooted in the community. Prior to the evening's proceedings, an appeal was made on behalf of Nat Williams, described by Johnny Best as one of the cleverest featherweights Liverpool had produced. The response to the appeal, made by Ted Broadribb, mirrors the solidarity boxing has for one of its own favoured sons. Williams had appeared on the first bill at Pudsey Street and later drew with top boxers such as Johnny Basham and Ted Lewis. Nat, a father of seven, had fallen on hard times and was in poor health, having been forced to give up his job as a second at the stadium. A total of £95 was raised in his support.

Top of the bill on the last night was Dom Volante, one of the boxers who had done so much to revive the fortunes of Pudsey Street after Best's takeover in 1928. His opponent was Teddy Brown of Forest Hall. Volante put on a typical, bustling performance, tearing into Brown with powerful punches to the body. Following seven punishing rounds, Brown was forced to retire in the eighth.

What followed next, however, almost made the evening's boxing irrelevant. Mr C. Shaw, the referee for the final contest, thanked Johnny Best for rescuing Liverpool boxing in 1928 and for restoring it to great popularity within the city. Best responded by saying that he was in negotiations for a new site and that there was every chance of Liverpool having a new permanent boxing hall within 12 months. In the meantime he would continue with promotions at New Brighton Tower.

Dom Volante roused the crowd with a mouth-organ rendition of 'For He's A Jolly Good Fellow' to great cheers from the crowd. He then praised Best for being the cleanest man in boxing. Best responded by saying that his biggest ambition was to bring a Lonsdale Belt to Liverpool.

The 4,000-strong crowd left the old arena not knowing that the new Liverpool Stadium, which would emerge within 18 months of the closure of Pudsey Street, would develop into an even greater boxing arena and host many title fights. However, before then Best would fulfil his dream of bringing a Lonsdale Belt to the city, albeit at a venue that had no links to boxing; a venue that had not even entered into his thoughts on the last night of boxing at Pudsey Street.

'The 4,000-strong crowd left the old arena not knowing that the new Liverpool Stadium, which would emerge within 18 months of the closure of Pudsey Street, would develop into an even greater boxing arena'

LIVERPOOL
STADIUM
1911 GRAND FINAL NIGHT 1931
Thursday, March 5th, 1931.

Under the direction of - - - - JOHNNY BEST.

SOUVENIR PROGRAMME.
THREEPENCE.

Henry Hughes & Co., Printers, 37-39, Vauxhall Road, Liverpool.

Farewell Performance At The Stadium

PROGRAMME.

1.—Six 3-Minutes Rounds Contest.
OS PARRY, Wrexham
versus
JOHNNY DRISCOLL, Liverpool

2.—Ten 3-Minutes Rounds Contest.
FRANKY HUGHES, Shotton
versus
BILLY BYRON, Walkden

3.—Fifteen 3-Minutes Rounds Contest.
Weigh in 9st. 4lb. at 2 p.m.
DOM VOLANTE
Liverpool
versus
TEDDY BROWN
Forest Hall

4.—Twelve 3-Minutes Rounds Contest.
Weigh in 9st. at 7 p.m.   £10 Aside.
BENNY HOWELLS, Wrexham
versus
BERT WALLACE, Liverpool

5.—Ten 3-Minutes Rounds Contest.
STAN HIGSON, Liverpool
versus
BILLY COOKE, Oldham

Official Timekeeper and Clerk of Scales:
Mr. CRICHTON SLIGHT.
"Cri" of the Liverpool Express.

Referee : Mr. TOM GAMBLE.

M.C. : Mr. C. SHAW.

It was a sad occasion for Merseyside sportsfolk when the Liverpool Stadium put on its final box... notable farewell—the last night at the old Stadium in Pudsey Street, which closed on March 5... faces in this group. In the centre is the late Mr. Johnny Best, with his youngest son, George, a... others are members of the Stadium staff, many of whom were still in service last week. On the... the late Dr. Regan.

PUDSEY STREET FAREWELL:
(Clockwise from top left) Final night programme cover and bill; how George Green saw it; boxers past, present and future pay their last tribute to the old arena. The ring from Pudsey Street was used at Anfield for the Tarleton v Cuthbert fight in 1931

★ ANFIELD STADIUM ★

ANFIELD SHOWPIECE: Jackie Jurich ducks to avoid Peter Kane during their world flyweight title bout in 1938

How Boxing Came to Anfield

Anfield is one of the great but forgotten British boxing stadiums. In a period when British title fights had only just been sanctioned outside London, Anfield hosted a dozen and more British title contests and eliminators, plus two world title fights. In all, over 600,000 spectators watched boxing at Anfield between 1931 and 1949. Moreover, many of the main attractions at the promotions were top Liverpool boxers such as Nel Tarleton, Ginger Foran, Alf Howard, Peter Kane, Ernie Roderick and Stan Rowan. Of this list, all bar Howard and Foran won a major title at Anfield. Perhaps the two stand-out boxers from the list are Nel Tarleton, who became the first Liverpool boxer to win a Lonsdale Belt in 1931; and Peter Kane, who won the world flyweight title, in 1938.

Boxing came to Anfield soon after the old Liverpool Stadium in Pudsey Street had been demolished. Between its closure and the first night at Anfield, on 1 October 1931, professional boxing within Liverpool took place under Johnny Best promotions at the Lyric Theatre, Everton Valley, and at St Martin's Hall, Scotland Road, which were promoted by Jack Dare. In addition to events at these venues, Best promoted a charity show at the HQ of the Liverpool Scottish that featured local favourite Alf Howard in December 1931. At this show Dixie Dean was the guest of honour, helping with a raffle that raised a further £30 for charity. Following the closure of Pudsey Street, Best had been looking for a large venue to host championship boxing but Anfield was not initially on his radar. The catalyst for staging boxing here was the British title fight between Nel Tarleton and Johnny Cuthbert of Sheffield. Tarleton and Cuthbert had met at Pudsey Street in 1930 for Cuthbert's title but the contest had ended in a draw. Both boxers were keen on a rematch and one had been scheduled for Sheffield, only for it to fall through after Ted Broadribb, Tarleton's manager, questioned certain details regarding the fight arrangements. Into this vacuum stepped

Johnny Best, who obtained the agreement of Cuthbert and Tarleton to stage the contest in Liverpool. However, Best did not have a venue suitable enough to stage such a huge fight, and until this could be resolved details could not be finalised.

Best, of course, had developed a big reputation for staging major championship fights during his short tenure at Pudsey Street. But despite his impressive reputation, without a suitable stadium Best could not host the fight that was destined to bring Liverpool its first Lonsdale Belt and fulfil Best's dream, which he expressed in the ring on the last night at Pudsey Street. The solution to his problem came via a chance discussion with Ernest 'Bee' Edwards of the *Liverpool Echo*, who suggested to Best that he try Anfield. To help Best, Edwards wrote a letter to the Liverpool board of directors offering £100 for the hire of the ground. Initially, the directors of Liverpool Football Club were not keen to host boxing because they feared encroachment by the crowd onto the pitch. However, these fears were allayed when Bee agreed to place a piece in his newspaper column appealing to the crowd not to walk or stand on the playing area. The hire agreement could not have included opening up the Kop as the Anfield minutes of 6 October 1931 reveal that Best was asked for an additional fee for use of the stand. Best offered £65, which was accepted by the board of directors.

For the Nel Talerton/Al Foreman contest on 17 March 1932, Best was charged £200, but his request to set up 400 ringside seats was

turned down by the board – they were concerned about damaging the playing surface. However, Best was obviously impressed with the facilities at Anfield because in April 1932 he contacted the board once more to request use of the ground during the summer months, offering the club 7.5 per cent of the gate receipts or a minimum of £75 for each occasion the ground was used. His request was duly accepted. Terms for the 1934 title fights were the same as for 1932, but this time Best's request for ringside seats was accepted.

An intriguing question arises from these events: would boxing have come to Anfield if the scheduled Sheffield promotion had fallen through, or if Best had not found the ideal venue via a chance conversation? The answer to this is of course inconclusive, but what is certain is that the Tarleton/Cuthbert fight changed the course of Liverpool's boxing history in more ways than one. Anfield provided a platform for Liverpool to stage world and British title fights on a consistent basis for the first time in its history. Moreover, the impact of promotions at Anfield paved the way for title fights to be staged at the soon-to-be-opened Liverpool Stadium.

Between 1931 and 1949 a total of 27 boxing promotions took place at Anfield. Pudsey Street may have offered Best a way into top boxing promotions while the Liverpool Stadium cemented his position as a top promoter, but it was Anfield that firmly established Best as one of the leading promoters in the boxing game. In the 1930s, prior to the outbreak of war, Best staged 20 ▶

'Would boxing have come to Anfield if the scheduled Sheffield promotion hadn't fallen through, or if Best had not found the ideal venue via a chance conversation?'

PRE-FIGHT TEST: One-time Liverpool striker Cyril Done (right), amongst the men in the ring at Anfield

promotions at Anfield, a further three were held during the war with another four held between 1946 and 1949. While the 1930s mark the high point for boxing at Anfield, it would be wrong to overlook the significance of open-air boxing in wartime or the importance of the British title fights that took place there in 1947 and 1949.

Open-air boxing had first been tried at Breck Park in 1928. However, its lack of cover for spectators meant that good attendances were too dependent upon the weather. The Tarleton/Volante contest in 1928 had drawn a big crowd but other promotions had been poorly supported. But because of its intimacy and its large capacity, Anfield was a different proposition to the open spaces of a greyhound track.

In 1928 the Kop, capable of holding 28,000 spectators, had been roofed making it the largest covered terrace in the country. Moreover, Anfield had been developing a reputation as a venue that would support sports other than football. For example, several years prior to its first boxing promotion in 1931, the Liverpool Marathon had finished at the stadium, the finish usually coinciding with half-time during the match. So a combination of good spectator facilities, a developing tradition of hosting other sports plus Johnny Best's desire to host another British title fight in Liverpool all led to Anfield becoming an established boxing venue.

The Tarleton/Cuthbert British featherweight title contest at Anfield was held on 1 October 1931. Preparations for the fight are worth recalling as they offer a unique insight into how early open-air boxing promotions were organised.

Firstly, there was the location of the ring to consider, preparations for which were meticulous. The ring was placed just past the players' tunnel towards the Kop. This enabled maximum use of the Paddock, the Main Stand and the Kop. The old ring from Pudsey Street was used, and was erected on a platform that was four feet from the ground. The ring height was calculated to give optimum vantage points to those standing on the terraces. The whole structure was mounted on duckboard to both protect the pitch and to ensure that the structure would not sink in case of heavy rain.

Having erected the ring, a gantry was built above it that could take 25 powerful spotlights, which would illuminate the fighting area. The lights that were used gave out light to the 'equivalent of 100,000 candle-power'. It has to be remembered that in the 1930s football grounds did not have floodlighting. Moreover, most open-air promotions had hitherto taken place in daylight hours, so illuminating an outside sporting event was pioneering work. Promotions at Breck Park, for example, took place in the summer and began at 7pm, finishing before darkness had set in.

Initially on fight nights at Anfield only two sections of the ground were used – the Kop and the Main Stand/Paddock areas. Although consideration for the safety of spectators was seen as essential during the fights, the terraces and the Main Stand were in the dark. The only lighting came from the spectators' matches as they lit their cigarettes. Indeed, the reports of the day comment upon the dramatic effect of these

lighted cigarettes flickering against the dark background of the terraces. The whole set-up was ready-made to generate a great atmosphere, and just like modern-day Anfield, which is at its best during night matches, the atmosphere on an Anfield fight night was something quite special.

During the 1930s Liverpool produced some of the finest boxers ever to grace the British ring. This meant that Liverpool boxers were often challenging for world, European, Commonwealth or British titles. Many such title fights took place at Anfield, and on most occasions the local boxer was victorious.

The great favourite of the Anfield crowd in the first half of the 1930s was Nel Tarleton, who appeared at the ground on seven occasions. Four of these contests were for British title fights, and on three occasions Tarleton emerged the victor, his first victory in 1931 being in a rematch against Johnny Cuthbert. Anfield's first world title fight in September 1934 saw Tarleton lose to the great Freddie Miller on points; a return nine months later at the Stanley Greyhound Track saw Miller prevail once more.

Following the great success of the Tarleton/Cuthbert promotion, Johnny Best was keen to continue professional boxing at Anfield, as it was one of the only Liverpool venues capable of hosting large boxing tournaments. Moreover, with plans for the new Liverpool Stadium well advanced, he was aware that he had to keep big-time professional boxing in the public eye. Therefore it is of little surprise that in 1932 Best promoted a total of six major tournaments at the ground – the last being just a month before the new stadium opened. Tarleton featured in two of these promotions against boxers of a high calibre. The first was against Al Foreman, the British lightweight champion, on the eve of the Grand National.

The Tarleton/Foreman contest, although a non-title fight, was billed as a meeting of champions. However, a dispute during the weigh-in nearly led to the meeting of champions being called off. It had been agreed beforehand that Foreman's weight would not be publicly disclosed. However, at the weigh-in it was revealed that Foreman was inside the 9st 9lbs lightweight limit, which meant that Tarleton could legitimately claim Foreman's title should he win. This resulted in the Foreman management team ▶

'While the 1930s mark the high point for boxing at Anfield it would be wrong to overlook the significance of open-air boxing in wartime or the importance of the British title fights that took place there in 1946 and 1949'

QUITE A DRAW: A preview of fight night 23 May 1932, from the *Liverpool Echo*

▶ immediately withdrawing from the contest. Best spent the rest of the day trying to salvage what was only his second promotion at Anfield. Failure to deliver the main attraction of the evening could have had long-term implications for staging top boxing tournaments at the ground. Right up to the last moment it looked like the fight would not take place, and news of the dispute spread around the city, a situation that adversely affected the attendance. Agreement between the parties was not reached until an hour before the two boxers were due to enter the ring. Eventually, to safeguard Foreman's title, it was agreed that the contest would be over 12 rounds instead of the championship-standard of 15. It was just as well that Foreman's title was not contested, because Tarleton produced what was for many contemporaries a masterclass of boxing to outpoint the lightweight champion.

Tarleton's second opponent of 1932 was Panama Al Brown, the world bantamweight champion. Once again the build-up to the fight was dogged with complications, this time solely in the Tarleton camp. A few days before the fight Tarleton was diagnosed with pleurisy and was advised not to enter the

Last Night's Boxing Show At Anfield

JACK DOYLE OF IRELAND. THE MOST DISCUSSED BOXER OF TO-DAY.

THEY SAY WITH EXPERIENCE DOYLE SHOULD BECOME A CHAMPION, BUT IF HE IS GOING TO KNOCK OUT ALL HIS OPPONENTS IN THE FIRST ROUND HOW CAN HE GAIN THE EXPERIENCE?

TH'T BROW OF A BHOY 'E IS ENTIORELY

GOOD-NIGHT EVERYBODY, GOOD-NIGHT.

THIS IS BOBBY SHIELDS WHO CAME FROM SCOTLAND TO MEET MR DOYLE.

I THINK THE JOURNEY MUST HAVE MADE HIM TIRED BECAUSE HE WENT TO SLEEP IN THE FIRST ROUND.

HOWARD DID GET HIS FAMOUS RIGHT HOME BUT IT WAS AFTER THE SHOW WAS OVER

BARNEY KIESWETTER RESEMBLES JIM DRISCOLL EVEN IF HE HAD BROUGHT HIS BIKE WITH HIM.

DON'T THINK HOWARD COULD HAVE CAUGHT KIESWETTER IN MORE WAYS THAN ONE.

TOON TIME: *Liverpool Echo* review of Anfield boxing on 22 July 1932

ring by his doctor. This was a serious condition for Tarleton as he only had one fully functioning lung, a condition he had had since childhood after contracting TB. Tarleton's condition was kept a secret but it did not prevent him putting on a fantastic display against a man with a much longer reach. After 15 rounds of high-level boxing the referee could not separate the boxers, declaring the contest a draw. The decision was not well received by the 30,000 crowd, which clearly felt that the home favourite had won.

It was not just Liverpool boxers that pulled in the crowds. Ireland's Jack Doyle was the big attraction at the July promotion of 1932. Doyle confirmed that he was a genuine contender for the British heavyweight title by knocking out his opponent, the Scottish champion Bobby Shields, in the first round. It was Doyle's 32nd knock out in 33 contests. The other big attraction was the home-based Alf Howard, who was soundly beaten on points by the South African Barney Kieswetter. Howard's career, following a series of injuries, was now in freefall and he failed to live up to his reputation as a possible British champion.

In the audience at the July meeting was Lord Lonsdale, who had been invited to the city to lay the foundation stone of the new Liverpool Stadium. The August promotion was scheduled to be the last-ever boxing night at Anfield, underlying the significance of Lord Lonsdale's presence at the previous meeting. Top of the bill was Barney Kieswetter, who defeated Joe Rostron of Heywood on points. Of local interest was the growing stature of Ginger Foran, making his fifth appearance of the year at Anfield, who stopped Bert Kirby of Birmingham in the 10th round. As it transpired there was another meeting in September 1932, this time an international affair that involved boxers from Canada taking on British boxers. The evening was dominated by the visitors, who won three of the four contests. When, one month later, the Liverpool Stadium opened its doors, no more boxing was planned for Anfield.

The opening of the Liverpool Stadium in October 1932 saw Johnny Best concentrate his efforts on promoting top-level boxing at the new venue. Weekly Thursday night promotions once again became a feature of the Liverpool sporting scene. Remarkably, the promotions were often headlined by local

boxing talent, including Volante, Tarleton, Foran and Roderick. Other boxers from outside the city, such as Johnny Cuthbert, Jack 'Kid' Berg and Jack London underpinned the programmes and ensured that the great hall was full to capacity.

However, nothing came close to a rematch between Tarleton and ex-Seaman Tommy Watson for the British featherweight title. Watson had beaten Tarleton at the first-ever title fight at the new stadium in November 1932. The rematch scheduled for June 1934 generated much interest, forcing Best to once more consider Anfield for promoting championship contests. The attendance of 30,000 again demonstrated the enormous potential for staging boxing at Anfield. Following Tarleton's defeat of Watson, Best was able to match Tarleton with Freddie Miller for the latter's world title.

Building on the success of the 1934 promotions, Best staged two further contests at Anfield in 1935. Both bills featured Miller, who took on and defeated Watson twice. The first contest in June saw Miller win on points over 10 rounds. Remarkably, just two weeks earlier Miller had met Tarleton for the second time at Stanley Track. Although Miller had Watson down in the fourth for a count of nine, the outcome of the contest was very close, with many pundits thinking Watson had won. The undercard featured, for the first time, Peter Kane, who stopped his opponent Billy Charnock in the second round. The other four contests on the undercard all featured local boxers, one being an all-Liverpool affair. There were victories for Merseyside boxers in every contest.

The return match the following month saw Miller knock out Watson in the second round. This was something of a sensational outcome because Watson had only been knocked out once before in his career, by Dom Volante. Once again the undercard was packed with quality boxing that strongly featured local fighters, with both Ginger Foran, returning after a 17-week lay-off, and Peter Kane winning inside the distance.

Tarleton returned to Anfield in 1936 for two defences of his British title, against Johnny King of Manchester on 6 May 1936 and Johnny McGrory of Glasgow on 24 September. Tarleton had won the Lonsdale Belt outright following a third successful defence against Dave Crowley at the Empire

Pool, Wembley, on 12 December 1934. Although Tarleton started as favourite for the Anfield defence of his title, he had met King twice since beating Crowley, losing one and drawing the other. On paper, the contest looked an even match but Tarleton dominated affairs from start to finish. Only once, in the fifth round, did he feel the power of King's punching but Tarleton's superb defence got him out of trouble. By contrast, King was down in rounds four, seven and 13 – Tarleton had promised to win by a knock out, and he almost did.

The Tarleton/McGrory match for the British featherweight title was a greatly anticipated event that had rival promoters in Glasgow competing with Johnny Best to host the contest. Glasgow had the ability to host the fight on a scale similar to Liverpool, having established Shawfield Park as an open-air venue capable of hosting crowds in excess of 20,000. In the end, Best's offer of a £1,250 purse, the largest ever at that time for a British featherweight title fight, secured the contest for Anfield for 24 September 1936. For Best, offering such a large sum was something of a financial gamble, as the Tarleton/King fight in May had not received support at the turnstile and resulted in a loss. Best, however, had big ambitions and was keen to keep himself in the public eye with a view to obtaining even bigger boxing matches in the future.

McGrory was regarded as a hard-hitting exciting boxer of great potential, and his match against Tarleton aroused great expectation around the country. Three days before the bout, 2,000 boxing fans gathered at the Liverpool Stadium to see Tarleton's final work-out. The build-up to the fight was heightened even further with the arrival of hundreds of fight fans from Glasgow.

Naturally Tarleton started as favourite for the fight, but some pundits felt that McGrory's youth, linked to his powerful punches, would see him home. The early rounds of the contest confirmed Tarleton's status as favourite, and in the fourth round he had McGrory down for a count of four. The fight took a decisive turn in the seventh when McGrory whipped a smashing hook to Tarleton's chin. The champion seemed out for the full count, but he somehow staggered to his feet at the count of eight. Fortunately for Tarleton, the bell sounded almost immediately to end the round. Round eight saw McGrory move in to finish the contest. Tarleton appeared groggy but his instinctive defence enabled him to survive the round without any further damage. By the following round the champion had regained his composure, and he began to dominate proceedings once more. Seemingly, he won each of the last six rounds.

At the final bell McGrory retreated to his corner while Tarleton stood in the middle of the ring in anticipation of his arm being raised. However, when referee Thomas had finished his calculations it was to the Scottish man's corner he went. Pandemonium broke out as dozens of ▶

ANFIELD WELCOME: Liverpool's Billy Liddell and Bob Paisley (second and fourth left respectively) are amongst the footballers welcoming the latest boxing star to Anfield

CHURCHMAN'S CIGARETTES

BENNY LYNCH

FIRST DEFEAT: Benny Lynch inflicted a world-title defeat on Peter Kane

WOE FOR THE SCOTS: Anfield impressions from 1932

McGrory fans stormed the ring. When order had been restored, Tarleton took the microphone and stunned the crowd by announcing his retirement.

Analysis of the fight brought surprise at the referee's decision, with both respected local and national journalists indicating that Tarleton appeared a clear winner. Nevertheless, for the second time in his career, Tarleton had lost his British title. He soon recanted his decision to retire from the ring, but the defeat to McGrory proved to be his last appearance at Anfield.

If it was Tarleton that enthused the Anfield crowd between 1931 and 1936 with his supreme boxing skills, it was the Golborne-born but Liverpool adopted boxer Peter Kane who had the fans cheering from the first bell in the second half of the decade. Between June 1935 and August 1937 Kane had six fights at Anfield, all of which he won. Only on one occasion, against Fortunato Ortega, did the contest go the distance. For the Ortega fight in March 1937, special trains brought 4,000 people from Golborne to Liverpool. In April of the same year, he stopped Phil Milligan of Oldham in the 11th round to win the Northern Area flyweight title. Still at the tender age of 19, this was Kane's 37th contest in two years, all of which had ended in victory for the Golborne blacksmith.

Later that year in a world title eliminator he stopped Jimmy Warnock of Belfast in the fourth round. The fight with Benny Lynch for the world flyweight title in Glasgow led to Kane's first defeat, with Lynch knocking him out in the 13th round. Also in this period Kane boxed at least 15 times at the Liverpool Stadium, indicating what an important draw he was for the promoter, Johnny Best. In March 1938 he took on Benny Lynch in a rematch, this time in a non-title fight. The contest went the 15-round distance and ended in a draw, much to the disgust of the Anfield crowd who clearly thought Kane had won. Just six months later Kane earned his world title fight against Jackie Jurich, and this time he won convincingly on points. Kane's ninth and last appearance at Anfield came in 1942 when he won by a knock out, once more against another local favourite, Joe Curran. In a total of nine fights Kane won eight, seven by KO, and drew the other with the great Benny Lynch.

Sandwiched between the Kane/Lynch contest

and Kane's tilt at the world title was a British lightweight championship fight between local favourite Jimmy Walsh and Dave Crowley of London. Walsh had won the title in 1936 at the Liverpool Stadium when he stopped Jack 'Kid' Berg in the ninth round. He made a successful defence in the same year against another top fighter, Harry Mizler, at the Empress Hall in Earls Court. This meant that Walsh was just one more successful defence away from securing the Lonsdale Belt. However, in the build-up to the fight Walsh had endured weight problems and just 24 hours before the contest he was four pounds overweight. Getting down to the required weight clearly affected his performance, enabling Crowley to dominate what was a drab affair. From Johnny Best's point of view, the smallness of the crowd was a worry, leading to a loss of £1,000 on the promotion.

Another Anfield stalwart was Ernie Roderick, who had a total of eight fights at the stadium. The highpoint of his fights at Anfield came in March 1939 when he knocked out the Glaswegian Jake Kilrain to win the British welterweight title. Two months later, Roderick took on Henry Armstrong at the Harringay Arena, London, for the world title but lost on points over 15 rounds. Roderick's last fight at Anfield came in wartime against Eric Boon. Anfield hosted three wartime promotions, all of which were held in daylight hours owing to wartime restrictions. In addition to the Roderick/Boon bill in 1940, there was a final Anfield appearance for Peter Kane in August 1942 against Joe Curran. Before a respectable crowd of 12,000, Kane knocked out Curran in the 11th round. The final wartime promotion, in August 1944, was an eliminator for the British bantamweight title between Jackie Paterson and Ronnie Clayton of Blackpool. Paterson took the honours, stopping Clayton in round 12.

In the post-war period, Anfield staged four more promotions, three of which were for British titles. Anfield's first post-war fight night took place in September 1946, with the top fight being between Stan Hawthorne of North Shields and Billy Thompson of Hickleton Main for the Northern Area lightweight crown. The contest was also an eliminator for the British lightweight title, the winner being due to meet the champion Ronnie James. The bout was greatly anticipated by the Liverpool boxing fraternity

Anfield Stadium

LIVERPOOL CLASH: Seaman Tom Watson evades an attack from Freddie Miller, 1935

as both boxers had outstanding records – Thompson was undefeated in 20 contests while Hawthorne had lost just once in 40 fights. Coming up to the final round, both fighters knew the contest was very close and both went all out for victory, making for an exciting finish. It took some time for the referee Hardwicke to tot up his score, but he eventually gave the decision to Hawthorne over the 12 rounds. The outcome would have pleased the Liverpool crowd as Hawthorne was a great favourite at the stadium.

The promised title fight against Ronnie James did not materialise, as James vacated the belt soon after losing a world title fight to Ike Williams at Ninian Park. The outcome was that the two leading lightweights, Hawthorne and Thompson, met each other once more 13 months later, but this time it was for the title vacated by James. Hawthorne was favourite to take the title because of the two boxers he undoubtedly had the harder punch. Fifty of Hawthorne's 57 victories had come inside the distance, while Thompson had stopped 15 opponents in his 30 victories.

In the build-up, Thompson had told the *Liverpool Echo* that he was now punching 100 per cent harder and it was hard hitting that would decide the outcome of the title fight. At the first bell Hawthorne clubbed a right to Thompson's chin but a steadfast Thompson responded in kind. After Hawthorne's early onslaught Thompson began to dominate and had Hawthorne down for a count of five. Thompson looked ready to end the fight there and then, but the bell prevented him finishing off a dazed Hawthorne. In the second round Thompson had Hawthorne down twice more and when the bell ended the round, Hawthorne looked a beaten man. From the outset of the third, Hawthorne's defence was becoming increasingly feeble and this, linked to cuts to his eyes, forced the referee to stop the fight. Against all the odds, Thompson had won the title inside three rounds. After the contest, Hawthorne said: "I have no excuses to make, the right man won. But there will be another time. The first punch I received on the chin in the first round bemused me and I never really recovered." There would not be another title challenge for Hawthorne, but Thompson would go on to win the Lonsdale Belt outright, and also become champion of Europe at lightweight.

A month before the Thompson/Hawthorne

title fight, on 11 September 1947, Al Phillips of London and Ronnie Clayton of Blackpool fought each other for the British featherweight title that had been vacated by Nel Tarleton. Clayton was a great favourite of the Liverpool stadium and it was anticipated that the crowd would be in the region of 30,000 – but once again bad weather affected the attendance, and only half that number turned up. The contest was the first £5,000 purse ever offered for a featherweight fight, and the poor attendance meant that Best lost £3,000 on the event. The contest itself was dominated by Clayton, who added aggression to his natural boxing ability to thwart Phillips' own aggressive style. At the end of 15 rounds the referee had little hesitation in giving the verdict to the Blackpool boxer. Clayton held the title until 1954, when he lost it to Sammy McCarthy at the White City, London. Also on the bill that night was Peter Fallon of Birkenhead, who outpointed Jarrow's Bert Duffy. Fallon was developing a reputation as one of the country's finest welterweights, and would go on to contest for the British title in 1953 against Wally Thom at Liverpool Stadium.

The last title fight at the ground resulted in another Lonsdale Belt for the city when Stan Rowan took both the British and

Commonwealth bantamweight titles from Jack Paterson of Glasgow. This was the last occasion that professional boxing took place at Anfield.

In 18 years of hosting boxing tournaments, Anfield had seen a Liverpool boxer win a Lonsdale Belt for the first time. Two other local boxers, Ernie Roderick and Stan Rowan, subsequently won British titles in their respective divisions. There had been great fights galore over the period, but perhaps the greatest night at the ground was when Peter Kane won the world title in 1938. At the time of writing, Liverpool boxing is on the up, with boxers such as Derry Matthews, the former world champion, capable of winning national and world titles. Moreover, in the amateur ranks there are many fine boxers challenging for national and international honours. Inevitably, some of these boxers will find themselves boxing professionally, and some are also capable of challenging for British and world titles. Anfield clearly forms an important part of Liverpool's boxing history and how fitting it would be if the ground was to hold one more world or British championship contest before it is demolished. Even more fitting would be if one of the present crop of promising Liverpool boxers was to win one such title.

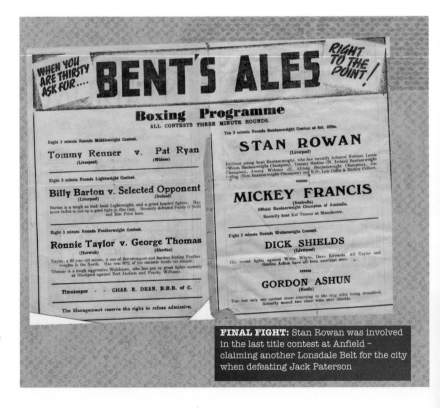

FINAL FIGHT: Stan Rowan was involved in the last title contest at Anfield – claiming another Lonsdale Belt for the city when defeating Jack Paterson

DONE AGAIN: Cyril and friends test the ring mic at Anfield

Boxing at Anfield 1931 – Liverpool's First Lonsdale Belt

The prospect of a Liverpool boxer winning a Lonsdale Belt generated great excitement in Liverpool in the autumn of 1931. That Anfield was the venue for Nel Tarleton's clash with champion Johnny Cuthbert, providing the base for the biggest-ever crowd for a boxing show in the city, only added to the excitement. Even Tarleton's training sessions at Moreton attracted large crowds, with many arriving at dawn to see Liverpool's great hope start his road work. Tarleton's sparring team, which included Dom Volante and Johnny Peters, was a great attraction in itself.

In those days the weigh-in for boxing matches took place on the day of the fight. Just like today, however, promoters used the event to generate publicity for the forthcoming promotion. The weigh-in for the Johnny Cuthbert v Nel Tarleton fight took place at 2pm at Lewis's department store in front of 1,000 excited boxing fans. Cuthbert was the first to get on the scales as onlookers, who had come in large numbers to wish Tarleton well, delayed challenger Nel Tarleton in the street outside the store.

The weigh-in was also attended by leading Lancashire and Yorkshire sportsmen. Included among them were many former boxers, all of whom had come to lend support to the fight build-up. Both boxers expressed quiet confidence in their abilities, with Cuthbert saying: "I hope to retain the featherweight title at Anfield tonight. It is my ambition, if only for this once." Tarleton responded respectively, stating: "I haven't much to say gentlemen, but I hope to be the first Merseyside boy to fetch a belt to Liverpool."

Following the weigh-in, the crowd called for Johnny Best, who responded by revealing his concerns about a pitch invasion during or after the main event. "If what Cuthbert and Tarleton say is true, we look like seeing a great fight tonight. I want to have future fights there, but everything depends on how you behave tonight. I appeal to you not to encroach on the playing pitch."

From the weigh-in many fans made their way to Anfield, where queues began to form as early as four o'clock, even though the evening's boxing was not due to start until 7.30pm. Reports of the day testify to an electric atmosphere from a crowd estimated at 30,000, with the Kop a complete sell-out.

It was clear from the outset that Tarleton had in the back of his mind his previous title fight at Pudsey Street, as he never gave up the pressure on Cuthbert for 15 rounds. Indeed, during the interval between the 10th and 11th rounds, Tarleton's corner advised him to ease up as the pace had been relentless. Tarleton responded confidently, saying: "I am well, I am winning, I am going on with it." Most commentators of the day had Tarleton well ahead on points at the end; some even indicated that he won every round. However, this does not tell the whole story, as in the first round the referee nearly ended his chances of defeating Cuthbert.

At the sound of the first bell the referee, Jack Smith, and Tarleton collided – the official trod on Tarleton's ankle. Although he was in discomfort from the injury, Tarleton shrugged off the incident and set about dismantling Cuthbert.

From the outset Tarleton's tactic was to go for the champion's waistline, as in their previous contest Cuthbert had shown he could not take a lot of punishment to the body. During the course of the fight Tarleton put in numerous rapier-like left hooks right on the belt line. It was a blow he had been practising for some time, and one he had learned in America.

In the third round one such blow put Cuthbert on the canvas for a count of five. There was some controversy in the fifth when a similar punch had the champion rolling on the canvas, indicating that he had been hit below the belt. The referee was unimpressed, however, and began counting, with Cuthbert struggling to his feet at the point of nine. Tarleton continued where he left off in subsequent rounds. In the seventh, Cuthbert was once again on the receiving end of severe body blows, while in the ninth Tarleton had the champion on the ropes – only for Cuthbert to be saved by the bell.

Cuthbert may have seemed all but defeated at this stage, but he was famed for his late surges. Tarleton, aware of this, did not back off but took the fight to Cuthbert once more. In the 11th he had Cuthbert down once more, with the champion again claiming a foul shot. The referee ignored his pleas once more and Cuthbert was forced to resume at the count of nine. In the final four rounds Tarleton got the better of Cuthbert, but his rasping blows did not seem to carry the same power. The reason ▶

TV TIMES: Dom Volante (second left) meets Len Harvey, Jock McAvoy and Teddy Baldock on board the Cunard liner Britannic. Volante had just been appointed as the gymnasium instructor on the vessel while the TV cameras were recording the TV programme 'It Happened to Me'

CUTHBERT (LEFT) V TARLETON:
Johnny Best is standing right of Tarleton, with Ted Broadribb – manager to Volante and Tarleton – next to him on the far right

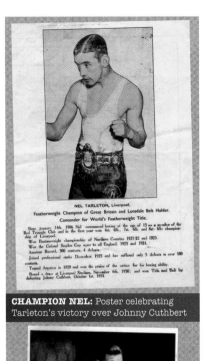

NEL TARLETON, Liverpool.
Featherweight Champion of Great Britain and Lonsdale Belt Holder.
Contender for World's Featherweight Title.

Born: January 14th, 1906. Nel commenced boxing at the age of 13 as a member of the Red Triangle Club and in the first year won 6st. 6lb., 7st. 6lb. and 8st. 6lb. championship of Liverpool.
Won Bantamweight championship of Northern Counties 1921-22 and 1923.
Won the Colonel Sugden Cup open to all England, 1923 and 1924.
Amateur Record, 300 contests, 4 defeats.
Joined professional ranks December, 1925 and has suffered only 5 defeats in over 100 contests.
Toured America in 1929 and won the praise of the critics for his boxing ability.
Boxed a draw at Liverpool Stadium, November 6th, 1930; and won Title and Belt by defeating Johnny Cuthbert, October 1st, 1931.

CHAMPION NEL: Poster celebrating Tarleton's victory over Johnny Cuthbert

DOM VOLANTE: The 'S' on the shorts stands for the boxing agency Sensational Snowball Star Scrappers

LOOKING BACK: Dom reminiscing with good friend Doug Yeadon. Yeadon was a Liverpool boxer, who ran the RAF boxing team in what is modern-day Iraq. He was also a member of the Merseyside Former Boxers' Association

▶ for this became clear at the end of the contest.

At the final bell the crowd yelled their delight, convinced that Tarleton had won. However, quietness prevailed the arena when the MC, Mr Nolan, approached the referee for his verdict. Following a short exchange between the two officials, Nolan moved forward and in a strong voice that could be heard at the back of the Kop, said:

"The featherweight champion of Great Britain and holder of the Lonsdale Belt is Nel Tarleton of Liverpool."

The crowd went wild with delight and Tarleton indulged in a slight fandango. Sportingly, Cuthbert said: "It had to come sooner or later. Champions are only made to be eventually beaten. I lost to a splendid fighter, and a clever one too."

A delighted Tarleton later revealed to 'Bee' (the pseudonym of sports editor Ernest Edwards) of the *Liverpool Echo* why he could not punch as hard in the final rounds of the contest: 'I won with two bad hands. Look at them Mr Bee', and the new champion

pulled off his bandages to reveal the truth of his words. Tarleton continued, saying: 'Cuthbert is a splendid fellow, and a credit to the game. Naturally I am delighted to be the first boy to bring honour to Liverpool. I hope one day to bring a world championship to the city.'

To loud cheers, Tarleton was congratulated by the Lord Mayor, the chairman of Liverpool Football Club Tom Crompton and by the club's vice-president, W.H. Cartwright.

When Tarleton reached his home in Gloucester Place later that night he was greeted by a large crowd made up not only of boxing fans but also women with babes in arms and young people, all of whom had come to see the man with the gold belt. They clamoured for a speech, but all the champion would say was: "Thank you very much, I will try to (go) on doing what I have done."

Clearly, as with most great sporting achievements, Liverpool's first Lonsdale Belt winner made a big impact on the people of Liverpool, who are always ready to salute a winner.

LIVERPOOL F.C. GROUND,
ANFIELD.

Thursday, 1st October. 1931.

JOHNNY BEST.

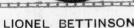
LIONEL BETTINSON.

Under the Distinguished Patronage of

THE LORD MAYOR OF LIVERPOOL
(Alderman EDWIN THOMPSON, J.P.)

THE NATIONAL SPORTING CLUB,
London, and

JOHNNY BEST,
Liverpool

PRESENT THE

15 Three-Minute Rounds Contest for **£100** Aside

FEATHERWEIGHT CHAMPIONSHIP

OF GREAT BRITAIN and

LONSDALE BELT.

Weigh in 9st. at 2 p.m.

JOHNNY CUTHBERT

Sheffield   *versus*   *Holder*

NEL TARLETON

Liverpool   *Challenger*

SOUVENIR PROGRAMME.

Price - - *THREEPENCE.*

Hy. Hughes & Co. (L'pool) Ltd., Printers. 37, Vauxhall Road.

Origins of the Lonsdale Belt

The Lonsdale Belt must rank as one of the finest individual trophies a sportsman can win. Belts have been part of boxing for a long time – the first boxer to be awarded one was Tom Cribb in 1809. Other boxers, such as Jem Mace, also earned a championship belt. But with the lack of a national governing body for boxing in those early days, the awarding of trophies for winning national titles was never standardised. Indeed, there was confusion as to who was a champion right up to the formation of the National Sporting Club in 1891. As the NSC gained more and more authority, it became accepted that a British title could only be won at a venue endorsed by the club. Up to 1930, all such British title fights took place in London.

In 1909, 100 years after Tom Cribb won his title belt, the National Sporting Club decided to issue a belt to the winner of a British championship title fight, the intention being to enhance the reputation of the club and the British title. Although it is not clear who was responsible for the idea of issuing a belt, it almost certainly was not Lord Lonsdale. The reason why the belt took his name was, quite simply, because he paid for the first belt to be made. At first the belts covered seven weight divisions, with the light-heavyweight division being added in 1914. Today there are 14 weight divisions. Until July 1936, Lonsdale Belts were issued by the NSC; since then they have come under the tutelage of the British Boxing Board of Control. In total, only 21 boxers won an NSC belt outright.

To win a belt outright, a boxer had to put three notches on the belt – in other words, he had to win three British title fights. Up until 1981, a boxer could win more than one Lonsdale Belt – Henry Cooper in fact won three. But to win a second belt a boxer would have to win a further three title fights. However, the rule now states that no boxer can receive more than one belt as his own property in any one-weight division. A further amendment to the rules in 1999 required a boxer to put four notches on a belt before winning it outright.

Nel Tarleton was not only the first Liverpool boxer to win a Lonsdale Belt, he is the only Liverpool boxer to win both an NSC and BBBofC belt. The belt Tarleton competed for against Johnny Cuthbert was in fact a newly issued NSC belt, as Cuthbert had won the previous belt outright when he defeated Dom Volante. Tarleton eventually won this outright in December 1934 when he defeated Dave Crowley at the Empire Pool, Wembley.

CHAMP: Tarleton v Al Foreman, 1932

ETCHED IN THE HISTORY BOOKS: Lord Lonsdale (above) and Nel Tarleton at his 1935 testimonial (left)

FUTURE CHAMPION: Les McAteer wearing the Lonsdale Belt after he claimed a revenge victory over Wally Swift in 11 rounds at Nottingham in 1969

Ernie Roderick – Liverpool's Finest Welterweight

In a career that spanned two decades, Ernie Roderick established himself as one of Britain's finest-ever welterweights. Roderick had something in the region of 140 professional contests, including 11 title fights (one for the world title), and came close to winning a second Lonsdale Belt. A modern-day boxer at the top of his profession would expect to contest a British, Commonwealth or world title in his first 20 fights. For Roderick, it took nearly 100 bouts before he got his chance to contest the British title at Anfield in 1939.

Roderick had a particularly tough opponent in the shape of Tony Butcher for his first contest in June 1931 at the Lyric Theatre in Everton Valley. Today few matchmakers would line a young boxer with potential against such a tough opponent. But Johnny Best knew all about Roderick's ability from Nel Tarleton, who had told Best about the emerging talent. Typically, Roderick did not disappoint his admirers and outpointed his more experienced opponent over 10 rounds. Moreover, in his first 17 fights Roderick lost only once, to Jimmy Stewart at Anfield in June 1932. It was the only time Roderick would lose at the ground in eight appearances. Throughout the 1930s, he was one of the biggest attractions on the bill at the football-ground promotions, initially supporting Tarleton and Kane but later as the main bout on the bill.

In 1933 Roderick travelled to Australia with Nel Tarleton where he had three tough fights for such a young boxer (he was only 19). After drawing with Bobby Blay and losing to Bobby Delaney and Cyril Pluto, all of them 15-round contests, he returned home a sick and sadly disillusioned young boxer. When, during the course of 1934 he lost seven of his 12 contests it seemed that his promising career was hitting the buffers (incidentally, one of his victories in this sequence was at

Anfield on the Tarleton/Miller bill, beating Charlie Baxter of Birmingham on points). During 1935 Roderick's form returned and over the next three years, up to his title contest with Jake Kilrain, he would have 70 bouts, losing just two to Jimmy Walsh and Sonny Jones.

Throughout the course of this period Roderick was continually talked about as a challenger for the British title, but he fell down the ranking following a six-month suspension imposed on him by the Northern Section of the British Boxing Board of Control. The ban resulted from Roderick using a new type of bandage on his hands in a contest against Bill Graham at Glasgow. Somewhat ironically, Roderick's last fight before his ban was against Jake Kilrain on 12 March 1936 in Glasgow, the very man he would have to overcome to win his British title some three years later. Roderick defeated Kilrain on points and scored another victory against him one year later when he stopped the now

British champion in the 10th round in a non-title contest. Kilrain had won the British welterweight title while Roderick was banned in June 1936 when he knocked out Dave McCleave of London in the eighth round at Shawfield Park.

Despite the delayed challenge for the British crown, when his chance did arrive, Roderick was in his prime. Still only 25, he had fought in nearly 100 contests when he met Kilrain for a third time at Anfield on 23 March 1939. The contest drew added significance when it became a world title eliminator, with the winner being matched with Henry 'Homicide' Armstrong at the Harringay Arena. Roderick dominated the contest from the outset, with each of the rounds having a certain predictability about them. Roderick would invariably open up with a series of lefts to the head followed by hooks to the body. These were damaging punches and it seemed just a matter of time before Kilrain would either be knocked out or forced to retire. Despite the ▶

WORLD WELTERWEIGHT FIGHT, 1939:
Henry Armstrong (left) and Ernie
Roderick afterwards at Harringay, London

ON THE ROAD: Early morning road work for Ernie in preparation for his world-title showdown with Henry Armstrong

KILRAIN V RODERICK: Programme for the welterweight championship fight, 1939

CHURCHMAN'S CIGARETTES

ERIC BOON

ERIC BOON: Roderick's final opponent at Anfield, in September 1940

AMBASSADOR: Roderick presents a prize to Terry Smith of Speke Boys' Club at a Liverpool Phoenix ABC show, 1970

▶ predictable outcome, the fight had an unpredictable end in the seventh round. Midway through the round, Kilrain was floored by a vicious right hook but he seemed to have recovered his control and was kneeling as referee Thomas was reeling off the count. Despite his apparent recovery Kilrain missed the count and was adjudged to have been knocked out. Kilrain was dismayed at the outcome and attempted to protest to the referee, but to no avail. For a few moments Roderick looked as surprised as Kilrain, but when he realised he was champion he jumped into the air in celebration.

Afterwards Kilrain explained that he had missed the count – not because he could not continue: "I was quite ready to go on," he said. Roderick countered, saying: "I knew I had got him with that right...All I am thinking about is the world title." Once again Anfield was the scene of joy for Liverpool boxing fans – it was the fourth time a Liverpool boxer had won either a British or a world title at the ground.

Just two months later, Roderick met Armstrong for the world welterweight title. It proved to be a tough contest for the Liverpool man as Roderick was to learn just why Armstrong had received the 'homicide' moniker. Armstrong dominated from start to finish, pummelling Roderick's body and when the challenger tried to punch his way back into the fight, the American just shrugged off the blows. Despite this, Armstrong complimented Roderick's performance, saying: "He is the greatest fighter I have ever met." This was a fine compliment from a man who won world titles in the feather, light and welterweight divisions. A return match with Armstrong was scuppered by the war, but Roderick always felt confident of beating the champion in any return match.

It was in wartime that Roderick made his final

appearance at Anfield against Eric Boon in September 1940. Roderick won the contest on points, but the scenes outside the ground were of greater significance. As more than 5,000 fight fans looked on, above their heads there were German bombers raiding the city, but amazingly no one in the crowd moved, no doubt torn at which battle they should watch. Ernie was to meet Boon once more, this time in defence of his British title at the Harringay Arena in 1947. Once again, Roderick was the winner on points.

Apart from four more appearances at the Stadium in 1941 and 1942, Roderick would not appear in Liverpool again. The shift towards title fights being held in London was gathering pace especially as Johnny Best was now the matchmaker at the Harringay Arena. When Roderick defeated Arthur Danahar at the Royal Albert Hall in September 1941, he became only the second Liverpool boxer to win a Lonsdale Belt outright. Remarkably, it would be 1947 before he would defend his welterweight title again. In between, he won and lost both the British middleweight title and the European welterweight title.

Like his brother-in-law Nel Tarleton, Roderick set his heart on winning a second Lonsdale Belt, one for each of his children. After beating Gwyn Williams in September 1947 and Eric Boon three months later, Roderick needed just one more defence to achieve his ambition. He met Henry Hall of Sheffield at Harringay in November 1948. Hall, the younger boxer by eight years, had established a big lead by the halfway stage of the contest but in the second half of the bout Roderick dominated, having Hall down in the 12th. In the last two rounds, Roderick went all-out for victory and was convinced he had done enough, but the referee gave the decision to Hall. A year later when he lost a title eliminator to Eddie Thomas, his dream of a second belt was over.

Did you know?
Ernie Roderick became the first-ever boxer to qualify for the British Boxing Board of Control pension of £1 a week in 1964. The pension level was set in 1936 and is awarded to all outright winners of the Lonsdale Belt when they reach the age of 50.

SPARRING: Roderick spars with Danny Mack in preparation for his 1937 fight with Jimmy Walsh; Roderick is pictured between his sparring partners (below)

Ginger Foran – Weight Problems Cost him the World Title

Ginger Foran was a great favourite at Anfield, boxing there eight times and losing on just one occasion. Foran made his debut at The Tower, New Brighton in 1931 against Nat Stewart, who he knocked out in the first round. Early in his career he developed a reputation of being a knock-out specialist, but as he came across opponents of higher quality he also showed that he had the boxing skill to defeat such opponents on points. He came of age at Anfield during 1932 when he boxed on all the promotions with the exception of the Canadian boxing night in September. Prior to boxing at Anfield, Foran had developed a strong local following but it was his first appearance at the ground in March 1932 that brought him national recognition. Foran took on George Anderson, the South African flyweight champion, over six rounds. Many thought that Foran had been overmatched, but he produced some of his best boxing to date and scored a convincing points victory.

Four more wins in four consecutive months at Anfield against Ginger McLeod, Arthur Killeen, Boy Walley and Bert Kirby established Foran as a boxer with championship potential. However, in the 1930s the flyweight division was packed with quality boxers. Top of the pile was Jackie Brown of Manchester who, already the British champion, won the world title in the same week that Foran knocked out Jim Maharg in the first round on the opening night of the Liverpool Stadium. Before Foran could face Brown for the world championship he would have to face several boxers of high calibre including Mickey Maguire, Jimmy Campbell, Harry Edwards and Tucker Winch. All these contests took place at the Liverpool Stadium, and before a home crowd Foran won each one comfortably.

Following this string of victories, the British Boxing Board of Control named Foran as the official challenger to Jackie Brown, and instructed his team to exchange contracts by 24 May 1933. The Brown camp, however, procrastinated (for what reason it is unknown), but it was becoming increasingly recognised that Foran was having trouble getting down to the required eight-stone weight limit for a flyweight. The Brown camp complained to the Board that Fred Bebington of Salford should also be considered a challenger. Bebington had been scheduled to meet Foran in March 1933 but had to pull out of the contest owing to a knee injury sustained in training. When the deadline of ▶

Ginger Foran
(LIVERPOOL)

Who returns to the ring, after 5 months lay-off. Ginger boxes here to-night against the promising Manchester Bantam, Boy Ellis, who recently won the Crystal Palace Bantamweight Competition.

Peter Banasko
(LIVERPOOL)

Who also returns to the ring after a 11 months lay-off caused through a hand injury during his contest against Fred Bebbington, whom he defeated on points.

24 May passed, the Board was forced to call another meeting for 30 June. At this meeting it was decided that Bebington and Foran should meet for the British Northern Area flyweight title; the contest would also act as the final eliminator for Brown's titles. Foran only agreed to this when his manager Ted Denvir received assurances that the winner would face Brown.

Foran met Bebington at the Liverpool Stadium on 27 July 1933, the outcome being an easy points victory for the Liverpool boxer. The way was now clear for Foran to meet Brown. Bids to host the fight were invited, with Belle Vue winning the honours. Before the fight could go ahead, another delay took place – this time because Foran had to have 11 teeth extracted owing to septic abscesses in his mouth. These delays were hurting Foran as his weight problem was becoming more acute, and following his operation he was unable to train properly, which led to him putting on even more.

Six weeks prior to the fight he was 10 pounds overweight. To get down to eight stone was possible, but at great cost to his body strength. Indeed, Johnny Best advised Foran to forgo his title challenge as he was in danger of damaging his health to get down to the required weight. But Foran had set his heart on boxing for the world and British championships.

Eventually the contest with Brown took place on 11 December 1933, but Foran's struggle to meet the weight had left him drained. His situation was exacerbated when on the eve of the challenge he had a bout of diarrhoea. Although he came in two pounds underweight at the weigh-in, any chance he had of winning the world and British titles had gone before he stepped into the ring.

In the corner with Foran that night was Johnny Best, so he certainly had an experienced man to help him through the contest. From the outset Foran's tactics were clear. He realised his only chance was to secure an early knock out, as the longer the fight continued the more his stamina would fail him. But Jackie Brown was a quality boxer and was able to fend off Foran's early threat. To his credit, Foran lasted the 15 rounds, but at the end Brown was the clear winner.

Such were Foran's weight problems that within 12 months following the Brown fight, he had moved through the bantamweight division into the featherweights. He quickly made his mark in the latter division, knocking out the British champion Johnny McGrory (breaking his jaw in the process) in March 1937 in a non-title fight. The injury was a tragedy for McGrory, as he had been lined-up for a world-title fight with Petey Sarron (McGrory would never get another chance for a world-title shot). There was an attempt by the Foran camp to get Ginger as a replacement for McGrory, but it failed to materialise.

Later in 1937, Foran left Liverpool for America where he continued his boxing career. He lived the rest of life in the USA and died there at the young age of 42 in November 1955. Johnny Best Jnr summed up how the boxing fraternity regarded Foran:

"He was one of the best flyweights Liverpool ever produced and a great favourite with the Stadium crowds."

GINGER FORAN   Liverpool
A local Flyweight who shows great promise has lost only one contest since turning professional

FORAN: The caption recognises the young boxer's "great promise"

MCGRORY: Johnny, who would be KO'd by Ginger Foran a year later, in action against Nel Tarleton, 1936

Tarleton v Watson – Tarleton Regains the British Title

After a gap of almost two years, championship boxing returned to Anfield on 26 July 1934. Many aspects of the programme reflected the first night of boxing at the ground. The main contest was for the British featherweight title and the challenger was Nel Tarleton once again. As with the 1931 Cuthbert fight, it was a rematch, this time against ex-Seaman Tommy Watson – Tarleton had lost his title to Watson at the Liverpool Stadium in November 1932.

Watson was a formidable opponent for Tarleton. Since outpointing Tarleton to take the Lonsdale Belt, Watson had made a successful defence of his title against Johnny McMillan of Glasgow, meaning that if Watson defeated Tarleton once more he would win the belt outright. Thus all the ingredients for a dramatic night's boxing were in place. The size of the purse, £1,000 for the winner, was the largest ever offered at a northern venue, only serving to heighten interest in the fight.

Following his defeat to Watson, Tarleton lost much of his former sharpness. Moreover, the old saying in boxing, 'they never come back', seemed applicable to the former champion. But after a difficult tour to Australia, Tarleton returned to something approaching his championship best, losing just one of his five contests in the build-up to the fight with Watson, against Sonny Lee of Leeds. Watson's form had also been excellent. He lost just twice in 17 contests after defeating Tarleton – once to the Cuban Kid Chocolate on points for the world title at Madison Square Gardens, and to Sonny Lee on a disqualification.

The different styles of the boxers made for an intriguing contest. From the waist to the shoulders Watson had the build of a middleweight. Watson's style was that of a fighter who liked to box at close quarters, making him a dangerous body puncher and earning himself the reputation of being the best in-fighter in his class. In contrast, Tarleton was tall and lithe with a long reach, regarded as one of the great boxing stylists possessing great speed, while his dazzling footwork enabled him to avoid many an attack from boxers such as Watson. Moreover, he had learned in America how to deliver the left-hook, a punch he could deliver with great speed to either head or body. It was this punch that undid Cuthbert when Tarleton had won the title in 1931.

Two contrasting styles, a British championship at stake, the winner to take on Freddie Miller for the world title, a passionate crowd and the atmosphere of Anfield all made for a great fight night. The 30,000-strong crowd were not to be disappointed. Tarleton summed up the home expectation, saying: "I am fighting for Merseyside and I am going to strive my utmost to bring back the title."

The contest itself followed the expected pattern, with the champion attempting to crowd the Liverpool man and hammer his ribs. However, Tarleton had learned not to underestimate his opponent, either escaping Watson's surges with good footwork or taking the blows on the arms. Such was the intensity of Watson's attacks that some blows did get through but they were met with powerful counter-punches from the challenger to Watson's body.

At the mid-point of the contest it was hard to separate the boxers, but in round eight Tarleton pulled one of his old boxing tricks. As he appeared to be hurt Watson came forward with too much confidence and was met with a series of counter-punches to the head and the body that clearly hurt the champion. The momentum was now clearly with Tarleton, who had Watson down in the 14th round for a count of six. Watson was a tough man and despite the punishment in the final round he survived Tarleton's attempts to knock him out.

Given that Tarleton had been on the wrong end of some refereeing decisions in the past there was a degree of nervousness, reflected in the almost complete silence of the crowd as the referee, C.B. Thomas, went to a neutral corner to add up the points. But as he walked across the ring to Tarleton's corner the roar swelled around the ground, reaching a crescendo when he raised the Liverpool man's arm in victory. Once again Tarleton was the proud bearer of the Lonsdale Belt.

There was no disputing the convincing nature of Tarleton's victory. Johnny Cuthbert told the *Daily Post* that "Tarleton won easily. He has never fought better in my opinion." Upon receiving the belt from Lord Lonsdale, a delighted Tarleton said:

"I always felt confident that I would win. I am naturally delighted at my success, and hope that I pleased the Liverpool public by my display. I am very proud to have won the championship again."

Watson was magnanimous in defeat, saying: "Tarleton fought splendidly. He is a great little fighter." The question now was could Tarleton take his improved form to his next fight and defeat the powerful Freddie Miller?

AT THE WEIGH-IN: Tarleton (left) and Watson

IN WITH HIS LEFT: Tarleton, with his back to the camera, launches an attack

Tarleton v Miller – Anfield's First World Title Fight

The world title fight between Nel Tarleton and Freddie Miller at Anfield on 20 September 1934 justified Johnny Best's vision. When Best had taken over Pudsey Street in 1928 there was little prospect of Liverpool ever hosting a title fight of any kind, let alone a world title contest. Indeed, many had thought that taking on Pudsey Street was folly and that Best's venture would not last too long. Yet in the space of a few years, 1930-34, Liverpool had hosted a European welterweight title bout and four British featherweight title fights. It must be stressed that such promotions were based on a growing pool of Liverpool boxing talent led by the talismanic Tarleton who, with the exception of the European title fight

that had been won by Alf Howard in 1930 at Pudsey Street, was involved in all the title fights promoted by Best in this period. Another factor was that this group of boxers were exceptionally proud of their Liverpool roots and were always keen to box their biggest fights in their hometown. This was an exceptional period for Liverpool boxing, a period that culminated in Freddie Miller defending his world featherweight title at Anfield a few months after Tarleton had regained his British title.

The Tarleton/Miller fight of September 1934 was the first time Liverpool had hosted a world title contest since the Ike Bradley/Digger Stanley fight in 1911. In the context of

the venue, the already great achievements of Tarleton plus the greater popularity of boxing in the 1930s meant that there was even greater mood of excitement around the city compared to 1911.

Freddie Miller had won the world title in January 1933 when he outpointed Tommy Paul. From the outset, Miller was out to prove that he was no ordinary champion. In the 20 months between winning the title and taking on Tarleton, Miller defended his title no less than six times, and in total had 34 contests. He believed in fighting often and getting paid rather than spending weeks training in the gym. In the build-up to the fight, he told the *Daily Post*: ▶

BEST'S VISION REALISED: Bill advertising the world title fight in 1934

Telegrams: "Stadium," Liverpool. *Liverpool* Telephone : BANK 4816 (2 lines)

STADIVM

Chairman :
MAJOR J. BENNETT,
O.B.E., T.D., C.C.

Managing Director
and Promoter.
JOHNNY BEST.

(PROMOTION)

(Present) at the

Liverpool Football Ground

ON

THURSDAY, SEPT. 20th, 1934

Commencing at 7-45 p.m.

The

Featherweight Championship of the World

Freddie Miller

(CINCINNATI, AMERICA)

(Official Featherweight Champion of the World)

v.

Nel Tarleton

(LIVERPOOL, ENGLAND)

(Official Featherweight Champion of Gt. Britain)

PROGRAMME - - - **PRICE THREEPENCE**

K

▶ 'A cheese champion will never get among the dollars. He must fight and keep on fighting if he is to have a bank balance at the end of his career.'

It was dollars that brought Miller to Liverpool. Johnny Best cabled Pete Reilly, Miller's manager, soon after Tarleton had beaten Watson with an offer to take on the British champion for a $1,000 purse, plus a percentage of the gate. Reilly responded with disdain, telling Best to "quit fooling, make me a real offer". After several more exchanges, Reilly laid out his terms, telling Best he wanted $13,000 free of all taxes.

Best agreed to the terms but he knew he was taking a financial gamble. The amount demanded by Reilly amounted to the total receipts from the Tarleton/Watson fight. To make the promotion a financial success Best would have to sell 30,000 tickets.

Miller arrived in Liverpool from New York just 10 days before the contest, and upon his arrival both Miller and Tarleton, in an unprecedented move, were invited to dinner at the Town Hall by the Lord Mayor. Indeed, a week before the fight, Miller and the Lord Mayor played a round of golf at Childwall Golf Club (see opposite page).

To the public eye it seemed that Miller was

MILLER CARTOON: Printed in the *Liverpool Echo* on 22 June 1935

not preparing for the fight in the correct manner. Moreover, when he did train he did not look too impressive. In contrast, Tarleton's preparations left nothing to chance. To adapt to boxing a southpaw, Tarleton engaged several southpaw sparring partners.

On the eve of the fight, both men did their final workouts before a large audience at the Stadium. Tarleton did several rounds with Dave Chadwick of Bridlington, Joe Bull of London and Nat Williams. Miller took on local boxers Jerry Costello, Billy Gannon and Peter Banasko.

Reporting on the workouts, the *Daily Post* commented that both boxers had amazing power in their punches and noted: 'One of his (Miller's) shots, a right-hand uppercut, looks to me a knock-out punch.' Reilly, who was one of the biggest leg-pullers in the game, seemed to be putting down his man's chances, telling the *Daily Post*: 'Tarleton looks marvellous. He is punching very hard.' Reilly also added that Miller would have to take off five pounds before the weigh-in to make the required weight.

On the eve of the contest, the scenes around the ground were chaotic. Two hours before the start, hundreds of people lined up outside the turnstiles. For the first time, to accommodate the expected large crowd, all parts of the ground were brought into use. Trams, coaches and trains brought boxing fans from as far as St Helens, North Wales, Warrington and Wigan.

So great was the crush to get in that even Johnny Best could not get near the official entrance, so he had to queue at the Kop and pay a 2s 6d entrance fee. Once inside he was recognised and escorted to the dressing rooms of the boxers.

A delay in starting the main bout of the evening led to slow handclapping by the crowd. However, once the referee entered the atmosphere lifted, with the crowd applauding as he announced the contenders. Loud applause developed into ecstatic cheering when the boxers threw off their dressing gowns.

At the first bell, Miller started on the attack with big blows to Tarleton's body. This became something of a pattern, but then Tarleton appeared to be gaining a foothold in

the contest when in round six Miller countered a left hook to his ribs with a powerful blow to Tarleton's body that put the challenger down for a count of eight. Despite this, Tarleton recovered his composure in the next round and had the better of Miller, who was cautioned twice by the referee. Hope grew brighter in round 10 when Tarleton seemed to be finding his form at last, but in the next three rounds Miller used all his power to dominate the contest. In the 12th, Tarleton was hindered by a cut to his nose and the following round once again was Miller's with the champion jabbing away at Tarleton's face. Remarkably, Tarleton came out for the 14th round with bounce and aggression, and landed some telling blows to the champion's head. But as the round progressed, Miller began to dominate once more with crushing blows to Tarleton's body. As the bell sounded for the final round, Tarleton needed a knock out to win, but it was Miller who forced the pace with vicious hooks and uppercuts. Tarleton responded once more with blows to the body, but Miller just kept powering forward, unleashing a fierce uppercut that put Tarleton on the ropes. To his credit Tarleton stayed on his feet, but at the final bell the referee had no hesitation in giving the verdict to the champion.

Despite his intensive sparring sessions with southpaws, Tarleton failed to master Miller's right lead. Miller perpetually poked an open right glove towards Tarleton's head not in the hope of kidding the referee, but for the purpose of preventing Tarleton from landing his own left-hand jabs. This tactic seemed to nullify Tarleton's reach advantage and allowed Miller to keep moving forward.

The big Liverpool crowd sportingly received the champion warmly. Miller, responding to the atmosphere, praised Tarleton for his efforts while a delighted Reilly said: "This is truly a world champion. He takes them all on and wins against them all." In the context of an seventh successful defence, it was hard to disagree.

Tarleton and Miller had a rematch at Stanley Greyhound Track in June 1935, with Miller once again emerging the victor. It was a much closer affair, with some pundits believing that Tarleton had actually won but a few weeks later Miller left for home after an eight-month stay in Liverpool with his world title intact.

PLAN OF GROUND

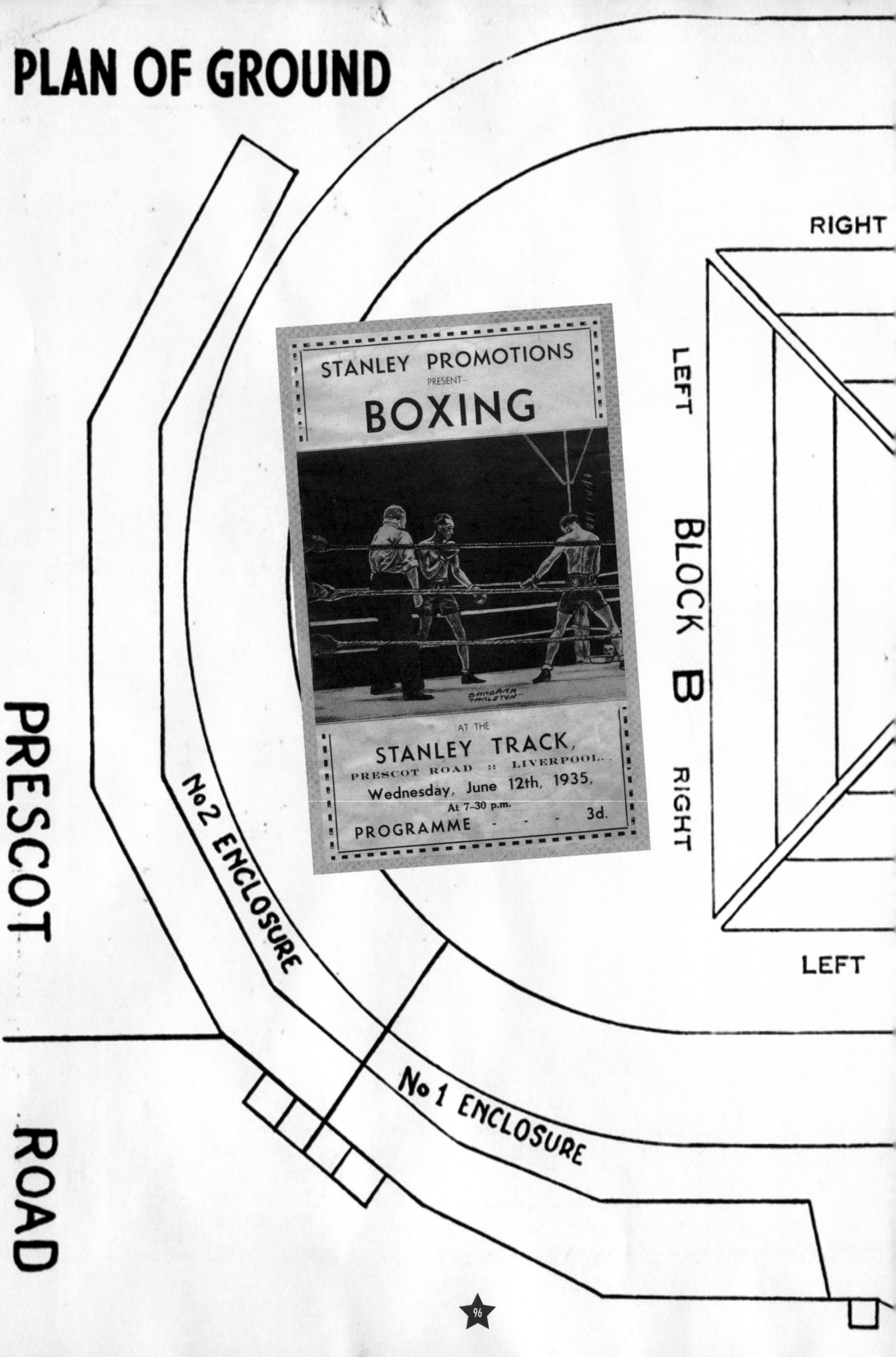
RIGHT
LEFT
BLOCK B
RIGHT
LEFT
PRESCOT ROAD
No 2 ENCLOSURE
No 1 ENCLOSURE
STANLEY PROMOTIONS
PRESENT–
BOXING
BARBARA TARLETON
AT THE
STANLEY TRACK,
PRESCOT ROAD :: LIVERPOOL.
Wednesday, June 12th, 1935,
At 7-30 p.m.
PROGRAMME - - - 3d.

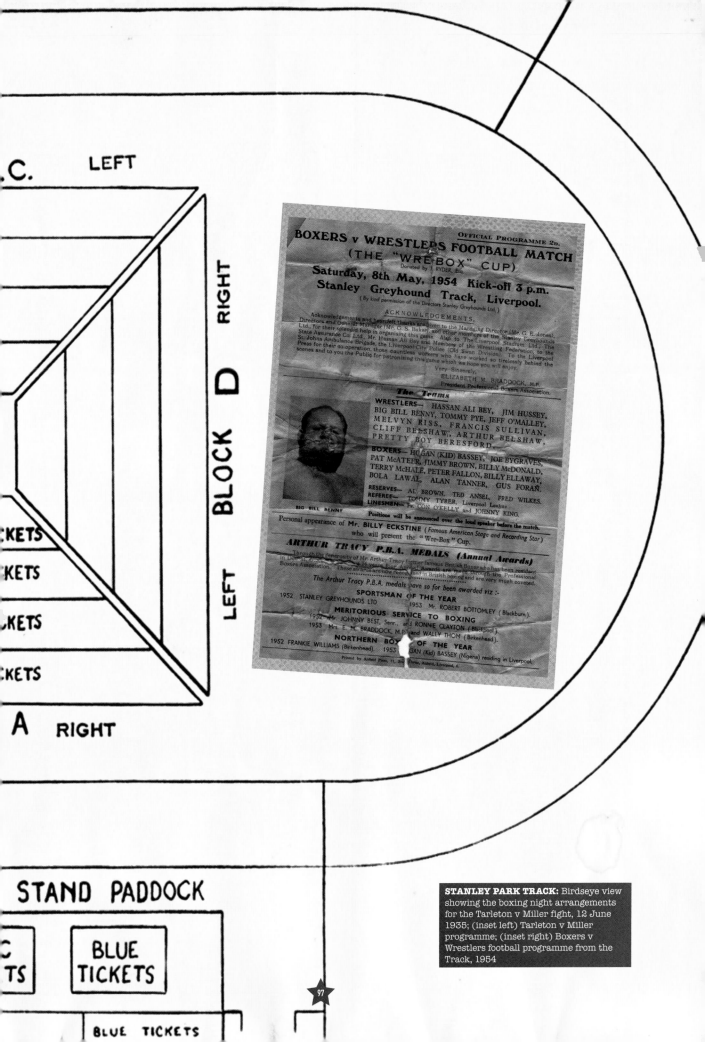

OFFICIAL PROGRAMME 2d.

BOXERS v WRESTLERS FOOTBALL MATCH
(THE "WRE-BOX" CUP)
Donated by T. RYDER, Esq.

Saturday, 8th May, 1954 Kick-off 3 p.m.
Stanley Greyhound Track, Liverpool.
(By kind permission of the Directors Stanley Greyhounds Ltd.)

ACKNOWLEDGEMENTS.

Acknowledgements and heartfelt thanks are given to the Managing Director (Mr. G. E. Jones), Directors and General Manager (Mr. G. S. Baker), and other members of the Stanley Greyhounds Ltd., for their splendid help in organising this game. Also to The Liverpool Stadium Ltd., The State Assurance Co. Ltd., Mr. Hassan Ali Bey and Members of the Wrestling Federation, to the St. Johns Ambulance Brigade, the Liverpool City Police (Old Swan Division). To the Liverpool Press for their co-operation, those countless workers who have worked so tirelessly behind the scenes and to you the Public for patronizing this game which we hope you will enjoy.

Very Sincerely,
ELIZABETH M. BRADDOCK, M.P.
President Professional Boxers Association.

The Teams

WRESTLERS— HASSAN ALI BEY, JIM HUSSEY, BIG BILL BENNY, TOMMY PYE, JEFF O'MALLEY, MELVYN RISS, FRANCIS SULLIVAN, CLIFF BELSHAW, ARTHUR BELSHAW, PRETTY BOY BERESFORD.

BOXERS— HOGAN (KID) BASSEY, JOE BYGRAVES, PAT McATEER, JIMMY BROWN, BILLY McDONALD, TERRY McHALE, PETER FALLON, BILLY ELLAWAY, BOLA LAWAL, ALAN TANNER, GUS FORAN.

RESERVES— AL BROWN, TED ANSEL, FRED WILKES.

REFEREE— TOMMY TYRER, Liverpool League.

LINESMEN— Fr. CON O'KELLY and JOHNNY KING.

BIG BILL BENNY

Positions will be announced over the loud speaker before the match.

Personal appearance of Mr. BILLY ECKSTINE (Famous American Stage and Recording Star) who will present the "Wre-Box" Cup.

ARTHUR TRACY P.B.A. MEDALS (Annual Awards)

Through the generosity of Mr. Arthur Tracy former famous British Boxer who has been resident in ... for ... years. Four Awards ... are made through the Professional Boxers Association. These awards are now recognised in British boxing and are very much coveted.

The Arthur Tracy P.B.A. medals have so far been awarded viz :-

SPORTSMAN OF THE YEAR
1952 STANLEY GREYHOUNDS LTD   1953 Mr. ROBERT BOTTOMLEY (Blackburn).

MERITORIOUS SERVICE TO BOXING
1952 Mr. JOHNNY BEST, Senr., and J RONNIE CLAYTON (Blackpool).
1953 Mrs. E. M. BRADDOCK, M.P. and WALLY THOM (Birkenhead).

NORTHERN BOXER OF THE YEAR
1952 FRANKIE WILLIAMS (Birkenhead).   1953 HOGAN (Kid) BASSEY (Nigeria) residing in Liverpool.

Printed by Anfield Press, 71, ... Anfield, Liverpool, 6.

STANLEY PARK TRACK: Birdseye view showing the boxing night arrangements for the Tarleton v Miller fight, 12 June 1935; (inset left) Tarleton v Miller programme; (inset right) Boxers v Wrestlers football programme from the Track, 1954

LEFT

.C.

BLOCK D

RIGHT

LEFT

A   RIGHT

CKETS

STAND PADDOCK

BLUE TICKETS

BLUE TICKETS

97

Nel Tarleton's Boxing Record:

No.	Date	Opponent	Venue	Result
1.	14th January 1926	George Sankey	Pudsey Street	Won on points (10 rounds)
2.	14th February 1926	Young Wilson	Leeds	Won on points (10 rounds)
3.	11th March 1926	Joe Martin	Pudsey Street	Won when Wilson retired in third round
4.	25th March 1926	Pat Malone	Pudsey Street	Won by eighth-round knock out
5.	6th May 1926	Les Tarrant	Pudsey Street	Won by seventh-round knock out
6.	17th June 1926	Kid Brooks	Pudsey Street	Won when Brooks disqualified in third round
7.	15th July 1926	Arthur Boddington	Pudsey Street	Lost on points (10 rounds)
8.	26th August 1926	Leo Kelly	Pudsey Street	Won when Kelly retired in 12th round
9.	9th September 1926	Kid Fitzpatrick	Pudsey Street	Won when referee stopped contest in fourth round
10.	23rd September 1926	Dom Volante	Pudsey Street	Lost on points (15 rounds)
11.	2nd December 1926	Chris Cairney	Pudsey Street	Won when Cairney retired in first round
12.	9th December 1926	Victor Crauc	Pudsey Street	Won when referee stopped contest in 14th round
13.	17th December 1926	Kid Pattenden	Premierland	Lost on points (15 rounds)
14.	23rd December 1926	Bert Mills	Pudsey Street	Won when referee stopped contest in 13th round
15.	13th January 1927	Frank Marcel	Pudsey Street	Won by seventh-round knock out
16.	3rd February 1927	Marcel Prudhomme	Pudsey Street	Won when referee stopped contest in eighth round
17.	17th February 1927	Mick Hill	Pudsey Street	Won on points (15 rounds)
18.	3rd March 1927	Dom Volante	Pudsey Street	Won on points (15 rounds)
19.	31st March 1927	Jerome Van Paemel	Pudsey Street	Won on points (15 rounds)
20.	14th April 1927	Peter Howard	Pudsey Street	Contest drawn (15 rounds)
21.	28th April 1927	Jack Ellis	Pudsey Street	Lost on points (15 rounds)
22.	19th May 1927	Jerome Vanpaemel	Pudsey Street	Won on points (15 rounds)
23.	23rd June 1927	Jack Kirby	Pudsey Street	Won when referee stopped contest in 11th round
24.	26th July 1927	Bert Saunders	Pudsey Street	Won by third-round knock out
25.	1st September 1927	Dom Volante	Pudsey Street	Won on points (15 rounds)
26.	8th September 1927	Johnny Brown	Premierland	Lost on points (15 rounds)
27.	22nd September 1927	Arthur Lloyd	Pudsey Street	Won by 15th-round knock out
28.	13th October 1927	Peter Howard	Pudsey Street	Won on points (15 rounds)
29.	17th November 1927	Enrico Venturi	Pudsey Street	Contest drawn (15 rounds)
30.	1st December 1927	Kid Socks	Pudsey Street	Won on points (15 rounds)
31.	29th December 1927	Alf Barber	Pudsey Street	Won when Barber retired in ninth round
32.	12th January 1928	Young Denain	Pudsey Street	Won by sixth-round knock out
33.	2nd February 1928	Donald Jones	Pudsey Street	Won by seventh-round knock out
34.	6th February 1928	Billy Hindley	NSC	Won on points (15 rounds)
35.	23rd February 1928	Louis Lepesant	Pudsey Street	Won by sixth-round knock out
36.	6th March 1928	Benny 'Kid' Carter	Pudsey Street	Won on points (15 rounds)
37.	15th March 1928	Robert Douillet	Pudsey Street	Won when Douillet retired in ninth round
38.	23rd March 1928	Jim McKenzie	Govan	Won on points (12 rounds)
39.	26th April 1928	Donald Jones	Pudsey Street	Won when Jones disqualified in fourth round
40.	17th May 1928	Billy Boulger	Pudsey Street	Won when Boulger retired in ninth round
41.	21st June 1928	Henri Pelemans	Pudsey Street	Won when referee stopped contest in eighth round
42.	26th July 1926	Dom Volante	Pudsey Street	Won on points (15 rounds) **Northern Area (vacant)**
43.	16th August 1928	Robert Obrecht	Pudsey Street	Won on points (15 rounds)
44.	16th October 1928	Kid Nicholson	Pudsey Street	Won on points (15 rounds)
45.	25th October 1928	Julian Verbist	Albert Hall	Contest drawn (10 rounds)
46.	11th November 1928	Robert Obrecht	Premierland	Won when referee stopped contest in 10th round
47.	18th November 1928	Billy Streets	Premierland	Won on points (15 rounds)
48.	25th November 1928	Rene Boitaert	Premierland	Won when referee stopped contest in 11th round
49.	6th December 1928	Julian Verbist	Pudsey Street	Won on points (15 rounds)
50.	11th December 1928	Lew Pinkus	NSC	Won on points (15 rounds)
51.	21st February 1929	Kid Pattenden	Crystal Palace	Won on points (10 rounds)
52.	22nd April 1922	Mick Hill	The Ring	Won when Hill retired in seventh round
53.	2nd May 1929	Billy Evans	Pudsey Street	Won on points (15 rounds)
54.	18th May 1929	Jack Kirby	West Bromwich	Won on points (15 rounds)
55.	3rd June 1929	Andre Beghin	NSC	Won on points (12 rounds)
56.	21st June 1929	Henri Poutrain	Clapton	Won on points (six rounds)
57.	25th July 1929	Henri Poutrain	Pudsey Street	Won on points (15 rounds)
58.	18th August 1929	Bugler Lake	Kilburn	Won when Lake retired in fourth round
59.	22nd August 1929	Robert Tassin	Pudsey Street	Won on points (15 rounds)
60.	11th October 1929	Archie Bell	New York	Won on points (10 rounds)
61.	2nd November 1929	Jackie Cohen	New York	Won on points (six rounds)
62.	11th November 1929	Pinky Silverberg	New York	Won points (10 rounds)
63.	20th December 1929	Al Ridgeway	New York	Lost on points (10 rounds)
64.	23rd May 1930	Joe Scalfaro	New York	Lost on points (10 rounds)
65.	24th June 1930	Frankie Marchese	New York	Won by seventh-round knock out
66.	3rd September 1930	Mickey Greb	Newark	Won on points (eight rounds)
67.	11th September 1930	Jimmy Slavin	New York	Contest drawn (eight rounds)
68.	6th November 1930	Johnny Cuthbert	Pudsey Street	Contest drawn (15 rounds) **British title and Lonsdale Belt**
69.	25th November 1930	Rene Boitaert	Paddington	Won when referee stopped contest in 11th round
70.	27th November 1930	Phil Claret	Pudsey Street	Won when referee stopped contest in ninth round
71.	1st December 1930	Tommy Dexter	Hull	Won on points (15 rounds)

No.	Date	Opponent	Venue	Result
72.	19th February 1931	Ernest Mignard	Pudsey Street	Won when referee stopped contest in 12th round
73.	10th March 1931	Louis Laseaux	Manchester	Won when referee stopped contest in 10th round
74.	26th March 1931	Ginger Jones	New Brighton	Won on points (15 rounds)
75.	23rd April 1931	Angelo Agatensi	New Brighton	Won by third-round knock out
76.	21st May 1931	Jack Garland	Olympia	Won on points (12 rounds)
77.	1st June 1931	Douglas Parker	Albert Hall	Won on points (eight round)
78.	13th June 1931	Albert Barker	Sheffield	Won on points (12 rounds)
79.	25th August 1931	Albert Barker	Southport	Won when referee stopped contest in 15th round
80.	1st October 1931	Johnny Cuthbert	Anfield	Won on points (15 rounds) **British title and Lonsdale Belt**
81.	9th November 1931	Nick Bensa	Albert Hall	Won on points (10 rounds)
82.	21st January 1932	Tommy Dexter	Birkenhead	Won when Dexter retired in 10th round
83.	24th January 1932	Young Josephs	Barnsley	Won on points (12 rounds)
84.	8th February 1932	Douglas Parker	Manchester	Won by seventh-round knock out
85.	29th February 1932	Francois Machtens	Leeds	Won on points (15 rounds)
86.	17th March 1932	Al Foreman	Anfield	Won on points (15 rounds)
87.	18th April 1932	Benny Sharkey	Newcastle	Won on points (15 rounds)
88.	13th June 1932	Al Brown	Anfield	Contest drawn (15 rounds)
89.	16th October 1932	Douglas Parker	The Ring	Won by 10th-round knockout
90.	10th November 1932	Seaman Tommy Watson	Liverpool Stadium	Lost on points (15 rounds) **British title and Lonsdale Belt**
91.	12th January 1933	Leon Mestre	Liverpool Stadium	Won when referee stopped contest in sixth round
92.	16th February 1933	Dan McGarry	Liverpool Stadium	Won on points (15 rounds)
93.	8th March 1933	Alec Law	Cheltenham	Won when Law retired in second round
94.	20th April 1933	Auguste Gyde	Liverpool Stadium	Won on points (12 rounds)
95.	21st August 1933	Jimmy Kelso	Sydney	Won on points (15 rounds)
96.	25th September 1933	Tod Morgan	Sydney	Contest drawn (15 rounds)
97.	12th October 1933	Young Llew Edwards	Melbourne	Lost on points (15 rounds)
98.	8th February 1934	Nick Bensa	Liverpool Stadium	Won when Bensa retired in 11th round
99.	12th February 1934	Norman Dale	Manchester	Won on points (12 rounds)
100.	1st March 1934	Gheorghe Covaci	Liverpool Stadium	Won when Covaci retired in eighth round
101.	9th May 1934	Harry Brooks	Blackfriars Ring	Won on points (15 rounds)
102.	17th May 1934	Sonny Lee	Liverpool Stadium	Lost on points (15 rounds)
103.	26th July 1934	Tommy Watson	Anfield	Won on points (15 rounds) **British title and Lonsdale Belt**
104.	20th September 1934	Freddie Miller	Anfield	Lost on points (15 rounds) **World title**
105.	10th December 1934	Dave Crowley	Wembley	Won on points (15 rounds) **British title and Lonsdale Belt**
106.	30th January 1935	Hal Cartwright	Wolverhampton	Won when referee stopped contest in 11th round
107.	4th February 1935	Norman Milton	Warrington	Won on points (10 rounds)
108.	25th March 1935	Johnny King	Manchester	Lost on points (12 rounds)
109.	12th June 1935	Freddie Miller	Stanley Greyhound Track	Lost on points (15 rounds) **World title**
110.	10th October 1935	Johnny King	Liverpool Stadium	Contest drawn (12 rounds)
111.	7th November 1935	Jimmy Walsh	Liverpool Stadium	Won on points (12 rounds)
112.	12th December 1935	Harry Edwards	Liverpool Stadium	Won on points (12 rounds)
113.	13th January 1936	Joe Connelly	Glasgow	Won on points (12 rounds)
114.	13th February 1936	George Williams	Liverpool Stadium	Won when referee stopped contest in seventh round
115.	26th March 1936	Raymond Renard	Liverpool Stadium	Won on points (12 rounds)
116.	6th May 1936	Johnny King	Anfield	Won on points (15 rounds) **British title and Lonsdale Belt**
117.	23rd July 1936	Maurice Baudry	Liverpool Stadium	Won on points (12 rounds)
118.	24th September 1936	Johnny McGrory	Anfield	Lost on points (15 rounds) **British title and Lonsdale Belt**
119.	11th February 1937	Frank Harsen	Liverpool Stadium	Won on points (12 rounds)
120.	22nd February 1937	Spider Kelly	Belfast	Lost on points (10 rounds)
121.	13th October 1938	Arnold Lagrand	Liverpool Stadium	Won on points (10 rounds)
122.	24th November 1938	Nipper Fred Morris	Liverpool Stadium	Won when Morris disqualified in eighth round
123.	2nd March 1939	Josef Preys	Liverpool Stadium	Won on points (10 rounds)
124.	30th March 1939	Billy Charlton	Liverpool Stadium	Won when Charlton disqualified in third round
125.	11th May 1939	Spider Kelly	Liverpool Stadium	Won on points (10 rounds)
126.	1st February 1940	Johnny Cusick	Liverpool Stadium	Won on points (15 rounds) **British and Empire titles and Lonsdale Belt**
127.	18th March 1940	Billy Walker	Earl's Court	Won on points (10 rounds)
128.	2nd November 1940	Tom Smith	Liverpool Stadium	Won on points (15 rounds) **British and Empire Titles and Lonsdale Belt**
129.	5th February 1941	Tom Smith	Newcastle	Lost on points (10 rounds)
130.	23rd February 1941	Bobby Watson	Liverpool Stadium	Won on points (10 rounds)
131.	28th August 1941	Billy Walker	Albert Hall	Won on points (eight rounds)
132.	19th September 1941	Jim Brady	Manchester	Lost on points (10 rounds)
133.	30th March 1942	Syd Worgan	Albert Hall	Won on points (eight rounds)
134.	21st April 1942	Pancho Ford	Watford	Won by fifth-round knock out
135.	8th October 1942	Syd Worgan	Liverpool Stadium	Won on points (10 rounds)
136.	15th March 1943	Syd Worgan	Nottingham	Won on points (10 rounds)
137.	24th May 1943	Len Davies	Birmingham	Lost on points (eight rounds)
138.	10th July 1943	Ben Duffy	Nottingham	Lost on points (eight rounds)
139.	4th February 1944	Ben Duffy	Manchester	Won on points (eight rounds)
140.	24th March 1944	Johnny King	Manchester	Lost when disqualified in second round
141.	5th May 1944	George Pook	Manchester	Won on points (eight rounds)
142.	7th August 1944	Johnny King	Manchester	Won on points (eight rounds)
143.	23rd February 1945	Al Phillips	Manchester	Won on points (15 rounds) **British and Empire titles and Lonsdale Belt**

ANFIELD PERFORMER: Fred Perry, here pictured at Wimbledon, appeared in an exhibition at Anfield in June 1937

Did You Know?

The tennis player Fred Perry, Wimbledon champion in 1934, 1935 and 1936 (and the last British man to win a Grand Slam tournament courtesy of his third All England Club success), played an exhibition match at Anfield on Saturday 12 June 1937 against Ellsworth Vines, Wimbledon champion of 1932. Both men had since turned professional and thus were unable to compete at Wimbledon and other major tournaments. Eleven thousand spectators turned up to watch a match whose start was delayed by rain, which fell until three o'clock: proceedings finally got under way at quarter past four. The *Daily Post* declared Perry to be in 'scintillating' form and opined that his game had improved by 'at least 25 per cent' since turning pro. A wooden structure was used as the court. It was a high-quality match, although neither player came to the net much (a tactic that was then highly unusual for natural grass court players) owing to the danger of being passed by his hard-hitting opponent. The first set went the way of Vines, 6-4, owing to the great speed with which he hit the ball. The seventh game of that set was a marathon, going to 10 deuces before finally being won by Vines. In the second set Perry bounced back with some good cross-court shots, dropping just one game en route to levelling the match. Perry was by now in full control, with Vines failing to consistently hit the ball as hard as he was capable and the Englishman ultimately prevailed 4-6 6-1 6-4 6-4. The singles match was followed by a doubles contest between the great Bill Tilden, who was partnered by L.R. Stoefen, and Fred Perry and Ellsworth Vines. The doubles was won by Tilden and Stoefen 6-3 11-13 7-5.

Peter Kane –
The Golborne Hammer

Although he hailed from Golborne in Greater Manchester, Peter Kane's boxing career will always be indelibly linked with Liverpool. He made his debut, aged just 16, at the Liverpool Stadium on 13 December 1934 against Joe Jacobs, who he knocked out in the fifth round. His debut typified much of his career. The following year he had a further 12 contests: two at Anfield and 10 at the Liverpool Stadium, that were all won by knock out. Indeed, in his first 13 fights, Kane only boxed in 38 rounds. The first boxer that took Kane the distance was Joe Curran, another Liverpool boxer of repute. He remained undefeated until his 41st contest, when he was knocked out by the great Benny Lynch in Glasgow in a world title fight. Just five contests and six months later, however, Peter Kane was crowned world flyweight champion at Anfield before a crowd of nearly 40,000, still the biggest-ever crowd for a boxing match on Merseyside.

From the age of 12, Kane served his boxing apprenticeship in fairgrounds and small halls around various Lancashire towns. On some occasions he boxed for as little as five shillings a night, yet by the age of 20 he became the youngest-ever flyweight to win the world title, for which he received a purse of £1,500. The records show none of these 'amateur' fights, but Kane thought they amounted to more than 100. Upon leaving school at 14 he became a blacksmith's striker, a job that gave him a magnificent physique, and he continued with this employment even

after he became world champion. Kane's hurricane style of boxing – he carried explosive power in both fists – made him a great crowd favourite.

By the end of 1936, Kane was being lined-up for a world championship bout. When he outpointed the IBU world flyweight champion Valentin Angelmann at the Liverpool Stadium on 23 November 1936 he showed a maturity that matched his explosive punching. His first contest outside of Britain was a return match against Angelmann, who he beat once again to confirm his world championship credentials. This contest took place in Paris before a crowd of 22,000 at the Palais de Sports.

During the course of 1937, Kane boxed three times at Anfield before ever-growing crowds. First he faced the Spanish flyweight champion Fortunato Ortega, who he beat on points over 12 rounds. Next up was a Northern Area flyweight title contest against Oldham-born Phil Milligan. In front of a crowd of over 20,000 Kane battered a sorry Milligan, whose corner threw in the towel in the 11th round, to take his first title.

The scene for Kane's third Anfield contest of 1937 must have been a wonderful sight for any sports fan. The attraction was a final eliminating contest against Jimmy Warnock of Belfast, for the right to meet Benny Lynch for the world title. Special trains brought thousands of people from Golborne to Liverpool, among them thousands of

Lancashire miners. Warnock was not short of support, with ferries bringing in a large Irish contingent complete with rattles, shillelaghs (wooden clubs), green berets and hats. Warnock's supporters occupied the Kemlyn Road terraces and the Paddock; Kane's support was largely on the Kop. With three other Irish fighters in the supporting contests the atmosphere prior to the main bout became increasingly electric.

When Kane emerged from the players' tunnel the roar was deafening. He was followed by Warnock, decked out in a green dressing gown. As he walked to the ring his supporters sang: 'Follow, follow, we will follow Warnock, anywhere, everywhere we will follow on.' Kane, however, brushed Warnock's challenge to one side, with the referee stopping the fight in the fourth round. The Irishman had previously taken five lengthy counts and was in no fit state to continue.

Having defeated Warnock, Kane was now the undisputed challenger for Benny Lynch's world and British titles. Johnny Best attempted to get the title fight for Anfield, offering a massive £7,500, but Lynch was contracted to Glasgow promoter George Dingley, who had the rights to stage all of his fights. Consequently, the fight was arranged for 13 October 1937 at Shawfield Park, Glasgow.

There was great anticipation for the Lynch/Kane contest, with some 1,200 travelling from Liverpool and other Lancashire towns to Glasgow. The villagers of Golborne decorated their houses and streets with bunting in anticipation of Kane bringing back the world title. In front of 40,000 fans, Lynch and Kane fought out one of the greatest-ever flyweight title fights. Kane was knocked down in the first round by the champion but recovered sufficiently to ▶

'...he boxed for as little as five shillings a night, yet by the age of 20 he became the youngest-ever flyweight to win the world title, for which he received a purse of £1,500'

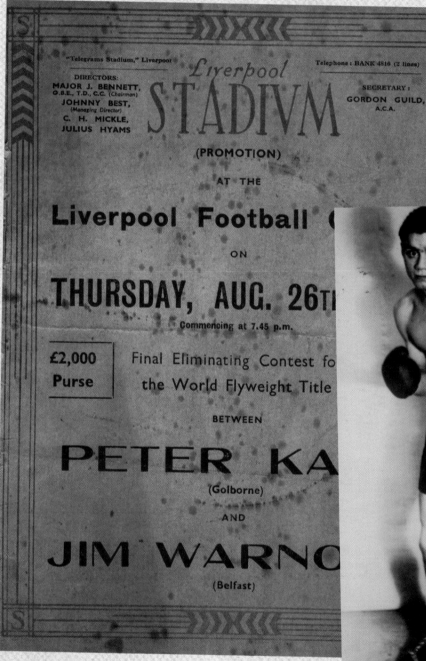

COVER SHOT: Programme from Kane's 1937 eliminator against Jim Warnock; (inset) Kane in fighting stance

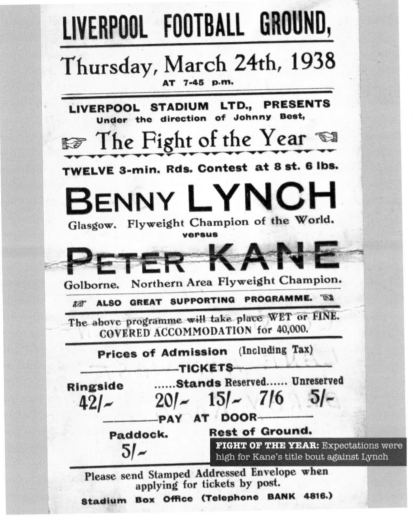

LIVERPOOL FOOTBALL GROUND,

Thursday, March 24th, 1938

AT 7-45 p.m.

LIVERPOOL STADIUM LTD., PRESENTS
Under the direction of Johnny Best,

☞ **The Fight of the Year** ☜

TWELVE 3-min. Rds. Contest at 8 st. 6 lbs.

BENNY LYNCH

Glasgow. Flyweight Champion of the World.

versus

PETER KANE

Golborne. Northern Area Flyweight Champion.

☞ **ALSO GREAT SUPPORTING PROGRAMME.** ☜

The above programme will take place WET or FINE.
COVERED ACCOMMODATION for 40,000.

Prices of Admission (Including Tax)

——————TICKETS——————

Ringside ......Stands Reserved...... Unreserved
42/- **20/-** **15/-** **7/6** **5/-**

——————PAY AT DOOR——————

Paddock. Rest of Ground.
5/-

FIGHT OF THE YEAR: Expectations were high for Kane's title bout against Lynch

Please send Stamped Addressed Envelope when
applying for tickets by post.

Stadium Box Office (Telephone BANK 4816.)

give Lynch a scare in the middle rounds. Overall, though, Lynch had too much experience for the challenger. As both boxers came out for the 13th round, Lynch caught Kane with a left hook to the jaw, rocking the challenger to the core. Lynch followed up his advantage by hitting Kane with a series of punches to the head; a tired and battered Kane was now incapable of fending off the champion's assault. Eventually the challenger dropped to the canvas to take a count of seven, and as he got up he was met with more heavy punishment and forced to go down on his knees again. This time he raised his head to hear the referee counting, but he was so exhausted that he could not get up. It was Kane's first defeat, a double disappointment as it also meant that his dream of winning the world title had ended in failure. Although well beaten, an appreciative crowd loudly cheered Kane as

he left the ring. It was recognition that he had participated in one of the greatest boxing contests ever seen in Britain.

Like all great boxers, Kane learned from his defeat. The following March Johnny Best secured a rematch at Anfield between the two top flyweights, although this time it was a non-title fight. As both boxers were having increasing difficulty getting down to flyweight, they agreed to box at 8st 6lbs, but at the weigh-in Lynch could not even get down to this weight. The contest itself, like their world title fight, was a full-blooded affair. On this occasion Kane acquitted himself much better and, by most judges of the time, should have been given the verdict, but to loud boos from the crowd the referee declared the contest a draw. A few weeks after the Kane bout, Lynch would have to relinquish his world title because of his

weight problems. With the world flyweight title now vacant, Best lined up a world title fight between Kane and Jackie Jurich, the American flyweight champion. It was to be another great Anfield boxing occasion.

Prior to the outbreak of World War Two, British boxing fans developed a great affinity with the flyweight division. World champions such as Jimmy Wilde, Jackie Brown and Benny Lynch excited crowds throughout the country. In the build-up to Peter Kane's second attempt to win the world flyweight title at Anfield on 22 September 1938, comparisons were drawn with the three great champions. This affinity with the flyweight division helps explain the great interest that the Kane/Jurich world title fight aroused. Throughout the Lancashire coalfields and within Liverpool itself, the public took a great interest in the contest. As for the contenders, it was felt that Jurich would win if the fight went the distance, as he was regarded as a classic performer who had great hand speed. In contrast, Kane carried enormous punching power in both hands, and it was thought he could only win by a knock out.

Kane began the fight in typically robust style, with powerful punches to head and body. However, one such body blow resulted in a broken right hand for Kane. Returning to his corner at the end of the first round he was advised to just use his left where possible. The injury changed the whole pattern of the fight as Kane had to adapt his style and instead of relying on explosive punches he now had to try to outbox Jurich. Despite his injury, Kane had Jurich down for a count of nine on three occasions in rounds two, 12 and 13, before going on to take the title on points. At the end Kane told the press: "He was a good, fast lad. I was handicapped by the injury to my hand. But I knew I was on top in the last round when Jurich made a desperate effort to clinch the fight with a knock out. I had to keep battling on."

When the referee raised Kane's hand he got a great reception from the crowd. He was the youngest boxer ever to hold the world flyweight title. Kane's victory also met with national acclaim. The *Daily Herald* commented that: 'Kane won a brilliant points victory over the American, Jackie Jurich. No greater demonstration of clean and clever all-round boxing has been seen in a British ring.' No less an authority than Jimmy Wilde said: "Kane has altered his style ▶

HOW IT WAS: George Green's cartoon depicts Kane's draw with champion Lynch

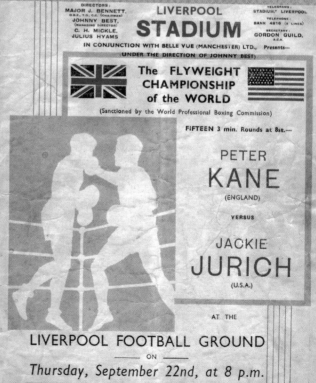

KANE V JURICH: The bill and programme from 1938

astonishingly. He has proved that he can box, and those who regard him as a purely tear-away type of fighter will have to re-adjust their ideas." Such acclamation was endorsed when Kane returned to Golborne to receive a civic reception in front of thousands of people.

The victory over Jurich was certainly the highpoint of Kane's career. A mixture of injury and weight problems meant that he never realised his full potential as a world champion. Three weeks after the Jurich fight the extent of his hand injury was revealed when Kane had to have the little finger of his right hand amputated. He resumed his career in 1939 with a series of victories, but all his contests were above the flyweight limit. Consequently Ted Denvir, Kane's manager, announced to the press in May 1939 that because of weight problems Kane was relinquishing his world title. However, Kane did eventually defend his title, in June 1943 against Jackie Paterson in Glasgow. Unfortunately, his problems getting down to the required weight were cruelly exposed when he suffered a first-round knock out, with the contest only lasting 61 seconds.

In March of the following year, Kane suffered a freak eye injury while on duty with the RAF that resulted in a discharge from the force. This led to a period of retirement from the ring, but following a successful operation he regained his boxing licence in 1946 and returned as a bantamweight under the management of Nel Tarleton. A run of impressive victories in 1946 and in the first half of 1947 led to a European bantamweight title fight against Theo Medina on 19 September. Kane outpointed the champion to win the title but lost it to Guido Ferracin on points just five months later. He tried to regain the title from Ferracin in July 1948 but this time had to retire in the fifth round. Just five months later Kane took on Stan Rowan in a final eliminator for the British bantamweight title, losing on points over 12 rounds. All these contests took place at Belle Vue, Manchester.

The fight with Rowan was Kane's last, a sad end to a great career. In his pomp he was a great favourite at the Liverpool Stadium and drew record crowds to Anfield. Kane may have hailed from Golborne, but it was the Liverpool boxing public that cheered him on as one of their own kind.

'The victory was certainly the highpoint...three weeks after the fight the extent of his hand injury was revealed when Kane had to have the little finger of his right hand amputated'

Stan Rowan – Liverpool's First Bantamweight Champion

'In terms of experience, Rowan was no match for the champion... Rowan had only had one scheduled 15-round fight'

Appropriately, the final night of boxing at Anfield brought another Lonsdale Belt to Liverpool. When Stan Rowan outpointed Jackie Paterson on 24 March 1949 to take the British and British Empire bantamweight titles, he became the first Liverpool boxer to take a national championship at the weight. It was the great Ike Bradley who began Liverpool's strong association with the bantamweight division, and given that the city had produced some of the country's finest bantamweights, it is somewhat surprising that it took so long for the British title to come here. Alan Rudkin would, of course, pick up the baton in the 1960s to take Liverpool's bantamweight tradition to an even higher level.

Paterson was a formidable opponent who, at one time, following his first-round knock out of Peter Kane, had been world champion at flyweight. At his peak he held five different championships, but a year before he met

Rowan he had lost his three flyweight titles to Rinty Monaghan in Belfast. Although he had lost all his flyweight titles prior to meeting Rowan, Paterson was still a potent boxer who carried a match-winning punch. Moreover, he was at his strongest at bantamweight, having found it increasingly difficult to boil down to flyweight.

Before he got his title shot, Rowan had to win three eliminators in the space of eight months. First he outpointed Ireland's Bunty Doran at the Liverpool Stadium on 18 March 1948, before beating both Danny O'Sullivan of London on 31 May and Peter Kane on 19 November, on points at the Harringay Arena and Belle Vue respectively. Prior to meeting these three strong opponents, Rowan had actually beaten Paterson convincingly at Harringay inside two rounds – he had Paterson on the canvas six times before the referee intervened to stop the contest. In this period he also took on, and beat, another

HOW HE SAW IT: Stan Rowan's success, captured by George Green in 1949

world-ranked rival in the form of Joe Curran at the Liverpool Stadium. These five contests alone demonstrate just how tough it was to get a chance to box for a British title in the 1930s and 1940s. There were plenty of quality opponents to beat before the BBBofC would consider a boxer suitable to challenge for a British title.

Following Rowan's defeat of Kane, Paterson upset the normally placid Rowan by telling him: "You'll have to do better than that to beat me." Rowan did not let his anger interfere with preparations, however, as he knew that Paterson would come to Anfield in much better physical shape, as this time his two titles were at stake.

In terms of experience, Rowan was no match for the champion. Paterson had competed in 14 title fights. In contrast, Rowan had only ever had one scheduled 15-round fight, against Joe Curran, but this had ended in a 10th-round knock out. From the outset, Rowan was aware that he had to use his superior boxing ability to beat Paterson. On several occasions in the past, Paterson had won a seemingly lost contest with a short right hook that usually put an opponent out for the count.

Rowan, however, was a cool, unhurried boxer with the ability to parry or avoid blows. Moreover, his left jab was capable of destroying an opponent's punch rhythm and this was precisely the method that Rowan employed in his Anfield title fight. Every time Paterson looked set to deliver a

knock-out blow, Rowan would unbalance the champion with a jab of sufficient force that resulted in the punch missing its target. In the 11th round, Rowan reminded the champion that he could also punch when he landed a right uppercut that lifted the champion off the canvas. Paterson had enough know-how to survive, but from this point Rowan, knowing what Paterson was capable of, was happy to box his way to the title.

Owing to weight problems, Rowan was forced to give up his British title without a single defence. Before relinquishing his title, he had lost his Empire title to Vic Toweel in Johannesburg at Wembley on 12 November 1949. Soon after, Rowan retired for a two-year period. When he did return, in August 1952, he made a winning comeback at the Liverpool Stadium against Jackie Briers, but Rowan was increasingly plagued with cuts to his eyes. Following a points defeat to Peter Keenan, who was then British bantamweight champion at the Kelvin Hall, Glasgow in March 1953, Rowan retired for good.

Rowan's professional career commenced at the Liverpool Stadium when as an 18-year-old he beat Eddie Douglas over four rounds. He quickly established himself as a firm favourite with the home crowd, who only saw him lose once prior to his championship-winning performance at Anfield. This is how Rowan should be remembered – the first Liverpool boxer to win the British bantamweight title.

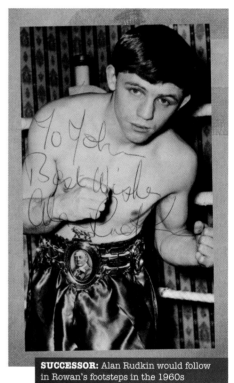

SUCCESSOR: Alan Rudkin would follow in Rowan's footsteps in the 1960s

Boxing Results at Anfield 1931-1949:

Opponents	Weight	Status of Contest	Rounds	Result
1 October 1931, attendance: 30,000, referee: Jack Smith				
Nel Tarleton v Johnny Cuthbert (Sheffield)	Feather	British Title	15	Tarleton won on points.
Dick Burke v Johnny Peters	Bantam	Non-Title	12	Burke won on points.
Billy Gannon v Tommy Hyams (London)	Feather	Non-Title	8	Hyams won on points.
Harold Higginson v Jack Mallon	Welter	Non-Title	8	Higginson won, the referee stopped the fight in the fifth round.
17 March 1932, attendance: 20,000				
Nel Tarleton v Al Foreman (Canada)	Catch	Non-Title	12	Tarleton won on points but had to fend off the hard-hitting Foreman towards the end of the fight.
Harold Higginson v Kid Farlo (London)	Welter	Non-Title	8	Higginson stopped Farlo in the third round.
Tommy Rose v Billy Renton (Hull)	Bantam	Non-Title	8	Renton won on points. Renton was one of Foreman's sparring partners.
Ginger Foran v George Anderson (South Africa)	Fly	Non-Title	8	Foran won on points, a good performance against the champion of South Africa.
23 May 1932, attendance: 12,000, referee: Jimmy Wilde				
Alf Howard v Willie Hamilton (Scotland)	Welter	Non-Title	12	Howard down four times in the ninth round. In 10th Hamilton hit Howard low and was disqualified.
Dom Volante v Harold Higginson	Light	Non-Title	15	Volante won by knock out in the third round, Volante whipped a right on the point that put Higginson on the canvas. The referee was then forced to stop the contest.
Ginger Foran v Ginger McLeod (Scotland)	Fly	Non-Title	10	Foran won on points against the very experienced McLeod. It was regarded as the best contest of the evening.
Ernie Roderick v Jerry Smith (Rock Ferry)	Welter	Non-Title	10	Roderick won in the ninth round, the referee stopping the contest. It was the first defeat for Smith the Rock Ferry 'Assassin'.
13 June 1932, attendance: 30,000, referee: Gus Platts				
Nel Tarleton v Al Brown (Panama)	Feather	Non-Title	15	Platts declared the contest a draw to the dismay of the home crowd.
Dick Burke v Kid Johns (Paris, France)	Feather	Non-Title	15	Burke knocked out Johns in the first round. It was the first time Johns had been knocked down.
Ernie Roderick v Jimmy Stewart	Light	Non-Title	10	Stewart won on points, Roderick was hampered by a cut inside the mouth from as early as the first round. It was Roderick's first defeat.
Billy Gannon v Mottee Kid Singh (British Guiana)	Feather	Non-title	10	Gannon won, referee stopped the contest in the seventh round.
Ginger Foran v Arthur Killeen (Bolton)	Fly	Non-Title	8	Foran knocked out Killeen in the fifth round.
Bob Nelson (Birkenhead) v Seaman Clayton (HMS Exeter)	Welter	Non-Title	6	Nelson won, referee stopped the fight in the fifth.
21 July 1932				
Jack Doyle (Ireland) v Bobby Shields (Scotland)	Heavy	Non-Title	15	Doyle knocked out the Scottish champion in two minutes 25 seconds. It was his 32nd first-round win in 33 contests.
Alf Howard v Barney Kieswetter (South Africa)	Welter	Non-Title	12	Howard well beaten on points, he could not cope with the skill of Kieswetter.
Steve McCall (Scotland) v Arthur Holsgrove	Middle	Non-Tilte	8	Holsgrove forced the Scot to retire in the fourth round after McCall hurt his shoulder.
Ginger Foran v Boy Walley (Singapore)	Fly	Non-Title	8	Foran won in the fifth round, Walley's corner threw in the towel.
Tommy Rose v Bud Walley (Singapore)	Bantam	Non-Title	12	Rose won on points, a close decision with some big hitting from both boxers.
Jerry Smith (Rock Ferry) v Charlie Smith (Birkenhead)	Welter	Non-Title	8	Jerry Smith won by KO in the fourth round.
18 August 1932				
Barney Kieswetter (South Africa) v Joe Rostron (Heywood)	Welter	Non-Title	12	Kieswetter won on points.
Ginger Foran v Bert Kirby (Birmingham)	Fly	Non-Title	12	Foran won in 10th round, Kirby forced to retire with a sprained ankle.
Jim Crawford (Wales) v Mottee Kid Singh (British Guiana)	Feather	Non-Title	10	Singh won in the fourth round when Crawford's corner threw in the towel. Crawford had been down several times.
Arthur Holsgrove v Bernard Cook (London)	Middle	Non-Title	8	Holsgrove won on a first-round KO.
Jimmy McGurn v Charlie Hazel (Wales)	Fly	Non-Title	8	McGurn knocked out Hazel in the third round.
Nat Williams v Young Martin	Light	Non-Title	6	Boxed a draw.
15 September 1932, referee: Jimmy Wilde				
Jackie Johnston (Canada) v Cuthbert Taylor (Wales)	Feather	Non-Title	10	Johnston won on points.
Tommy Bland (Canada) v Harold Higginson	Light	Non-Title	10	Bland knocked out Higginson in the second round.
Johnny Goodrich (Canada) v Tommy Rose	Bantam	Non-Title	N/A	Goodrich won, referee stopped the contest in the sixth round. Rose had a badly cut eye.

Opponents	Weight	Status of Contest	Rounds	Result
Jack Dane (Canada) v Arthur Holsgrove	Cruiser	Non-Title	6	Contest drawn.
Jimmy Stewart v Bryn Edwards (Tonypandy, Wales)	Light	Non-Title	8	Stewart won on points.
Jack Fraser v Billy Cooper (Birkenhead)	Light	Non-Title	6	Fraser won on points.

26 July 1934, attendance: 15,000, referee: C.B. Thomas

Opponents	Weight	Status of Contest	Rounds	Result
Nel Tarleton v ex-Seaman Tommy Watson (Newcastle)	Feather	British Title	15	Tarleton won on points.
Al Burke (London) v Cock Moffit	Middle	Non-Title	10	Burke won on points.
Bob Rimmer v Nipper Hampston (Batley)	Bantam	Non-Title	6	Hampston won on points.
Billy Gannon v Mottee Kid Singh (British Guiana)	Feather	Non-Title	6	Gannon won on points.
Tom Routledge (Seaforth) v Joe Horridge	Light	Non-Title	6	Routledge won on points.

20 September 1934, attendance: 31,213, referee: C.H. Douglas

Opponents	Weight	Status of Contest	Rounds	Result
Nel Tarleton v Freddie Miller (Cincinatti, USA)	Feather	World Title	15	Miller won on points
Ginger Foran v John Ellis (Manchester)	Feather	Non-Title	10	Foran boxed with great skill. He landed a right hook to Ellis' jaw in the fifth round that dropped Ellis for the full count.
Ernie Roderick v Charlie Baxter (Birmingham)	Welter	Non-Title	10	A close encounter won by Roderick on points.
Peter Clarke v Ralph Lenny (USA)	Light	Non-Title	8	Described as a rough, crude contest. Lenny, Miller's sparring partner, won on points.
Peter Banasko v George Sanderson	Welter	Non-Title	6	Banasko was the clear winner on points.
Bob Nelson (Birkenhead) v Tim Shean (Merthyr, Wales)	Welter	Non-Title	4	Contest drawn.

27 June 1935, attendance: 11,200, referee: Jack Smith

Opponents	Weight	Status of Contest	Rounds	Result
Freddie Miller (USA) v ex-Seaman Tommy Watson (N'castle)	Catch	Non-Title	10	Miller won on points.
Billy Gannon v Douglas Kestrell (Cardiff, Wales)	Feather	Non-Title	10	Gannon won on points.
Joe Curran v Peter Miller (Gateshead)	N/A	Non-Title	8	Curran won on points.
Peter Clarke v Tommy Routledge (Seaforth)	Light	Non-Title	8	Clarke won. Contest stopped in the sixth round. Clarke showed great sportsmanship: when Routledge was unable to defend himself he appealed to the referee to stop the fight. Routledge's corner threw in the towel to safeguard their man.
Billy Hughes (Birkenhead) v Len Wickwar (Leicester)	Light	Non-Title	6	Hughes knocked out Wickwar in the fifth round.
Peter Kane (Golborne) v Billy Charnock (Manchester)	Fly	Non-Title	6	Kane won, referee stopped the contest in the second round.

25 July 1935, attendance: 11,450

Opponents	Weight	Status of Contest	Rounds	Result
Freddie Miller (USA) v ex-Seaman Tommy Watson (N'castle)	Catch	Non-Title	10	Miller knocked out Watson in the second round.
Vernon Cormier (USA) v Cuthbert Taylor (Merthyr, Wales)	Feather	Non-Title	10	Taylor won on points, a surprise result.
Ginger Foran v Stan Jehu (Wales)	Feather	Non-Title	10	Foran stopped Jehu in the eighth round.
Peter Kane (Golborne) v Jackie Shea	Fly	Non-Title	6	Kane knocked out Shea in the second round.
Les Carter v Billy Charlton (Newcastle)	Light	Non-Title	6	Charlton stopped Carter in the second round.

6 May 1936, referee: Jack Hart

Opponents	Weight	Status of Contest	Rounds	Result
Nel Tarleton v Johnny King (Manchester)	Feather	British Title	15	Tarleton won on points.
Reg Gregory v Gaston Kinsabelle (Belgium)	Middle	Non-Title	10	Gregory won on points and maintained his unbeaten record.
Peter Kane (Golborne) v Praxille Gyde (France)	Fly	Non-Title	8	Kane knocked out the French flyweight champion in the third round.
Peter Clarke v John Finnerty (Scotland)	Light	Non-Title	6	Finnerty won on points.
George Powell v Mick Howard	Bantam	Non-Title	6	Powell won on points.
Ken Robinson v George Foort (Burnley)	Middle	Non-Title	6	Robinson knocked out Foort in the fifth round.

24 September 1936, attendance: 13,000, referee: C.B. Thomas

Opponents	Weight	Status of Contest	Rounds	Result
Nel Tarleton v Johnny McGrory (Glasgow, Scotland)	Feather	British Title	15	McGrory won on points.
Jimmy Walsh (Chester) v Billy Hughes (Birkenhead)	Light	Non-Title	10	Walsh won in the fifth round when Hughes' corner threw in the towel.
Ginger Foran v Gustavo Ansini (Italy)	Feather	Non-Title	10	Ansini won on points.
Peter Banasko v Bob Williamson (Glasgow, Scotland)	Welter	Non-Title	10	Banasko won on points.
Peter Clarke v Tommy Hyams	Light	Non-Title	8	Clarke won in round four when Hyams was disqualified.
Larry Bonar v Jerry Durante (Warrington)	Welter	Non-Title	4	Durante won on points.

18 March 1937, attendance: 15,000

Opponents	Weight	Status of Contest	Rounds	Result
Peter Kane (Golborne) v Fortunato Ortega (Spain)	Fly	Non-Title	12	Kane won on points.
Ernie Roderick v Ercole Buratti (Italy)	Welter	Non-Title	10	Roderick won on points.
Charlie Smith (Birkenhead) v Pat Murphy	Welter	Non-Title	10	Smith stopped Murphy in the fifth round.
Joe Curran v Al McCoy (Bargoed, Wales)	Fly	Non-Title	8	McCoy won on points.
Tommy Griffiths v Nat Stewart (Birkenhead)	Fly	Non-Title	6	Griffiths knocked out Stewart in the second round.
Sammy Shaw (Beverley) v Young Glimmer	Bantam	Non-Title	4	Shaw knocked out Glimmer in the second round.

Opponents	Weight	Status of Contest	Rounds	Result
29 April 1937, attendance: 20,000, referee: Jack Smith				
Peter Kane (Golborne) v Phil Milligan (Oldham)	Fly	Northern	15	Kane won in the 11th when Milligan's corner threw in the towel.
Vincent Homulos (Canada) v Franky Erne (Scotland)	Welter	Non-Title	8	Erne won on points.
Herbie Clarke v Tut Whalley (Hanley)	Light	Non-Title	8	Whalley won on points.
Pat Desmond (Ireland) v Stan Kirby (Leicester)	Cruiser	Non-Title	8	Kirby won, the referee stopped the fight in the fourth round.
Charlie Wilson (Manchester) v Dick Hughes	Bantam	Non-Title	6	Wilson won. The referee stopped the fight in the first round.
Charlie Smith (Birkenhead) v Bob Moorcroft	Welter	Non-Title	6	Smith won on points.
26 August 1937, attendance: 35,361, referee: Len Hardy				
Peter Kane (Golborne) v Jim Warnock (Belfast, N. Ireland)	Fly	Eliminator – British flyweight	15	Kane won in round four. The referee stopped the fight with Warnock on the canvas. He had previously taken five lengthy counts.
Jimmy Walsh (Chester) v Les McCarthy (Manchester)	Light	Non-Title	10	Walsh won on points.
Tommy Rose v Tommy Stewart (Belfast)	Bantam	Non-Title	8	Stewart won on points.
Dan McAllister (Belfast, N. Ireland) v Jim Chadwick (Bolton)	Light	Non-Title	8	McAllister won on points.
Jimmy Devitt v Tommy Elliot (Belfast, N. Ireland)	Feather	Non-Title	8	Devitt won on points
Boy McCann v Marvin Harte	Bantam	Non-Title	6	McCann won on points.
24 March 1938, attendance: 22,000, referee: C.H. Douglas				
Peter Kane (Golborne) v Benny Lynch (Glasgow, Scotland)	Bantam	Non-Title	12	Drawn contest.
Kid Tanner (British Guiana) v Jim Reilly (Glasgow, S'land)	Bantam	Non-Title	8	Reilly was disqualified in round five.
Con O'Kelly (Manchester) v Cal Rooney (Belfast, N. Ireland)	Heavy	Non-Title	8	O'Kelly won on points.
Herbie Clarke v Johnny McManus (Glasgow, Scotland)	Light	Non-Title	8	McManus, Lynch's sparring partner, won on points.
Joe Connolly (Scotland) v Ginger Murphy (Manchester)	Bantam	Non-Title	6	Connolly won, the referee stopped the fight in the second round.
Joe Kiely (Limerick, Eire) v Charlie Wilson (Manchester)	Bantam	Non-Title	6	Kiely won on points.
23 June 1938, attendance: 6,000, referee: E. Henderson				
Jimmy Walsh (Chester) v Dave Crowley (London)	Light	British Title	15	Crowley won on points.
Ernie Roderick (Ammanford, Wales) v Dai Jones	Catch	Non-Title	10	Roderick gave 12lbs to Jones but still won on points.
Kid Tanner (British Guiana) v George Marsden (Nottingham)	Bantam	Non-Title	8	Tanner won in the fifth round when Marsden's corner conceded.
Dan McAllister (Belfast, N. I.) v Frank Kenny (Scotland)	Light	Non-Title	8	McAllister won on points.
Bert Chambers (Widnes) v Patsy Quinn (Belfast, N. Ireland)	Welter	Non-Title	6	Chambers won on points.
Jimmy Stubbs (Runcorn) v Tommy Allan (Manchester)	Fly	Non-Title	4	Stubbs won on points.
22 September 1938, attendance: 40,000, referee: E. Henderson				
Peter Kane (Golborne) v Jackie Jurich (San Jose, USA)	Fly	World Title	15	Kane won on points.
Ernie Roderick v Roy Mills (Sunderland)	Catch	Non-Title	8	Roderick knocked out Mills in the second round. Mills had a 10 lbs weight advantage over Roderick.
Dan McAllister (Belfast, N. I.) v Young Beckett (Wales)	Light	Non-Titlle	8	McAllister won on points.
Herbie Clarke v Harry Edwards (Birmingham)	Feather	Non-Title	8	Clarke won, the referee stopped the bout in the seventh round.
Charlie Wilson (Lancaster) v Tommy Rose	Bantam	Non-Title	6	Rose won on points.
Jimmy Stubbs (Runcorn) v Young McCann (Golborne)	Fly	Non-Title	4	Stubbs won, contest stopped in the third round.
23 March 1939, attendance: 12,000, referee: C.B. Thomas				
Ernie Roderick v Jake Kilrain (Bellshill, Scotland)	Welter	British Title	15	Roderick KO'd Kilrain in the seventh round to take Kilrain's title.
Kid Tanner (British Guiana) v Johnny Holt (South Africa)	Bantam	Non-Title	8	Holt won on points, the decision was a controversial one.
Jimmy Stubbs (Runcorn) v Johnny Badhams (Birmingham)	Fly	Non-Title	8	Stubbs won on points.
George Daly (London) v George Bridges (Manchester)	Light	Non-Title	8	Daly won on points.
Alf Edwards (Birmingham) v Johnny Monaghan	Feather	Non-Title	8	Edwards won on points.
Harry Topliss v Basil Magee	Bantam	Non-Title	6	Magee, in his first contest, won on points.
21 September 1940, attendance: 5,000, referee: E. Henderson				
Ernie Roderick v Eric Boon (Chatteris)	Catch	Non-Title	10	Roderick won on points.
Harry Kid Silver (London) v Johnny Cunnigham	Welter	Non-Title	8	Silver won on points.
Basil Magee v Jimmy Wilde (Wales)	Bantam	Non-Title	6	Magee won on points
Johnny Downes (Manchester) v Kid Ash (Bootle)	Welter	Non-Title	6	Downes won on points. Kid Ash an alias for Gordon Ashun.
Joe Samuels v Stucargt Milan (Czechoslavakia)	Middle	Non-Title	6	Samuels stopped Milan in the third round.
3 August 1942, attendance: 12,000, referee: D. Richards				
Peter Kane (Golborne) v Joe Curran	Fly	Non-Title	12	Kane knocked Curran out in the 11th round.
Ronnie Clayton (Blackpool) v Les Johnson	Feather	Non-Title	8	Clayton won on points.
Buster Osborne (London) v Frank Duffy (Bootle)	Middle	Non-Title	8	Osborne won on points.

Opponents	Weight	Status of Contest	Rounds	Result
Danny Mack v Mick Gibbons (Haydock)	Light	Non-Title	8	Mack won on points.
Bob Hopwood (Bolton) v Tommy Gibbons (Wigan)	Light	Non-Title	6	Hopwood stopped Gibbons in the third round.

12 August 1944, attendance: 12,670

Opponents	Weight	Status of Contest	Rounds	Result
Jackie Paterson (Scotland) v Ronnie Clayton (Blackpool)	Bantam	Non-Title	15	Paterson stopped Clayton in the 12th round.
Mick Gibbons (Haydock) v Frank Gilhooley (Glasgow, S'land)	Light	Non-Title	8	Gibbons won on points.
Tommy Hendry (Glasgow, Scotland) v Bert Hornby (Bolton)	Welter	Non-Title	8	Contest drawn.
Bobby Hinds (Barnsley) v Danny Wood (Glasgow, Scotland)	Light	Non-Title	8	Hinds won, referee stopped the bout at the end of round three.
Billy Cottrell (Bermondsey) v Alf Gidman	Middle	Non-Title	8	Cottrell won on a first-round knock out.

12 September 1946, attendance: 18,000, referees: B. Hardwicke, Jack Curphey, Dave Richards

Opponents	Weight	Status of Contest	Rounds	Result
Stan Hawthorne (N. Shields) v Billy Thompson (H. Main)	Light	Eliminator – British Title	12	Hawthorne won on points.
Peter Fallon (Birkenhead) v Ernie Stapleton (Wood Green)	Welter	Non-Title	8	Fallon won on points.
Gerry Smyth (Belfast, N. Ireland) v Bert Hornby (Bolton)	Light	Non-Title	8	Smyth won on points.
Stan Hibbert (Battersea) v Dan McAllister	Light	Non-Title	8	Hibbert won, referee stopped the contest in third round.
Dick Grant (Barnsley) v Willie Rigby (Southport)	Feather	Non-Title	6	Grant knocked Rigby out in the second round.
Ernie Thompson (Nuneaton) v Jim Hurst (Blaydon)	Light	Non-Title	6	Thompson knocked-out Hurst in the second round.

11 September 1947, attendance: 20,000, referees: C.B. Thomas, Jack Curphey

Opponents	Weight	Status of Contest	Rounds	Result
Ronnie Clayton (Blackpool) v Al Phillips (Aldgate, London)	Feather	European, British & British Emp.	15	Clayton won on points.
Peter Fallon (Birkenhead) v Ben Duffy (Jarrow)	Light	Non-Title	8	Fallon won on points.
Ric Sanders (Leicester) v Dick Shields	Welter	Non-Title	8	Sanders won on points.
Freddie Hicks (Bermondsey) v Willie Rigby (Southport)	Feather	Non-Title	6	Hicks won on points.
Ronnie Taylor (Horwich) v Dave Sharkey (London)	Feather	Non-Title	6	Taylor stopped Sharkey in the fourth round.

16 October 1947, attendance: 12,000, referees: Peter Muir, Jack Curphey, Jack Hanlon

Opponents	Weight	Status of Contest	Rounds	Result
Stan Hawthorne (N. Shields) v Billy Thompson (H. Main)	Light	British	15	Thompson won, the referee stopped the contest in the third round.
Johnny Molloy (St Helens) v Bert Jackson (Fleetwood)	Feather	Non-Title	12	Molloy won on points.
Jackie Hughes v Frankie Kelly (Birkenhead)	Feather	Non-Title	8	Kelly won on points
Emmet Kenny (St Helens) v Ernie Stapleton (Wood Green)	Light	Non-Title	8	Contest drawn.
Danny O'Sullivan (Finsbury Park) v Ernie Ormerod	Bantam	Non-Title	6	O'Sullivan won, referee stopped the bout in the sixth round.

24 March 1949, attendance: 17,000, referee: Andrew Smyth

Opponents	Weight	Status of Contest	Rounds	Result
Stan Rowan v Jackie Paterson (Glasgow, Scotland)	Bantam	British & British Emp.	15	Rowan won on points.
Bert Hornby (Bolton) v Billy MacDonald	Light	Non-Title	8	Hornby won stopping MacDonald in the fifth round.
Mickey McLaughlin (N. Ireland) v Joe Murphy (Scotland)	Fly	Non-Title	8	McLaughlin knocked-out Murphy in the fourth round.
Jackie Fairclough (Preston) v Frankie McCoy (Lisburn, N. I.)	Bantam	Non-Title	6	Fairclough won on points.
Bernard Pugh v Terry Riley	Feather	Non-Title	6	Pugh won on points.

NB: Unless otherwise stated all boxers are from Liverpool

PRE-FIGHT: Thompson and Hawthorne weigh-in for their British lightweight title contest at Anfield, 10 October 1947

3245687   3245687

★

LIVERPOOL STADIUM

Liverpool's BOXING Venues

★

BIG PICTURE: Preparations ahead of John Conteh's WBC defence against Len Hutchins

Liverpool Stadium –
The Cockpit of Champions

It is often assumed that St Paul's Square, site of the Liverpool Stadium, was the only one considered for Liverpool's new boxing arena in 1932. Following the sale of the site around Pudsey Street to property developers in February 1929, it became increasingly clear that the area was being considered for demolition and redevelopment. In the ensuing period up to the closure of the stadium, various rival groups sought to find an alternative site on which to build a modern boxing stadium.

Building sports complexes was a big debate in Liverpool in the late 1920s and early 1930s. The city council had sent a delegation to Cologne to see what had been developed there, and drew up serious plans for a 'Wembley of the north' to be built in Liverpool. Although this did not materialise, this was the background to the first proposal that came forward to build a sports complex that could accommodate 6,000 seated spectators, and that would include a boxing stadium, ice hockey rink and dance floor, on a site in the Gildart Street area near the top of London Road.

The consortium behind the project was led by J.H. Layton and John Henry Haigh, who initially had the support of Johnny Best. The plans for the stadium were drawn up by A.E. Shennan architects, who were based in North John Street. The whole proposal, which was to cost in the region of £60,000 including £15,000 for a refrigeration plant, received planning permission in January 1931 and seemed set to become part of the Liverpool

landscape. However, problems with raising the capital led to the demise of the project.

Another possibility that emerged in this period was a giant stadium complex that would include a boxing stadium and an open-air swimming pool in the Norris Green area. Once again, costs and logistical problems could not be overcome.
The proposal with the best chance of success was a draft plan drawn up in the autumn of 1930 by Johnny Best and Lionel Bettinson, of the National Sporting Club, with the aim of incorporating Liverpool in a scheme to establish several national boxing centres. Bettinson was keen to include ice hockey in a similar way to the London Road proposal. Talks reached an advanced stage and the whole project seemed a natural extension of the programme to have British championship contests in the regions. From Johnny Best's point of view, the linking up with the NSC:

"...would enable me to get all the best boxers to Liverpool. Again there would certainly be other championship fights taking place here and the hall could be used for the eliminating contests. ▶

'Building sports complexes was a big debate in Liverpool in the 1920s and 1930s. The city council had sent a delegation to Cologne to see what had been developed there, and drew up serious plans for a "Wembley of the north"'

"I hope when we get the new stadium to make Liverpool the principal provincial boxing centre."

Clearly Best was very ambitious and hoped that links with the NSC could put boxing in Liverpool on a much higher level. Although no formal links between Liverpool and the NSC were established, one only has to look at the number of championship fights hosted at both Anfield and the Stadium in the 1930s to understand that Best had achieved his aims without such links.

The final proposal to come forward was to build a boxing stadium on St Paul's Square and although this was eventually successful, it was met with stiff opposition from certain elements within the Church. Best had made initial enquiries about leasing the site soon after Pudsey Street had closed. When he met with a positive response he then engaged Kenmure Kinna, a leading city architect, to draw up plans for the stadium and asked Gordon Guild to pull together costings in support of the overall project. In addition to Kinna, who became one of the directors, Best secured three other directors: Major James Bennett, Harold Mickle and Julius Hyams. Guild became the secretary and Johnny Best was established as the managing director. These six became known as the 'Harmony Six' because of the way they worked together to secure their goal of building the biggest boxing stadium in Britain.

St Paul's Church was built in 1763 on a site known as Dog Field. Coursing, and bull and bear-baiting events had taken place there probably since the time of the restoration of the monarchy in 1660. The church had closed in 1901 and was demolished in 1930, and in the period between closure and demolition it had become badly dilapidated. Demolition of the church had been controversial as the site was also a graveyard and any grave could only be disturbed with the permission of the Ecclesiastical Commissioners. When the planning application for the boxing stadium was made, there were several objections from certain church quarters, who thought that using the site for boxing was inappropriate. Another complication was that the land was owned by the London, Midland ▶

RINGSIDE ENTRANCE TO NEW LIVERPOOL STADIUM.

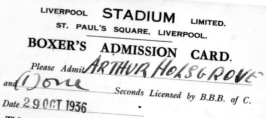

STADIUM MEMORIES: Tarleton faces McGrory in 1936 at Anfield (above) – the Liverpool Stadium still staged promotions at Anfield after the new Stadium was built. Below, the interior and exterior of the Stadium

and Scottish Railway Company. So before any planning permission could be approved, LMS had to obtain permission from the Church authorities. Fortunately for Best and his fellow directors, the Bishop of Liverpool acceded to the change as long as the graves were removed to another site and re-consecrated.

Some Interesting Facts About the STADIUM

by the Architect : Kenmure Kinna, Esq., A.R.I.B.A.

THE NEW STADIUM, unique in conception and design, is an example of the modern style building, which has emanated from the necessity of economy in undertakings of this character.

The building is steel framed (of British Steel) and clothed with brickwork of a pleasing grey colour, with a large central feature faced in Terra Cotta. The roof is supported on steel trusses, and is the largest span of its kind in Liverpool being 120 ft. between supports. The planning of the building presented some interesting difficulties, as the axis of the main entrance at Bixteth Street does not coincide with the centre of the site, while the site itself is not square with the axis. The levels of the main hall have been decided so that everyone has a clear view of the ring from any part of the building, and thus has arisen the saucer shape which was prevalent in the days of the gladiators.

The Contestants are provided for, with several dressing rooms, baths and showers, while the gymnasium will be replete with every modern training device. The whole building is heated with low-pressure water system, and ventilated by natural means and extractor fans in the roof.

The lighting is worthy of special mention, the ring fitting being an entirely new departure, the round indicator forms a very effective protection from the glare of approximately 35,000 candle power, while the rays are concentrated on to the ring by means of specially designed baffles.

The ring is unusual in construction, with steel corner posts and tightening devices, while the usual parade of buckets will be absent, there being a water supply with sink arranged under the ring side. The whole ring can be dismantled in an hour leaving the space for use for other purposes.

A word should be said for the contractor, Mr. John Lewis, and his sub-contractors and work-people, who have all pulled together so willingly to complete this Stadium in so short a time, and to all, our warmest thanks are tendered.

COMPLETED: Letter posted by architect Kinna explaining the stadium's design

However, this was not the end of the complications. The business quarter of Liverpool objected as they thought that such a venue would devalue the area around Exchange Station. Another objection came from the chairman of the planning authority, who felt that more money should be spent on the building. The proposal from the Liverpool Stadium partners was to raise capital of £20,000, £18,000 of which was to be spent on building the stadium. In response to the planning authority, Gordon Guild, who made the application on behalf of Best, explained that LMS would only grant a 21-year lease on the land so it would not be a satisfactory commercial proposition to spend more than £18,000 on the building.

Having listened to all objections and explanations from the various bodies, the planning authorities formally endorsed the plans to build a boxing stadium at their meeting of 23 October 1931. Work eventually began on the site the following February. On 2 February 1932, Liverpool Stadium Limited was incorporated. Many leading sportsmen of the day bought shares in the company, including the leading footballer and English baseball player Louis Page, and Nel Tarleton.

On 22 July 1932, when the building was two-thirds complete, a ceremony to lay the foundation stone was performed, with Lord Lonsdale given the honour of unveiling it. Prior to the stone being unveiled a ceremony was performed that involved placing a steel casket – containing the programme of the previous night's boxing at Anfield and copies of all the local newspapers of the day – alongside the foundation stone.

The Lord Mayor, Alderman J.C. Cross, opened the proceedings, revealing that he had a double interest in the ceremony in that he had been christened in the now-demolished church and that he was also a keen sportsman. The church, he said:

"Had served a useful purpose and I believe the new stadium will serve a useful purpose for many years to come.

"I should like to congratulate the new directors of the stadium on the efforts to bring boxing to the position that boxing should hold in the British Empire. No city has made greater progress to place boxing on a clean footing than Liverpool."

Unveiling the stone, Lord Lonsdale said: "It gives me great pleasure to lay this foundation stone, and I hope your stadium will prove one of the finest boxing stadiums in the world."

Four cornerstones were also placed around the foundation, bearing the names of the directors. However, a proposed tour of the stadium had to be postponed as heavy rain had flooded parts of the newly completed arena.

Just three months later, and only eight months since building had begun, on 20 October 1932, the stadium was opened for its first night of boxing. Once again the ceremony was given a civic presence, a sure indication that the public authorities considered sport as an important part of Liverpool's cultural heritage. The opening ceremony was conducted by the Lord Mayor, and alongside him were the Mayors of Bootle, Southport, Birkenhead, Chester and Wrexham. The Mayor of Wrexham, Councillor Dodman, was the former manager of Johnny Basham, one of Pudsey Street's favourite boxers. Various sportsmen were also present, including Ike Bradley, Nel Tarleton, Jimmy Wilde, the chairmen from the city football clubs and numerous professional footballers. Upon opening the stadium, the Lord Mayor declared: "Boxers are part of a great city and do serve their purpose in the scheme of things."

"'I should like to congratulate the new directors of the stadium on the efforts to bring boxing to the position that boxing should hold in the British Empire. No city has made greater progress to place boxing on a clean footing than Liverpool'"

LIVERPOOL
STADIUM
Adjoining Exchange Station.

GINGER FORAN   NEL TARLETON   JIMMY STEWART

THURSDAY, MARCH 1st, 1934, at 7-45 p.m.

GRAND
BOXING TOURNAMENT
PROCEEDS IN AID OF
Liverpool Jewish Charities.

Twelve 3-Minute Rounds Contest at 9st. 9lbs.   Twelve 3-Minute Rounds Contest at 8 st. 6 lbs.

GINGER
NEL TARLETON   FORAN
Liverpool   Contender for Featherweight Title   VERSUS   Liverpool   Contender for Bantamweight Title   VERSUS

AUREL
GEORGE COVACCI   THOMAS
Lightweight Champion of Roumania   Flyweight Champion of Roumania

Twelve 3-Minute Rounds Contest at 9st. 11 lbs.

JIMMY
STEWART
Liverpool   Contender for Lightweight Title.   VERSUS

GEORGE
REYNOLDS
Wolverhampton

GEORGE COVACCI, Roumania.   AUREL THOMAS, Roumania.

ALSO OTHER CONTESTS.

LADIES ADMITTED.   Tickets obtainable at the STADIUM, 'Phone Bank 4816 (2 Lines), and Agencies.

	RESERVED All Bookable Seats.				
	Ringside	Extension	Circle	Outer Circle	Unreserved Pay at Door
Prices of Admission (Including Tax)	15/-	10/-	5/-	3/-	2/6

ORIGINAL SITE: St Paul's Church, which occupied the Liverpool Stadium land until its demolition in 1930

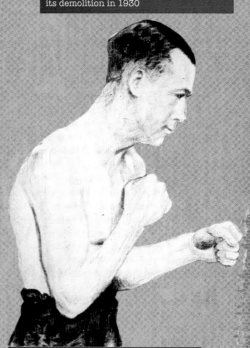

LIVERPOOL LINE-UP: A bill from March 1934 featuring Tarleton, Foran and (above) Jimmy Stewart

The Opening Night at Liverpool Stadium

The return of regular Thursday fight nights generated great excitement throughout the city. With tickets competitively priced, it was no surprise that thousands were locked out for the first night. The old Liverpool Stadium in Pudsey Street was known as the graveyard of champions. Remarkably, the opening night's boxing at the new Liverpool Stadium saw three champions and one former champion being defeated.

Top of the bill was a final eliminating contest between Alf Howard, former European welterweight champion, and Stoker Reynolds. The winner was to meet Jack Hood, the British welterweight champion, for the British title. Hopes were high that Howard would regain his old form after his defeat to Barney Kieswetter at Anfield. However, Reynolds beat him convincingly and had Howard on the canvas 11 times before the referee stopped the contest in the fourth round.

The sensation of the night came in the chief supporting contest between Ginger Foran and the Scottish flyweight champion Jim Maharg. Maharg was regarded as a tough opponent for Foran, but the contest only lasted two minutes, during which time the Scottish champion was down six times before he was eventually counted out by referee Jimmy Wilde.

Another Scottish champion, Jim Hunter, was knocked out by the Liverpool lightweight Jimmy Stewart in the sixth round, while Ernie Roderick beat the Welsh lightweight champion Billy Quinlan on points over 10 rounds. The two other contests on the opening night were both local affairs, with Teddy Jones defeating Danny Weston in three rounds and the young Nat Williams outpointing George Simcock over six. In all, the first night at the new Liverpool Stadium presented six bouts of high quality that involved eight Liverpool boxers. This gives an indication of the quality in depth of Liverpool boxing in the 1930s.

Three weeks after opening, the Stadium hosted its first major title fight between Tarleton and ex-Seaman Tommy Watson. To the surprise of many, Tarleton lost his British featherweight title and it did seem to confirm that the new Stadium was maintaining the Pudsey Street tradition of being a graveyard of champions. However, it should also be stated that both Liverpool stadiums were also nurseries for many fine Liverpool boxers to develop their professional careers. The list of such boxers is too long to reproduce here, but Harold Higginson, Dom Volante, Alf Howard, Jimmy Stewart and Joe Curran were all capable of taking on and beating top-class boxers. It was fighters of such calibre that excited the crowds at both stadiums in the 1920s and 1930s; boxers that could fill a stadium in their own right.

Throughout the 1930s the Liverpool Stadium, in conjunction with its promotions at Anfield, served up a wonderful diet of world and British championship boxing to many thousands of boxing fans. It demonstrated that it was both the graveyard of champions and the cockpit of champions.

'Throughout the 1930s, the Liverpool Stadium, in conjunction with its promotions at Anfield, served up a wonderful diet of world and British championship boxing to many thousands of fans. It was both the graveyard and cockpit of champions'

JIM MAHARG (Scotland).
(Flyweight Champion of Scotland).
Recently boxed Jacky Brown for the Flyweight Championship Belt, and lost on a foul.

GINGER FORAN (Liverpool).
Liverpool's most promising Flyweight, who has defeated Bert Kirby, Ginger McLeod, Geo Anderson (Flyweight Champion of South Africa), Boy Walley, Arthur Killeen, and many others.

OPEN FOR BUSINESS: Cover and cartoons from the first programme (1932)

Johnny Best – The Man Who Made Champions

Crowds flock to stadiums to see top-class sportsmen and women. In team games such as football, managers can often be a crowd hero, respected by the players and within the game generally. Ultimately, however, it is the player who excites the crowd and draws the fan to the ground. Likewise, in boxing it is the boxer with the knock-out punch who excites the crowd. Boxing and boxers, as with other sports, need promoters and managers while the matchmaker will try to arrange a contest that will draw the crowds to the stadium. Rarely in boxing though is the promoter or the manager seen as a sporting hero by boxing fans. But Johnny Best was the exception to this rule. The crowds and fighters loved him, while other promoters often took their lead from him.

Best's first sporting love was football. He was a fine footballer whose playing career started with Orrell Football Club. At Orrell he played alongside Arnold Wilson, the man who would eventually manage Pudsey Street Stadium. He later played in goal for Tranmere Rovers; he also played in goal for a boxers' XI against Everton, who had just won the FA Cup for the first time, at Goodison Park in 1906. Best did not lose contact with football, but following a visit to the Adelphi Theatre, to see Yank Kenny take on Philadelphia Jack O'Brien, he became a big boxing fan. The fight only lasted four rounds, but it ended dramatically on disqualification when Kenny hit the referee with a left hook.

That night changed Best's life. Inspired by what he saw, he, along with a few other enthusiasts, formed a boxing club in a cellar close to Pudsey Street. This was the very place where Wilson saw the raw talent of Nat Williams and the place that cemented his relationship with Johnny Best. Wilson went on to open Pudsey Street Stadium in 1911 – a venue where Williams often performed. Following the opening of Pudsey Street Best, like Wilson, concentrated on the business side of the game although he still involved himself as a boxer and a trainer on an occasional basis.

Throughout his career in boxing Best often expressed, publicly and privately, his belief that the small boxing halls were the breeding grounds of champions. Best, of course, spoke from a position of strength after he had created one of the finest boxing stadiums in the world, but he recognised that without the small halls such as the Drill Hall in Birkenhead, his supply of boxing talent would be difficult to maintain. Moreover, the great boxing venues in London such as Harringay, Earls Court and the Albert Hall were dependent upon boxing halls such as the Liverpool Stadium to produce boxers that could compete on a national and international level.

When he took over Pudsey Street at the end of 1928, Best made it clear that Liverpool would never be in need of quality boxers in his lifetime. Indeed, he is on record as saying:

"If any Liverpool boy has the ability, I have to bring it out. I will give him a chance to reach the top of the ladder in the end."

It was a philosophy that saw Merseyside develop many champions in the 30 years he promoted shows at Pudsey Street, New Brighton, Southport, Anfield and the Liverpool Stadium. Moreover, he was always ▶

'Best had created one of the finest boxing stadiums in the world, but he recognised that without the small halls, such as the Drill Hall in Birkenhead, his supply of boxing talent would be difficult to maintain'

JOHNNY BEST, Esq.
Liverpool Stadium.

LIONEL BETTINSON, Esq.
The Popular Manager of
National Sporting Club.

CHURCHMAN'S CIGARETTES

HENRY ARMSTRONG

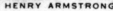

CLOCKWISE FROM TOP LEFT: Best with former *Liverpool Echo* sports editor Ernest 'Bee' Edwards; boxer Henry Armstrong, who fought Roderick; Peter Kane after defeating Marino in 1947

▶ on the look out to bring over international talent. He was the first promoter to introduce Larry Gains to this country, and was associated with the many black boxers that came to Liverpool from British Guiana, Jamaica and Nigeria between the 1930s and 1950s. He was also the only boxing promoter to run weekly shows through the Second World War years.

Best's great entrepreneurial and organisational skills enabled him to bring title fights to Liverpool on a regular basis for the first time. It was his ability that established both Anfield and the Liverpool Stadium as venues capable of hosting world and British championship fights. Many of these vital contests involved local boxers. In fact, up to the time of his death in December 1956, aged 70, Best had produced more champions than any other promoter working in Britain over the same period. Despite these achievements, Best was a very modest man who shunned the limelight. Throughout his tenure at the Stadium, Best was assisted by his son, also called Johnny, in the promotion of boxing. Indeed, it was Johnny Best Jnr who flew to America to sign up Henry Armstrong to fight Ernie Roderick for the world title, although it was the father who had done the matchmaking.

Liverpool boxing owes a great debt to Best. His legacy is as great as those of Nel Tarleton, Peter Kane, Wally Thom, Pat McAteer, Johnny Cooke and John Conteh. Boxers trusted Best implicitly. An example of this trust is that Nel Tarleton and Best never had a contract between them except for title fights, when it was compulsory to have one. Many of the other named boxers had a similar relationship with him during their professional careers. In the modern-day sport it would be hard to find a parallel relationship between boxer and promoter; and it is even harder to imagine a promoter having the public acclaim of fight fans in the way that Best had.

Public recognition of his contribution to Liverpool sport is long overdue.

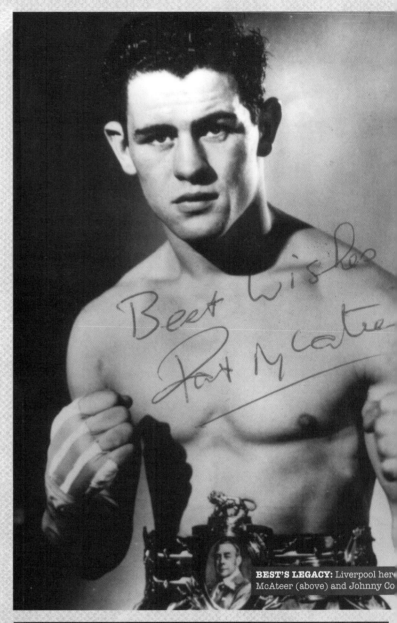

BEST'S LEGACY: Liverpool her McAteer (above) and Johnny Co

Two Pioneers –
Peter Banasko and Kid Tanner

CONTENDERS: Gordon 'Kid' Ashun (above, 1940s) and Allan Tanner (1950s)

ALLAN TANNER (British Guiana)
Contender for Featherweight and Lightweight Empire Title
Managed by:- DON & TONY YARO England's Premier Boxing Managers.

Black boxers have featured strongly in Liverpool's boxing history. Jim (Jem) Butler, who also put on promotions at the Lyceum Theatre in the 19th century, was one of several fine black boxers to emerge from the city in the 1890s. Reflecting Liverpool's position as the world's trading hub, many black boxers also came here from America to ply their trade. These included world-ranking fighters such as Sam McVea, Joe Jeanette and The Dixie Kid. During the 1930s, two boxers emerged to take this great tradition to a much higher level. The first was Liverpool-born Peter Banasko, who like Butler was a fine boxer, and who developed into one of Liverpool's most significant boxing managers. The second was Ritchie 'Kid' Tanner, who came to Liverpool at the age of 22 from British Guiana (modern-day Guyana) in 1938.

Banasko's career started in St Malachy's gym in Dingle. By the time he was 14 he had more than 100 amateur contests under his belt. As an amateur he won the six-stone schoolboy championship of Britain, making him the first Liverpool boxer to win a national title.

He turned pro in 1932 and after a losing start he ran up 40 straight wins, beating some quality opponents on the way. He had the ability to box for the British title, but because the BBBofC had a bar on blacks

fighting for the British titles, he could never fulfil his ambitions. The black bar was not lifted until 1948. His career was further hampered by a series of hand injuries that at one point kept him out of boxing for a year. The onset of war in 1939 also had an adverse affect upon his career. When the war ended, Banasko realised that his days as a boxer were coming to an end, so he decided to take out a manager's licence. Banasko's managerial career was to change the face of Liverpool boxing. Using his Nigerian contacts, he played a big role in bringing over boxers such as Hogan Kid Bassey and Dick Tiger, both of whom were managed by Banasko in the formative years of their boxing careers in Britain.

In this context, Ritchie 'Kid' Tanner can be regarded as a pioneer, as in the 1930s his success in the boxing ring paved the way for other black boxers to come to Liverpool in the late 1940s and early 1950s.

Tanner was introduced to boxing at the age of 14 whilst working as a junior clerk in an auctioneering mart. One of the porters there was a former boxer named 'Fighting Babe', who used to spar with work-mates during the lunch hour. The young Tanner tried a spell with the gloves one day, and it was immediately spotted that he had a natural boxing talent. The sparring sessions with 'Fighting Babe' became a part of his daily routine, and within two years he was able to outbox the fighting porter. Meanwhile Tanner began reading about other boxers and began to wonder if one day he could become a champion.

Fortunately for him, his employers took an interest in his boxing skills and he was entered by them into some local championships. He beat all his opponents convincingly, going on to win the Georgetown Championship some weeks later. It was at ▶

'Ritchie "Kid" Tanner can be regarded as a pioneer, as in the 1930s his success in the boxing ring paved the way for other black boxers to come to Liverpool in the late 1940s and early 1950s'

PIONEER: Ritchie 'Kid' Tanner - his success paved the way for others

KID TANNER (MIGHTY MIDGET OF THE SOUTHERN CARIBBEAN)
FLY, BANTAM & FEATHERWEIGHT CHAMPION OF BRITISH WEST INDIES AND BRITISH SOUTH AMERICA.
Under Direction of **TONY & DOM VAIRO, 39 Thurston Road, Liverpool, 4.**
'Phone: **ANFIELD 288.**
London Representative **JOHN S. SHARPE, 3 Edwin St., London, E.1**
'Phone: **STEPNEY GREEN 2933.**

LEADING THE WAY: 'Kid' Tanner (left) and Peter Banasko

this point, with the support of his parents and his employers, that he was encouraged to turn professional. Before long, Tanner was a triple champion in his homeland at fly, bantam and featherweight. These titles were held by 'Kid' Gums, who was considered unbeatable, but Tanner knocked him out in the second round.

Boxing was booming in Guiana at this time with Tanner, who was now affectionately known as 'Our Kid', beating all comers with ease. A point came, however, when no one would face him despite high purses being offered to opponents. This forced Tanner to consider his future and after a short spell in Trinidad, where he also beat the champion – albeit at the second attempt – he decided to go in search of big money. At first Tanner

was unsure whether to go to America, but he realised that it would be easier to make a career in Britain because getting a passport to the 'mother' country would be much easier.

He arrived in Liverpool in 1938 and immediately called upon Johnny Best. Best, who was always keen to welcome new talent, was impressed by Tanner's press cuttings and directed him to the Brothers Vario, who swiftly realised that they had stumbled on an enormous talent.

Tanner quickly became a big favourite with the Stadium crowd. His first contest at the Stadium, 3 March 1938, saw him outpoint the experienced Tut Whalley. Such was his progress – he won 18 fights in 1938 – he was being mooted as a possible contender for

the world flyweight title. However, after losing to Jackie Paterson in a British Empire flyweight title fight in July 1940, and to Jim Brady six months later for the bantamweight version, his record became somewhat mixed, and in the post-war years his career went into freefall. Tanner eventually retired in 1950 after a 19-year boxing career during which he had 150 fights.

The significance of Peter Banasko and 'Kid' Tanner's contribution to Merseyside boxing should not be underestimated. Their efforts in the ring, and Banasko's excursion into management, paved the way for other boxers to come here from British Guiana and Africa in the post-war period.

Two Great Stadium Favourites of the 1930s – Jimmy Stewart and Jimmy Walsh

Johnny Best's policy of discovering and developing unknown boxers into fine fighters bore fruit in the 1930s, with Merseyside developing some of Britain's best boxers. Two such men from that period, Jimmy Stewart and Jimmy Walsh, have disappeared from many boxing fans' thoughts, but they both deserve to be part of any Mersey Boxing Hall of Fame.

Jimmy Stewart did not take up boxing until he was 21 and did not turn professional until he was 25. Despite this, Stewart fought, and beat, some of the country's finest lightweights. He was a no-compromise, hard-hitting boxer who became a great favourite with the Liverpool boxing fans. Throughout his boxing career he worked for Liverpool's *Evening Express* and turned down the opportunity of a fighting career in America as he wanted long-term job security.

Stewart was the first man to beat Ernie Roderick, at Anfield in 1932 – a victory that enhanced his growing reputation. He also appeared on the first night's boxing bill at the Liverpool Stadium – an indication that Best regarded him as a big attraction for the fans. He did not disappoint, knocking out the Scottish lightweight champion Jim Hunter in the sixth round.

However, he is best remembered for two remarkable fights at the Stadium against Sunderland's Douglas Parker and Jack 'Kid' Berg. Stewart's contest with Parker on 16 March 1933 was described by Johnny Best Jnr as "sensational thrilling action" that involved "murderous punching...by both men", with advantage swinging "first in one then in the other's favour".

The contest lasted eight rounds, during which the crowd were in a constant frenzy. In the opening round, Parker crashed a left hook to Stewart's chin, putting him down for a count of nine. Stewart showed his grit and powers of recuperation by coming back at Parker towards the end of the round. Round three saw Stewart hurt once more with a punch to the body that put him down for another count of nine. Stewart fought back in the next round but was down again for a count of eight. When he got to his feet this time, he went toe-to-toe with Parker, a situation that had the crowd cheering on both boxers. This was a turning point in the contest as from now it was Stewart who dominated, dropping Parker in the fifth, who inadvisably got up too quickly. Both men had given and taken punches that would have finished off most boxers, and as they both came out for the eighth round Parker threw a left hook but Stewart anticipated the move this time and caught Parker with a right to the chin. Parker got up at nine but Stewart was quickly on top of him, raining punches on Parker's head and body. During this onslaught, Parker's corner threw in the towel. Stewart had won, but so fierce had been the punching that he was unaware of what round he had won in. Remarkably, just three weeks later he was back in the ring again at the Stadium, this time against Johnny Cuthbert who beat him on points over 15 rounds. In the fight with Cuthbert, Stewart broke his hand – an injury that kept him out of the ring for nearly a year and severely jeopardised his chances of fighting for the British title.

Upon returning to the ring the following March, Stewart had three contests in quick succession before taking on the legendary Jack 'Kid' Berg at the Stadium on 31 May 1934. Berg had returned to Britain after establishing himself as one of the best lightweights in the world. Berg's reputation was so good that he was able to bring one of the best trainers, Ray Arcell, over from America to be in his corner on the night of the fight. The odds on Stewart winning were long, but many astute local punters knew where to put their money. Berg came out in his usual attacking style from the first bell and had Stewart on the ropes, but many of Berg's punches landed on the arms of his opponent. Stewart fought back and caught Berg with a powerful punch to the head that had the crowd on its feet. The second round went to Berg and when the bell went, Stewart slumped onto his stool. During the interval between the rounds, Berg's corner could be seen urging their man to go out and finish off the contest. However, a weary Stewart was often a deceptive sight, and so it proved in the third round. The third round saw Berg coming forward once more, pumping lefts and rights into Stewart's face. But Berg came forward once too often, as Stewart backed away and landed a terrific punch to Berg's chin. Berg got up at the count of nine, but once on his feet Stewart came forward to land the decisive blow and knock out the ▶

'Stewart's contest with Parker on 16 March 1933 was described by Johnny Best Jnr as "sensational thrilling action" that involved "murderous punching...by both men"'

THE JOY AND THE PAIN: Dave Crowley beats Jimmy Walsh for the British lightweight title in 1938 (top); Jimmy Stewart defeats Jack 'Kid' Berg at the Liverpool Stadium on 31 May 1934

champion boxer. The crowd roared its approval as yet another champion had been defeated at the graveyard of champions.

The Berg victory demonstrated that Stewart was capable of boxing for the British title. His chance came nine months later when Stewart met fellow Stadium favourite Jimmy Walsh in an eliminator for the British lightweight title.

Jimmy Walsh – Chester's first and only champion boxer

Although he was born in Chester, Jimmy Walsh was essentially a product of the Liverpool Stadium. At the young age of 16 he walked from Chester to Dom and Tony Vario's gymnasium in Transport House, Liverpool, where he presented himself to the two brothers saying: "Hello, I'm Jimmy Walsh and I want to be a boxer."

Some weeks earlier, the Varios had seen Walsh put on a fine display at an amateur tournament and tried to persuade him to turn professional, but Walsh's parents would not hear of it. However, Jimmy later persuaded his parents to let him become a boxer, hence the walk to Liverpool.

Walsh began his career as a featherweight and had his first contest at Pudsey Street in 1929, when he was disqualified. Johnny Best quickly recognised his talent, however, and made him a regular on the bill at the new Stadium where he quickly became a crowd favourite. During the course of 1933, after several victories over capable boxers during the previous year, Walsh was matched with tougher opponents including Benny Sharkey, Dave Crowley and Johnny McMillan. All three were comfortably beaten, but it was the victory over McMillan that opened up even greater opportunities for Walsh. McMillan, after beating Dick Burke of Liverpool at the Stadium, was in the running for a crack at the British featherweight title, but Walsh outclassed the Scot before the referee stopped the fight in the 12th round.

Walsh further demonstrated his pedigree when he met Harry Mizler in a non-title fight at the Stadium in March 1934. Just two months prior to the fight, Mizler had won the British lightweight crown, defeating Johnny

Cuthbert at the Royal Albert Hall. Despite his championship status, Mizler was no match for Walsh, who outpointed the champion over 12 rounds. Walsh was now being talked of as a future champion, declaring after the contest that he was after Mizler's title. Before he could realise his ambition, however, he would have to fight other boxers in contention for the British title – most notably Jimmy Stewart.

The Stewart/Walsh title eliminator took place at the Stadium on 14 February 1935. The record of both boxers was superb, while their contrasting styles aroused great excitement among boxing fans in the build-up to the contest. Stewart's best chance of victory was via a knock out, but he surprisingly changed his style in an attempt to outbox Walsh. However, Walsh's ringcraft was too great for Stewart and whenever Stewart did attempt to land a knock-out punch, Walsh was able to dance away. Walsh emerged as the clear winner over 15 rounds. Following the defeat, Stewart's career went into decline. He eventually retired after losing to Harry Craster in 1937 at the New St James Hall, Newcastle.

It would be 14 months before Walsh would eventually get his title fight against Jack 'Kid' Berg, and once again it was to be held at the Stadium. Berg had won the title from Harry Mizler in October 1934; the fight with Walsh was to be his first defence. After beating Stewart, Walsh's record was mixed: out of 16 contests he won just 10, losing five and drawing the other.

Although Berg's performances since winning the title were also mixed, he entered the contest as the overwhelming favourite. At the time of the fight Berg was nearly 27, had been boxing for 12 years, and had 138 contests including a long spell in America under his belt. In comparison, Walsh was 23 with just 43 recorded bouts to his name, most of which had been in Liverpool. No one gave the Chester man a chance.

However, from the outset Walsh was the dominant boxer, decking Berg twice in the first round, once in the third and twice more in the sixth. In the eighth round Berg was outpunched; at the sound of the bell, a weak

Berg turned towards his corner and seemed to turn his ankle. He came out for the ninth round but could not continue – the referee had to escort the champion back to his corner by the hand. Yet again the Stadium had seen a champion defeated, and once more a Liverpool-based boxer was a British champion.

Six months later, on 19 October 1936, Walsh defended his lightweight title against Mizler at the Empress Hall London, on the opening night of the rejuvenated NSC. Walsh emerged as the clear winner on points, with Mizler finding it difficult to cope with the diversity of Walsh's attack. The referee, C.H. Douglas, in a throwback to the early days of the NSC, did not referee from inside the ring but sat in a ringside seat. During the course of 15 rounds he did not need to intervene or raise his voice when telling both boxers to break. After the fight he praised Walsh for his efforts, saying: "(Walsh) had done more to uplift British boxing in that contest than had been done by dozens of others."

It would be nearly two years before Walsh would defend his title. During this period he fought 22 bouts, of which he won 16. However, by the time he met Dave Crowley at Anfield he was not in the best condition, owing to problems of meeting the weight, and lost on points in front of a small crowd. His defeat meant that he failed to win the Lonsdale Belt outright.

Following his defeat to Crowley, Walsh seemed to lose interest in boxing: after five more bouts he hung up his gloves. In retirement he became a successful businessman.

Stewart and Walsh typified the reservoir of talent that developed around the Liverpool stadiums in the 1920s and 1930s. Such boxers were quite capable of challenging for national titles; that Walsh did and Stewart did not is no reflection on Stewart's ability. There was great competition in all the weight divisions at this time – this is why boxers had to fight for several years before they would be considered for a British title fight.

CHESTER'S CHAMPION: Jimmy Walsh in the Stadium – photo printed in the *Evening Express*

The Liverpool Stadium in the 1940s

War brought great change in the way sport was organised. The Football League and FA Cup, for example, were immediately suspended and replaced with regional competitions. Likewise, boxing had to adapt as many of the best boxers signed up for the war effort. Remarkably, however, Liverpool was one of two places, the other being Blackpool, where boxing took place on a weekly basis throughout the war. However, things could have been different when the Stadium received a direct hit during the Blitz. Fortunately, the bomb passed between the girders of the roof and embedded itself in the earth of the old graveyard before it exploded, thereby limiting the impact upon the building. The bomb created a 10-foot crater and dislodged about 20 tons of earth. Every piece of glass in the roof was shattered, while inside several seats were blown onto the girders. Remarkably, Best got a team of boxers and boxing fans together (obtaining hired labour was just not possible in wartime) who worked all through the night to ensure that the arena was ready for the next promotion.

For the first two years of the war, promotions took place on various days in the week including Sundays, before becoming regularised to the traditional Thursday night slot. The backbone of the promotions comprised Merseyside boxers such as Nel Tarleton, Peter Kane, Joe Curran, Gus Foran, Jimmy Molloy, Ernie Roderick and Stan Rowan, among others. Tarleton had two British title fights in 1940, while Freddie Mills made two appearances in 1940 and 1941. In August 1944, the great Jackie Paterson stopped Stadium favourite Ronnie Clayton in the 12th round in a British bantamweight eliminator.

Perhaps one of the most remarkable nights at the Stadium was a private showing on 4 July 1944, American Independence Day, when the heavyweight champion of the world

Joe Louis appeared in an exhibition of boxing for the American forces based in the area. Louis, using heavy sparring gloves, took on Sergeant George Nicholson in a three-round exhibition bout. While in Liverpool, Louis played a round of golf at Formby Golf Club and 'signed' amateur terms with Liverpool Football Club.

During the war it was quite common for boxers to pull out of a fight owing to commitments to the service to which they belonged. This gave relatively unknown boxers opportunities to fight at the Stadium. One such example was in August 1940 when an army corporal took on Jock McAvoy, the British middleweight champion. The unknown corporal completely outboxed the champion over 10 rounds and received a great reception from the crowd. His name? Freddie Mills.

Another example was in 1941 when Basil Magee, who was being managed by George Tarleton, was asked to choose an opponent from three lads who were standing outside hoping to get a contest. Magee chose a sailor who was promptly asked to strip, and Magee's

opponent went on to knock him out in the third round. The name of his opponent? Al Phillips, who was barely known outside Aldgate at the time but went on to win the British featherweight title in 1947 – his first attempt in 1945 saw him lose to Tarleton.

Such contests were typical during the war years, but they were no substitute for scheduled title fights and once again these featured the ubiquitous Nel Tarleton. Tarleton was seemingly entering the twilight of his career, but this did not stop him regaining the featherweight title and making a successful defence during 1940.

Peacetime brought great optimism among the population – unlike the years that followed 1918, the post-1945 years brought prolonged economic prosperity and rising incomes. After five years of wartime restrictions, people began to enjoy themselves once more and as a consequence attendances at sports events boomed. Boxing was no exception to this, and in Liverpool there was still enough local talent to present quality promotions.

IN FROM THE COLD: Freddie Mills was virtually unknown in boxing circles until he outclassed British champion Jock McAvoy at the Stadium in 1940

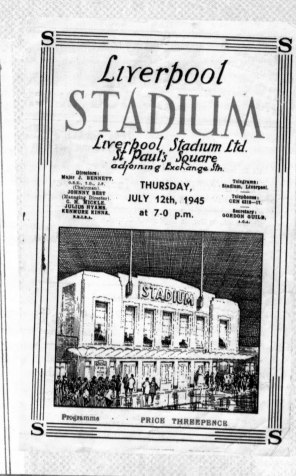

WAR GAMES: Stadium programmes from 1941 and 1945, and a ticket to the Joe Louis exhibition fight

LIVERPOOL STADIUM
(Adjoining Exchange Station)

TUESDAY, JULY 4th 1944, at 6.30 p.m.

Special Exhibition by

JOE LOUIS (U.S. Army)

Heavyweight Champion of the World

Courtesy extended to the Holder of this Ticket by the U.S. Army Chiefs and the Directors of the Liverpool Stadium, Ltd.

Seat must be taken before commencement.

Tarleton Wins a
Second Lonsdale Belt

Nel Tarleton is among the all-time greats of British boxing. He became the first boxer to win two Lonsdale Belts outright when he beat Al Phillips at Belle Vue, Manchester in 1945. The title fight with Phillips was the 10th time he had fought for the British title over a 14-year period. During this period, he had regained the title twice, a feat no other contemporary boxer could match and had twice lost narrowly to Freddie Miller for the world title. Moreover, before he retired, Tarleton had been matched to fight for the world title once more against Willie Pep but injury forced Pep to withdraw. No other Liverpool boxer, with the exception of Ernie Roderick, had come close to the remarkable achievements of Nel Tarleton.

Tarleton was born in 1906 in Anfield. In his amateur days he won two gold medals, one of which he gave to his mother. Before turning pro in 1926 he was working as a plasterer,

but he soon realised that he could earn more money from boxing. His first paid fight was when he was still registered as an amateur: he earned £6 for a contest that took place in Birmingham. Despite using a pseudonym, Nat Nelson, when he got back home he found that the story of his fight was in the local papers, with the press clearly stating that Tarleton had boxed under an assumed name. This rendered his position as an amateur untenable, forcing him to turn professional.

Subsequently, he went to meet Pa Taylor at Pudsey Street who, upon seeing Tarleton, remarked:

"There's one thing, if you stand edge-on no opponent will see you."

Despite Taylor's initial impressions, he soon realised that he had a special talent on his hands. Throughout his long career, very few

of Tarleton's opponents would get near him, not because he was too thin and could not be seen, but because of his stinging left jab that kept many opponents at bay. Tarleton also had quick feet, an attribute he used to great effect to get out of trouble. He also had a remarkable knack of scoring points when being forced back, while no one could surpass him when he had his back on the ropes. It would seem that Tarleton knew the 'rope-a-dope' technique long before Muhammad Ali used it.

These were the skills that enabled him to have longevity in the ring. When he lost his British title for the second time to Johnny McGrory, it seemed that Tarleton's career had finally come and gone. When in 1937 he contracted pneumonia, it seemed even less likely that he could rebuild his ring career. But once he recovered from his illness, Tarleton put together a string of victories that kept him in contention for another shot at the title. In this period Tarleton beat Jim 'Spider' Kelly, who had won the British title in November 1938 in a non-title fight at the Stadium. A few weeks later, Kelly would lose his title to Johnny Cusick of Manchester. This sequence of events made Tarleton the natural challenger to Cusick, but the outbreak of war seemed to scupper any chance of such a contest taking place.

Tarleton joined the RAF as a PTI at the outbreak of war, a position that enabled him to maintain his fitness. Within the first few months of the war, a stroke of good fortune gave Tarleton the chance to take on Cusick for the featherweight title. Liverpool newspapers had established a war fund and wanted to put on a major sports event to raise money. Out of this came Cusick's defence of his British and British Empire titles against Tarleton at the Stadium on 1 February 1940.

Tarleton was now 34, 10 years older than the

TITLE FIGHT: Tarleton takes on Johnny Cusick for the British and Empire featherweight title on 1 February 1940. Tarleton won on points

CHAMP: Tarleton sports his belt

champion. Cusick was regarded as a skilful fighter, and despite his age was very experienced. However, he was outboxed by the veteran, who had Cusick down for a count of nine in the sixth round. Tarleton resisted the temptation to go all-out for a KO, realising that if this did not come off, he would expend too much and enable the younger man to regain the initiative. In common with all his title fights, this one went the distance with Tarleton emerging a clear winner over 15 rounds. He had become the oldest British champion and the first British boxer ever to regain a British championship twice. As usual, Tarleton showed great humility when addressing the public:

DOING BATTLE: Another shot from Tarleton's fight with Cusick

"I should like to pay tribute to all those who have helped to regain my title, particularly all my sparring partners – Peter Kane, Basil Magee and others who have helped me in my preparations – and Mr Johnny Best, who made the fight possible.

"Johnny never lost faith in me, and it was owing to his efforts that the fight was brought about. I am glad that I was able to justify the faith in me."

Tarleton defended his titles nine months later, once again at the Stadium. His opponent this time was Sergeant Tom Smith of Sunderland, who was 12 years younger than him. Smith came with a reputation of being a highly skilled opponent, but he had yet to meet a boxer with the ringcraft of Tarleton. During the fight, Smith adopted the

wrong tactics: rather than take the fight to Tarleton he chose to box on the retreat and rely on counter-punches. However, this was Tarleton territory; in effect, Smith played into Tarleton's hands and at the end of the contest Tarleton was a clear points winner.

Tarleton should now have had his second Lonsdale Belt. To win the first he had beaten Cuthbert, Watson and Crowley. Following his victory over Crowley, he had successfully defended his title against Johnny King in May 1936. However, in this period there was a changeover in the body that was issuing the Lonsdale Belt – the BBBofC was taking over from the NSC. For the Tarleton/King fight the Board did not issue a new belt; as a consequence the victory over Cusick counted as his first notch on the belt.

Wartime conditions made it increasingly difficult to organise British title fights. Because of this, it was more than four years until Tarleton could make his defence of the title and win that elusive second belt. His opponent this time was Al Phillips, known as the 'Aldgate Tiger'. Phillips was 14 years younger than Tarleton, who was now 39.

From the outset it looked as if Tarleton would fail in his attempt to win a second belt. Phillips attacked furiously for 11 rounds; in the 10th he caught Tarleton with a dangerous punch that rocked the champion. However, Tarleton, using all his old skills, was able to draw his opponent onto counter-punches that scored heavily in his favour. Moreover, Phillips' punches looked menacing but he was unable to penetrate Tarleton's defence with any regularity. In classic fashion, the champion grew stronger towards the end of the fight: in the 12th round he caught Phillips with a right to the jaw that put Phillips down momentarily. Later he caught Phillips with a shot to the ribs that had Phillips' legs shaking. Tarleton's counter-punches sapped the remaining strength from Phillips and towards the end of the fight he began to suffer from cramp in his right leg – from this point onwards, Tarleton was able to coast to a points victory. Tarleton had secured his second belt, and he remains the only Liverpool boxer to achieve such a feat.

Tarleton did not retire immediately. Indeed, in February 1947 he returned to training to prepare for a rematch with Phillips. However, after a few days of hard training he realised

that his body was not up to the task and announced his retirement, saying:

"I have never made any secret of the fact that I would never stay in boxing and take a hiding, and perhaps a permanent injury, no matter the size of the purse, and realising that I could not do myself full justice against Phillips, wrote to the Board of Control to the effect that I wished to relinquish my two titles. It is a big wrench but I think I am the best judge."

It is fitting that one of the finest featherweights seen in a British ring retired as a champion.

Is Tarleton Liverpool's greatest ever boxer? Sports people love comparisons. We love to compare a sportsperson of yesteryear with a present star. Such comparisons, while enjoyable, are almost impossible to judge because the sportsman or woman plies their trade under different circumstances. The centre-forward in the age of Dixie Dean received greater wing service, and played at a time when football was more attack-minded. Likewise with boxers, in the 1920s many professionals had to share their time with a full-time job or box far too regularly to make a living. Today a top professional boxer spends months preparing for a top fight, and the fitness levels are consequently much greater.

Tarleton was compared to the great Welsh boxer Peerless Jim Driscoll during his career. Sadly, we have no film of Driscoll and very little of Tarleton. We have their records, the press reports and recorded memories of the great boxers, which demonstrate that both were very fine boxers. What is certain is that there is no modern-day equivalent of Tarleton in the featherweight division today. We can also say that Nel Tarleton was one of the finest boxers to emerge from Liverpool; he was the finest British featherweight of his generation. If Liverpool ever develops a Hall of Fame for its finest sportsmen and women, the name of Nel Tarleton would be among the first to be enrolled.

Tarleton died just a few days short of his 50th birthday on 12 January 1956 at his home in Waterloo. At his funeral, more than 300 boxing fans crowded the grounds of the Anfield crematorium to pay tribute to one of Liverpool's finest sportsmen.

FROM TOP LEFT: Tarleton v King at Anfield in 1936; a cartoon of Tarleton v Foreman in 1932; Tarleton delivering a body punch to Freddie Miller at Anfield in 1934; receiving his testimonial in 1935

Jimmy Molloy v Emile Delmine – Great Fight, Poor Attendance

According to Johnny Best, Liverpool has not produced a tougher fighter than Jimmy Molloy. When Molloy appeared on the scene in 1939, Best had great hopes for him. He was, in his opinion, one of the best deliverers of a left hook ever seen in a Liverpool ring. Added to these attributes were his toughness and durability – attributes that enabled him to survive rough passages during a fight and come from behind to win. His contests were often toe-to-toe slugging matches, but Molloy was the one who usually prevailed. To say he was a great favourite of the Stadium underestimates the excitement he generated when he entered the ring.

In a career that spanned 13 years, he beat many top welterweights and was at one time the number one contender to Ernie Roderick. However, the only title fight he ever had was for the Central Area welterweight title, against Wally Thom in 1950 at the Stadium, which he lost on points. He met Thom again 10 months later and this time he emerged the winner, with Thom being stopped in the second round. However, by this time his career was drawing to a close and any chance of a shot at the British title had gone.

As a promoter, Johnny Best would try to match boxers who would produce top-class, hard-hitting contests. His ability in producing such matches over a period of time had enabled him to present some of the finest boxing nights ever seen in Britain. He knew what type of contest would fill the Stadium, and when he matched Jimmy Molloy against Emile Delmine, the Belgian knock-out specialist, in June 1949, he was sure that the Stadium would be a sell-out. Like Molloy, Delmine was a terrific puncher – such was his quality, he had dispensed with Stan Hawthorne, who himself was a contender for the British welterweight title, in three rounds at the Stadium.

Under normal circumstances the hall would have been packed out with 5,000 fight fans as boxing was booming in this period, yet on the night only 1,100 turned up to watch. The reason? On the same night Freddie Mills met Bruce Woodcock for the British heavyweight title at the White City, London. Jack Solomons the promoter had granted permission for the BBC to televise the fight live, and it was the first ever Solomons promotion to take place on a Thursday, the traditional night for boxing in Liverpool. Such was the interest in the Mills/Woodcock contest that many thousands of fight fans opted to stay home to watch boxing on TV. It was in many ways a harbinger of times ahead, as throughout the 1950s the Stadium would have to compete with the live broadcast of boxing. For the record, Mills was knocked out in the 14th round.

As for the Molloy/Delmine contest, it lived up to all expectations. At the first bell Molloy came at Delmine only to be met with a left hook that would have finished off most fighters. But Molloy came back, hitting Delmine with punches of similar quality. In the third round Delmine floored his opponent, but once again Molloy

demonstrated his powers of recovery. From the sixth round onwards Molloy changed tactics, aiming his punches to the body rather than the head, and this proved to be the turning point in the contest. Although Molloy had to take considerable punishment to get close in, his tactics eventually paid off. Remarkably, given the ferocity of the contest, the fight lasted until the ninth round when Molloy side-stepped a long right by Delmine and countered with a left hook to the body of the Belgian knock-out specialist. Delmine fell heavily to the canvas; he never had a chance of meeting the count.

One of the finest fights ever seen at the Stadium had the crowd on their feet; it was the type of contest that Liverpool fight fans had been brought up on. However, there was a more significant contest developing outside the boxing halls, and that was the impact television was having on live sporting events. From the 1960s onwards many sports would face similar difficulties, but in the 1950s it was the regional boxing halls that had to contend with declining attendances as the best fights became regularly broadcast into people's living rooms.

> 'Best knew what type of contest would fill the Stadium, and when he matched Jimmy Molloy against Emile Delmine, the Belgian knock-out specialist, in June 1949, he was sure that the Stadium would be a sell-out'

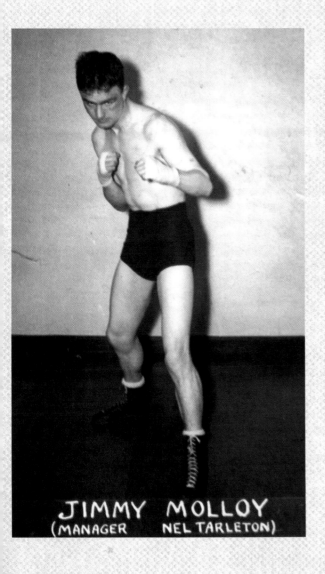

JIMMY MOLLOY
(MANAGER NEL TARLETON)

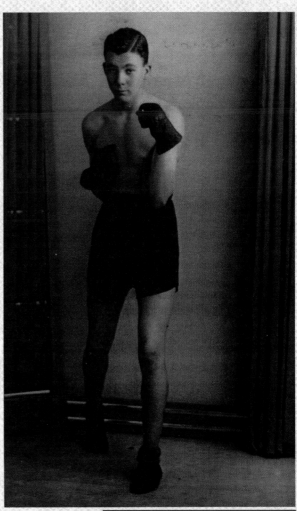

MOLLOY, MAN AND BOY: Molloy v Delmine didn't pull the crowd expected

1950s – From Optimism to Closure, to New Hope

At the onset of the 1950s, there seemed little in the way to stop the growth of the Liverpool Stadium. Merseyside was still developing top-notch fighters, while a flow of quality boxers coming from Africa, British Guiana and Jamaica seemed to ensure that the full-house signs would be maintained.

However, in the background there were three barriers emerging that would halt this growth, and they revealed their significance as the 1950s progressed. These factors were the Entertainment Tax; the fall in the number of boxers; and the impact of television upon live boxing shows.

The Entertainment Tax was introduced in 1939 to supplement government revenue at a time of exceptional expenditure. In the immediate post-war period the tax was not removed, but at a time of booming attendances it did not appear that the tax was affecting sport. Contradictorily, as the post-war boom gathered pace and disposable incomes grew, attendances at sports events peaked and then began to fall. Economic prosperity brought access to other forms of leisure such as annual holidays, while television was becoming an alternative home-based form of leisure. In 1950 about

one in 20 people watched television, but just 20 years later these figures were reversed, with just one in 20 people not watching the TV. Moreover, in this period there was an increasing number of sports programmes, including live broadcasts of boxing, initially on the BBC and later on ITV.

In the early 1950s, however, the big problem appeared to be the amount of money the Entertainment Tax was taking out of boxing. This became particularly acute in 1952 when the tax was doubled. Before 1952 it took 16 per cent of gross receipts, but following the budget of 1952 this was increased to 32 per cent. While doubling the tax for boxing and other sports Rab Butler, Chancellor of the Exchequer, proposed to exempt cricket clubs from the tax in recognition that many were struggling.

Bessie Braddock, Labour MP for Liverpool Exchange, raised the issue in Parliament in May 1953 pointing out that the Stadium had hosted 28 shows between September 1952 and April 1953. From gate receipts, she told the House and the Chancellor of the Exchequer, the Stadium had paid £4,272 in tax but made an overall loss of £2,804. By 1956, the Exchequer's take had risen to

£14,000, one-third of the Stadium's annual gate receipts. Soon after the tax was doubled, Johnny Best met Treasury officials and warned them that raising the tax would close the bulk of the country's small halls.

Alas, his prediction proved all too correct. Prior to the war, in Manchester there were at least three weekly shows in small boxing halls. From these halls came boxers such as Johnny King and Jackie Brown. On Merseyside, fight fans could go to boxing shows almost every night of the week. In addition to the Thursday night Stadium shows, fight fans could choose from several halls on the Wirral, including the Birkenhead Drill Hall, the Birkenhead Stadium, the Bebington Stadium, the Labour Hall at Ellesmere Port and Central Hall Hoylake.

While Merseyside might have been exceptional, boxing was vibrant in other parts of the country such as Glasgow, the North East of England and Yorkshire, while London was the main hub. These halls could draw from a pool of more than 3,000 boxers, but by the early 1950s the number was halved and the total dropped to around 1,100 by 1956. There was also a corresponding drop in the number of boxing promotions from around 1,000 per year in 1952 to approximately 300 in 1956. Other sports were also being affected: the city's football clubs, for example, had paid more than £200,000 in Entertainment Tax between 1950 and 1955.

The effect was that promoters in the regional halls were not able to pay boxers good purses, so new layers were not being attracted to the sport. This had an impact at grassroots level, with gymnasiums unable to attract young men. Another factor was full employment, unlike the inter-war years, which meant that young men could now make a living without recourse to the boxing ring. ▶

'Young men could now make a living without recourse to the boxing ring. In the 1950s, only a handful of boxers earned their living as professionals – the great majority were part-time boxers with jobs outside the ring'

COVER DESIGN: Big-time boxing at the Stadium, in 1955

In the 1950s, only a handful of boxers earned their living as professionals – the great majority were part-time boxers with jobs outside the ring. They were dependent upon the employer to give them time off work. However, as boxers increasingly had to travel greater distances to shows because the small halls were closing, employers became more reluctant to grant facility time. This was another factor in the decline in the number of boxers – rather than lose their job, they gave up boxing.

The small hall, which had been the backbone of British boxing in the inter-war years, went into serious decline in the post-war period. Even in London the smaller halls were suffering. In 1952 there was a total of 708 promotions in Britain, and by 1956 this had dropped to just 299. The most important regional boxing hall was the Liverpool Stadium which in 1956, for example, held 33 shows compared to seven in Glasgow, four in Newcastle and one in Leeds. Remarkably Sheffield, the city that produced boxers such as Johnny Cuthbert, had no promotions at all. With the decline of the small boxing hall, the supply of boxers with championship credentials declined. And with top-line boxers in short supply, the purse money of the top boxers grew, making it increasingly difficult for places like the Stadium to promote championship fights.

Another factor was the increasing pull of London, which in the 1950s began to take a higher proportion of championship fights. This meant that promoters like Jack Solomons became increasingly powerful and championship boxing became more and more located in London at venues such as the Harringay Arena, the Empress Hall and, for really big promotions, the Royal Albert Hall. But even Solomons could not make his promotions pay on gate receipts alone; to make a profit, he had to have the show broadcast on TV.

The changing nature of boxing in the post-war period was also reflected in the amount of fights a boxer would take part in before being lined-up for a title fight. Prior to the war, it took great boxers such as Tarleton and Roderick five and seven years respectively before they got a chance of a ▶

Telephone : CENtral 6316

BOXING

STADIUM

LIVERPOOL STADIUM LIMITED
Directors :
C. H. MICKLE (Chairman) JOHNNY BEST (Managing Director)
KENMURE KINNA, JOHN MOORES, G. E. Jones, A. D. Fisher

THURSDAY, 1st MARCH, 1956, at 8 p.m.   SIXPENCE

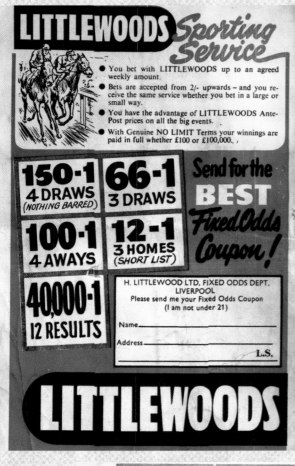
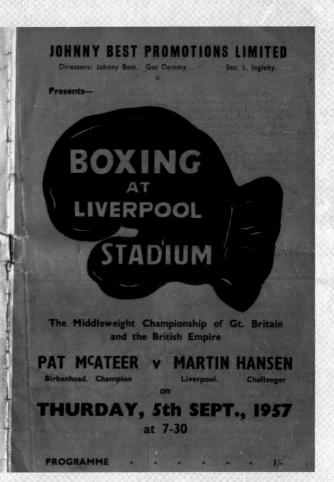

JOHNNY BEST PROMOTIONS LIMITED
Directors: Johnny Best. Gus Demmy.   Sec. L. Ingleby.

Presents—

BOXING
AT
LIVERPOOL
STADIUM

The Middleweight Championship of Gt. Britain and the British Empire

PAT McATEER v MARTIN HANSEN
Birkenhead. Champion   Liverpool. Challenger
on
THURDAY, 5th SEPT., 1957
at 7-30

PROGRAMME - - - - - 1/-

Middleweight Championship of Gt. Britain and the British Empire

Fifteen 3 minute Rounds Contest at 11 st. 6 lbs.

PAT McATEER
(Birkenhead)   (Champion)
versus
MARTIN HANSEN
(Liverpool)   (Challenger)

Officials appointed by the B.B.B. of Control
Steward in Charge   L/Col. J. W. Graham
Referees   Andrew Smyth (Belfast)
                  Geo. Balshaw (L'pool)
                  Fred Hampson (Batley)
Timekeepers   Jack Turner (Preston) and C. E. Dean (Liverpool)

PAT McATEER
(Photo by courtesy of Liverpool Echo)

MARTIN HANSEN

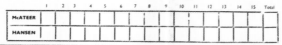

	1	2	3	4	5	6	7	8	9	10	11	12	13	14	15	Total
McATEER																
HANSEN																

This Stadium is Disinfected Daily by "WHITTAKERS" (Disinfectants) LTD. of Lark Lane, Liverpool 17.
Telephone LARK LANE 3037

BEST FIGHTS ON: Programme from 1957 for the McAteer v Hansen bout

SEPTEMBER PASS: McAteer v Hansen at the Stadium, 1957

COVER UPDATE: The programme given a revamp for a Stadium show, 1958

title fight. In the 1950s, as the number of boxers declined, it was not uncommon for a boxer to reach championship status after a score of contests. Today it is not uncommon for a boxer to challenge for a British or world title before he has had 20 contests.

Weekly shows suspended, Stadium closes and re-opens under new ownership

It is not uncommon for an advertised boxing bill to be changed – boxers pull out through injury and a suitable substitute is usually found. After all, the term 'Mugs Alley' arose from a place where a reserve boxer would be asked to wait in case he was needed to replace someone on the bill who had dropped out through injury. However, the fall in the number of licensed boxers from 1945 reduced the number of suitable reserves, making it increasingly difficult for promoters such as Best to make a match should a boxer withdraw.

This situation became so acute that on a number of occasions in the 1950s Best had to cancel promotions. The following two examples, from January and April of 1955, reflect the growing difficulty of sustaining weekly promotions. In the first instance six boxers withdrew for various reasons, mainly injury or unavailability, and when no suitable replacements could be found Best decided to scrap the event rather than put on a 'scratch' programme. On the second occasion in April the top two contests were affected when Willie Armstrong, the Scottish middleweight champion, had to withdraw owing to a hand

injury leaving Abe Quarley of the Gold Coast without an opponent. When the chief supporting contest, between Charlie Hill of Glasgow and Teddy Black of Trinidad had to be pulled, owing to the withdrawal of Black, Best felt that the lack of quality contests would affect attendance so he decided to cancel the show.

Explaining the situation, Best said:

"It is harder today to get men for supporting bouts than it is to get top-liners. At one time you could go to almost any gym and pick half a dozen in full training who were ready to step into the breach. That is not so today."

Moreover, even though there was a shortage of opponents, boxers were becoming choosy about the type of opponent they would meet. This was illustrated in the *Daily Post* of 12 April 1956 when it reported that 'the position is made more difficult because so many refuse to either meet coloured boxers or "southpaws"'.

Another factor was the growing financial demands of boxers, which made it increasingly difficult for regional promoters such as Johnny Best to make a profit on shows. Pat McAteer was one fighter capable of filling the Stadium in the 1950s, but in 1956 finding a suitable opponent at the right price proved difficult. Best Jnr revealed:

"We did inquire about Dutch champion Leen Jansen, but Jansen's demands were too high." ▶

'The fall in the number of licensed boxers from 1945 reduced the number of suitable reserves, making it increasingly difficult for promoters such as Best to make a match should a boxer withdraw...on a number of occasions Best had to cancel promotions'

WEIGH-IN: (Left to right) Pat McAteer, Dick Tiger, Alan Dean, Leen Jansen, 1957

▶ Best was able to match McAteer with Willie Armstrong in May 1956 – it was just as well that McAteer was not worried about meeting the Scottish champion despite his southpaw style. Best did secure a match with Jansen 14 months later, but this came after the abolition of the Entertainment Tax, a situation that gave more room for manoeuvre with regard to paying boxers.

As 1956 progressed the problem deepened, and when it was announced, on 9 November, that boxing at the Stadium would now take place every three weeks, it came as little surprise to Merseyside fight fans. The Stadium would never hold weekly boxing again, and had it not been for the income derived from wrestling, and classical and rock music concerts, the Stadium would not have survived as long as it did.

Indeed, just four weeks later, on 6 December, the Stadium closed its doors for a four-month period. It was feared that the hall would not stage boxing again. The problem, according to Charles Mickle the chairman, was that they were having difficulties meeting "weekly overhead expenses whether there is boxing or not…". The truth was that the shows were losing money and every time the doors were opened for boxing, the Stadium was subject to paying Entertainment Tax.

The hall finally re-opened for the traditional eve of Grand National meeting in March 1957, and featured four prominent local boxers: Billy Ellaway, Syd Greb and Tommy and Leo Molloy. However, prior to the show, a meeting of shareholders held on 22 March decided to put the hall up for sale. The shareholders announced that following the promotion on the eve of the Grand National, boxing would be discontinued until further notice. The statement from the shareholders read as follows:

'At a shareholders' meeting this evening, 22 March 1957, it was with regret resolved that boxing be discontinued following the show on 28 March 1957, and that wrestling be continued pending the sale of the hall.'

Explaining the statement, Benny Carter, a Stadium official, said:

"People will pay to see the big names but not to watch budding talent. With the Stadium running weekly shows, you can't have champions or title contenders every week. For 80 per cent of the time your shows must consist of budding talent, which has been the Stadium modus operandi."

LIFELINE: John Moores was able to attract big-time boxing to the Stadium

Carter also made it clear that even when big contests were held it was hard to make a clear profit. The Pat McAteer/Johnny Sullivan British middleweight title fight of 1955 was given as an example:

"We took £10,350 that night – the biggest 'gate' ever at the Stadium – but we didn't even cover our weekly expenses. Naturally, a large slice went to the boxers, but tax took £3,440…Even if the tax is reduced it will take at least three years to put British boxing back on its feet. Halls are closing all the time, and gymnasiums too. Consequently, there are fewer boxers."

An approach was made to the city council to buy the building, but this did not materialise, even though the council leader Jack Braddock was a big supporter of boxing. The council did have reserves of more than £1 million, but legally it could only acquire a business that was viable. However, two weeks after closure a lifeline was delivered when the majority of the Stadium shares were bought by John Moores, the pools magnate. The background to the purchase was the abolition of the Entertainment Tax in the 1957 budget. The proms and wrestling formed part of the business plan but the hope of reverting to weekly shows by the winter never materialised.

Moores had been a director of the Stadium since 1949, being appointed to the board following the death of Major Bennett. Under Moores' stewardship, the Stadium was still able to attract important title fights. For example, Pat McAteer successfully defended his British and Empire titles there in September 1957 against Martin Hansen. The following year, when McAteer lost his Empire title to Dick Tiger, world heavyweight champion Floyd Patterson made a guest appearance. Such nights brought big crowds but there was no longer the quality in depth, as had been the case in the 1930s, to draw full houses every week. In an attempt to boost crowds the Stadium tried various promotional ideas, one example being that for 6 May 1959 the show was held on the Wednesday instead of the usual Thursday, and escorted women were admitted free. However, the reasoning behind the promotion said a lot about how society was changing – a situation that was underlined by the local press:

'…the plan is to attract the public to boxing. The change to Wednesday is made because there are so many counter attractions on Thursday.'

Boxing was facing increasing competition from other leisure pursuits and without quality shows, the return to weekly Thursday night slots was just not a viable business proposition.

PREPARATION: Dick Tiger with boss Tony Vairo, 1957. "I took a new manager and since then I have never looked back."

The Nigerian Connection

As one of the world's great trading centres, Liverpool has long provided a home for many people from around the world. Some have come because of economic displacement; others have come in search of employment and a better life. A diverse population has contributed to Liverpool's unique character and has certainly shaped the identity of its people. In the post-war period a unique community settled in Liverpool, a community that extended the city's worldwide reputation as a sporting hotbed and a centre of boxing excellence. Many of these boxers came from Nigeria, most notably Hogan 'Kid' Bassey and Dick Tiger, while several adopted the city as their home. Both Bassey and Tiger would establish themselves as boxers of international repute at the Liverpool Stadium.

The first of the two to arrive in Liverpool was Bassey in December 1951. Bassey came here after winning the Nigerian and West African titles at fly and bantamweight. The problem for Bassey was that at the age of 18 he had fought all the best boxers on the west coast of Africa and to progress he needed to find stiffer opposition. Moreover, at the time it was not possible to make a living in Nigeria as a professional boxer. It was at this point that Bassey considered leaving Nigeria for Britain to continue his boxing career, but he could not afford to pay his passage. However, in Lagos at the time were two men, Jack Farnworth and Douglas Collister, who had links with Peter Banasko in Liverpool. Following his retirement from boxing after the war, Banasko had established himself as a manager and had already taken on another West African, Israel Boyle. When Farnworth offered to pay Bassey's passage, he readily accepted with the promise that he would pay back his benefactor. Upon arriving in Liverpool, Bassey was met at the docks by Banasko and Boyle – Bassey had previously met Boyle in Lagos at various boxing shows.

It was Boyle who was to play a key role in settling Bassey into his new home.

Bassey was to live in Liverpool for nearly 10 years. During his time in the city he became a great favourite of the Stadium crowd. However, in the early stages of his stay he was subjected to some racism. Looking back on his career in the mid-1960s, Bassey remembered how his boxing prowess was able to break down such attitudes towards him:

"It was very pleasing to me to know that I had practically buried the racial prejudice, which definitely existed in my early days; though it was perhaps not so much in evidence on Merseyside as elsewhere, since Liverpool is more cosmopolitan than most cities in Britain."

Bassey was subject to some overt racial prejudice, however, prior to his fight with Bobby Boland in April 1952. Although the contest was catchweight, Boland had scaled over the agreed weight limit and as there was a forfeit clause in the contract, Boland had to lose the weight or pay the forfeit. Boland was forced to do extra training to shed the weight, and as his frustration grew, so did his anger: "Why should I have to bother with

all this for a n*****", he was heard to shout. Unacceptable though Boland's comments were, it must be remembered that the black bar on boxers fighting for a British title had only just been lifted. Bassey, meanwhile, had to be restrained from taking on Boland there and then, but he eventually saved his anger for the ring by knocking out Boland in the fifth round.

Bassey is a shining example of how sport can break down racist attitudes. From the beginning, his style of boxing endeared him to Mersey fight fans. Indeed, Johnny Best Jnr regarded his fights with Johnny Butterworth of Rochdale and Jean Sneyers in 1954 as two of the finest seen at the Stadium.

Unlike many other Liverpool boxers of the time, Bassey's greatest achievements came at venues other than the Stadium. The reasons for this are twofold. Firstly, being Nigerian he was unable to fight for a British title, and secondly, by the mid-1950s, when Bassey was on the verge of becoming recognised at world level, Johnny Best was finding it increasingly difficult to attract boxers with a worldwide reputation to the Stadium. Moreover, boxing itself was in ▶

"It was very pleasing to me to know that I had practically buried the racial prejudice, which definitely existed in my early days; though it was perhaps not so much in evidence on Merseyside as elsewhere, since Liverpool is more cosmopolitan than most cities in Britain."

HOGAN 'KID' BASSEY: Shaking hands with Cherif Hamia in June 1957 before fighting for the world featherweight title (right), and receiving an award from D.J. Collister in 1957 (above)

'Bassey took on Cherif Hamia for the vacant world featherweight title in Paris, stopping Hamia in the 10th round to lift the crown. Upon returning home to Liverpool, Bassey received a hero's welcome'

▶ something of a recession owing to the punishing Entertainment Tax and the declining number of quality boxers. In this situation, Bassey was forced to find a full-time job as a motor mechanic's assistant to supplement his income from boxing.

Bassey now recognised that if he was to realise his growing boxing ambitions, he would have to seek international opponents. Although he won the British Empire featherweight title under Banasko, beating 'Spider' Kelly in Belfast in November 1955, there were growing disagreements with his manager. Indeed, Bassey broke with Banasko immediately after the Kelly fight, moving to the George Biddles camp. A disillusioned Banasko decided to withdraw from boxing altogether, even though he had just signed up Dick Tiger.

Success over Kelly had given Bassey a worldwide reputation, and following a successful defence of his Empire title at Nottingham on 1 April 1957 (defeating Percy Lewis), he turned his attention to the world title. Three weeks after beating Lewis, Bassey outpointed Miguel Berrios in America in an eliminator for the world title. Just two months later, Bassey took on Cherif Hamia for the vacant world featherweight title in Paris, stopping Hamia in the 10th round to lift the crown. Upon returning home to Liverpool, Bassey received a hero's welcome.

Following his world-champion status, Bassey would only make one more appearance at the Stadium – against Jean Pierre Cossemyns ▶

STADIUM MEMORIES: Bassey pictured in 1958 when he was world champion (top), and at the Town Hall in 1957

KING OF THE WORLD: Bassey returns home to Liverpool with the world featherweight trophy. Charlie Fox, his trainer, is holding it aloft

READY TO WIN: Training for the Hamia fight in St Helens, June 1957

▶ in January 1958. His final Stadium appearance was in effect a warm-up for his first title defence against Ricardo Moreno in California. Bassey beat Cossemyns and subsequently knocked out Moreno in the third round to retain his title. However, 11 months later he lost his title to Davey Moore in Los Angeles when the referee stopped the contest in the 13th round. A rematch at the same venue on 19 August 1959 had a similar outcome, with Bassey unable to answer the bell for the 11th round.

Defeated he may have been, but when Bassey returned to Liverpool, crowds greeted him at his home with placards saying 'Welcome Home to Hogan Our Champ'. Bassey had clearly earned the admiration of his fellow Liverpudlians.

Bassey returned to Nigeria in 1960, where he became the national boxing coach. Under his guidance, Nigeria won two gold medals at the 1964 and 1972 Olympic Games. When Bassey died in 1992, he was mourned not only in Nigeria but in his adopted home of Liverpool.

Dick Tiger

Unlike Bassey, Dick Tiger, born Richard Ihetu, did not arrive in Liverpool with a Nigerian title to his name. In fact, his first four contests in Britain all resulted in defeat and it seemed that he was just going to be a journeyman boxer who would not progress beyond local halls. After losing Peter Banasko as his manager, Tiger came under the management of Tony Vairo. However, under the guidance of his new manager and his trainer Maurice Foran, Tiger rapidly developed into a world-ranking middleweight.

In his fifth contest, Tiger knocked out Dennis Rowley in the first round. He had at last displayed the attribute that was to be his hallmark throughout the rest of his career: a boxer with a knock-out punch. Over the coming years, several top British middleweights would succumb in similar fashion. These included Terry Downes in five rounds, Billy Ellaway in two rounds and Pat McAteer in nine rounds. The most important of these victories was for McAteer's Empire title at the Stadium on 27 March 1958.

McAteer was British champion at the time,

and he was favourite to keep his Empire belt. However, Tiger was to knock out the champion in the ninth before a stunned but admiring crowd. After his next contest, in which he knocked out Ellaway in the second round, Tiger was advised by his trainer Foran that he could be a world champion if he went to America. This meant a change in manager as well as trainer.

Tiger soon established himself as a force across the Atlantic, but he had trouble in getting a world title shot as both middleweight world champions – Paul Pender, the WBC champion and Gene Fullmer, the WBA champion – were reluctant to meet him. However, by 1962 Tiger's championship credentials could not be ignored and Fullmer was forced to meet him on 23 October in San Francisco. Tiger battered the champion for 15 rounds and received the unanimous decision of the judges. After a return contest, just four months later in Las Vegas, resulted in draw, a third and deciding contest was held in Tiger's homeland, Nigeria, on 10 August 1963. This time both the WBA and WBC versions of the world title were at stake – Paul Pender having retired after regaining the WBC title from Terry Downes. Once again Tiger prevailed, but this time Fullmer's manager would not let the former champion continue as he was receiving too much punishment.

Just four months later, Tiger lost his titles to Joey Giardello in New Jersey. Now aged 34, many thought Tiger would retire, but instead he had a series of bouts, including a victory over Rubin Carter, that once again gave him the chance to fight Giardello for the world title. The pair met in New York in October 1965, with Tiger once again emerging as world champion. After losing his titles at his first defence to Emile Griffith, he moved up to light-heavyweight. In December 1966 he took on and beat the world light-heavyweight champion Jose Torres. After two successful defences – one against Torres, the other against Roger Rouse – Tiger lost these titles to Bob Foster in May 1968 when he was knocked out in the fourth round.

Although he continued to fight on, he finally retired after losing to Griffith again in 1970. Tragically in July 1971 he was diagnosed with liver cancer. Just five months later, he died in Nigeria at the age of 42.

Remarkably, Nigeria's two greatest boxers had learnt the fundamentals of professional boxing at the Liverpool Stadium. Although they both had to leave their country of birth and their adopted home of Liverpool to attain world-champion status, both were always conscious of where they learnt their boxing.

IT WOULD ONLY LAST TWO ROUNDS: Tiger and Ellaway at the weigh-in 1958

WINNING COMBINATION: Bassey (left) with Tiger. Bassey is holding the World Trophy, Tiger the Empire Trophy he received when beating Pat McAteer

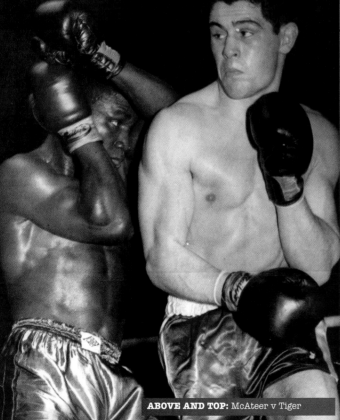

ABOVE AND TOP: McAteer v Tiger

TIGER TEAM IN GYM: Back row: Joe Jackson (timekeeper), M. Foran (trainer) and N. Elliot (member of the PBA). Front row: Tiger and Roy Jacobs

Wally Thom – Underrated, but not Forgotten

Like Liverpool, Birkenhead has a magnificent boxing tradition. Few other towns of comparable size have produced champions as regularly as Birkenhead. The post-war period was a particularly fruitful one for the town, with boxers such as Wally Thom and Pat McAteer bringing home British titles in the 1950s. Moreover, both boxers had big local rivals: Thom v Fallon and McAteer v Ellaway were regarded as local 'derbies', and served to heighten the atmosphere at the Stadium.

Thom's background is very similar to other Merseyside fighters, brought up in a working-class area where sport was a part of everyday life. Thom was born in 1926 in the North End area of Birkenhead, the same place as the great Dixie Dean. Thom's links

with Dean go back to childhood when his father bought him his first punch-ball from Dean's sports shop on Grange Road.

It was at school that Thom first got the opportunity to box in an organised way. The headmaster asked for a boy to box for the Blake Cup at Byrne Avenue Baths. Four boys came forward and were asked to demonstrate their boxing skills, and Wally got the nod – a sure sign that Dixie Dean's punch-ball played a formative role in Thom's development. Needless to say, Wally won his contest and received his first boxing medal.

Soon afterwards, Thom joined the Birkenhead Amateur Boxing Club. When the building was bombed in the war, most boys joined Alex Powell's club on Egerton Street. Overall, Thom had a successful amateur career, reaching two ABA finals but losing each time to the great Randolph Turpin in 1945 and to Alan Buxton in 1947.

Thom turned professional in 1949, with his first contest being at the Stadium against Rex Bryan of Wrexham. This was the first of 22 straight victories, all bar one at the Stadium, that brought him the chance take on Eddie Thomas for his British and British Empire welterweight titles. Among these 22 wins was a stirring 12-round contest with Bootle boxer Jimmy Molloy, and a final eliminating contest for the British welterweight title against Cliff Curvis.

Thom's fight with Curvis disproved the old ring maxim that two southpaws cannot put on a good contest. From the start until the ninth round, when Curvis was disqualified, the fight gripped the audience. The bout was ended following a clash of heads between the two fighters. The referee first spoke to Curvis and then turned to speak to Thom, and as he did so Curvis stepped round the

referee and hit Thom on the chin. Referee Muir had no other course of action but to disqualify Curvis for striking his opponent before being told to box on.

Before meeting Eddie Thomas for the British and British Empire titles at Harringay, Thom experienced his first defeat at the hands of Molloy. Worryingly for Thom, he was stopped in the second round following an eye injury. It was a big turning point in Thom's career, as from this point on he had to deal with persistent cuts around the eyes – a problem that would ultimately curtail his career.

The fight with Thomas took place at Harringay on 16 October 1951 – with the exception of one bout in Blackpool, it was Thom's first contest outside the Liverpool Stadium. Thomas was overwhelming favourite to win, but Thom put on a trademark display of forceful boxing and beat the champion on points over 15 rounds. Thom brought back to Merseyside the title held for so long by the great Ernie Roderick.

However, Thom lost the titles at his first defence against Curvis before a record crowd at the Stadium just nine months later. The contest started sensationally, with Curvis putting Thom on the canvas for two counts of four and nine. Throughout, Thom was no match for the challenger, and like their first bout it ended in the ninth round, although this time it was Curvis who won via a knock out.

One of the hardest tasks in boxing is to regain a title, so often defeat to an up-and-coming challenger signals the end. Moreover, Thom's lethargic performance against Curvis seemed to spell the end of his championship hopes. This situation was reinforced when he lost to his local rival Peter Fallon in a final eliminating contest at the Stadium in February 1953. ▶

WALLY THOM
British Welterweight Champion

WELTERWEIGHT CHAMPIONSHIP OF EUROPE

FIFTEEN 3 MINUTE ROUNDS AT 10 st. 7 lbs

GILBERT LAVOINE
(France)
(WELTERWEIGHT CHAMPION OF EUROPE)

VERSUS

WALLY THOM
(Birkenhead)
(WELTERWEIGHT CHAMPION OF GT. BRITAIN)

OFFICIALS (APPOINTED BY THE B.B.B. of C.)
Steward in charge—Lt. Col. J. W. GRAHAM.
Referee—Mr. A. KOCH (Sweden)   Timekeeper—Mr. C. E. DEAN

	1	2	3	4	5	6	7	8	9	10	11	12	13	14	15	TOTAL
LAVOINE																
THOM																

Boxing News Photograph
WALLY THOM

Boxing News Photograph
GILBERT LAVOINE

PAGES FROM A 1954 PROGRAMME:
Thom features in the main event (above),
while Ellaway's fight is previewed (below)

— SUPPORTING CONTESTS —

Eight 3 minute Rounds Lightweight Contest

MICKEY FLANAGAN
(Birkenhead)
Has wins over Mickey O'Neill, Cliff Anderson, Ronnie Wormall, etc.
versus
ALAN TANNER
(British Guiana)
The clever British Guianan has put up many excellent displays in this hall.

Eight 3 minute Rounds Welterweight Contest

SANDY MANUEL
(Nigeria)
Boxing in great form. Scored a fine win over Peter King in this hall.
versus
PETER KING
(Manchester)
The Manchester boxer recently K.O'd Ken Regan in one round at Belle Vue.

Eight 3 minute Rounds Lightweight Contest

LEO MOLLOY
(Birkenhead)
Another fine young prospect from Birkenhead. Has won all his 10 professional contests.
versus
KEVIN DUFFY
(Haslington)
Has lost only 1 of his 14 professional contests.

Six 3 minute Rounds Lightweight Contest.

Emrys Jones v. Del Willis
(Oswestry)   (Manchester)
Contender for the Welsh lightweight title.

WALLY THOM
Welterweight Champion of Gt. Britain.

THURSDAY, 2nd SEPTEMBER, at 7·30 p.m.
Eight 3 minute Rounds Middleweight Contest.

Billy Ellaway v. Selected Opp.
(Liverpool) One of the hardest
hitting middles in the country.

PRICES 20/- 10/- 7/6 (Reserved) 3/6 pay at door.

Carter & Nuttall (Printers) T.U., 134 Breck Road, Liverpool, 5

BIRKENHEAD V BOOTLE: Clipping previewing Thom's fight with Gordon Ashun in December 1949

'Curvis' shock decision to retire without a single defence brought Thom an unexpected opportunity to fight for the title once more. His opponent was none other than his great local rival Peter Fallon'

city.
Wally Thom, the former Northern Count amateur welterweight champion from Birk head, who has a 100 per cent. profession record, is matched · over eight rounds w: the strong Bootle lad, Gordon Ashun, whe we have not een 'or some time.
Thom has had five professional contes winning four inside the distance. Rex Bry was Thom's first opponent and succeeded going to a points decision.
Over six rounds the welterweights, Ja Scott, of Burnley, and George Day, of Hu both of whom lost to Jim Allsopp here; a paired, while Billy Gray, the Bootle lig weight, meets a selected opponent.

▶ Fallon was a very fine boxer who possessed a powerful left hook. To get the opportunity to meet Thom he had beaten some very good welterweights, including Israel Boyle, Kit Pompey, Joe Corcoran and, earlier in his career, the champion Cliff Curvis. The Fallon/Thom contest was another of the great nights at the Stadium. The local rivalry only served to heighten the tension and lift the crowd to a frenzy; for 12 rounds the action was fierce and relentless, with Thom down for three counts and Fallon for one. At the bell for the final round, it was hard to separate the two but it was Fallon who dominated events, staging a powerful rally prior to the final bell. Fallon took the decision and earned the right to meet Curvis for a second time – this time for the British title.

It looked all over for Thom; his chance of regaining the title now looked even more remote. However, Curvis' shock decision to retire without a single defence brought Thom an unexpected opportunity to fight for the title once more. His opponent was none other than his great local rival Peter Fallon.

Once again, Johnny Best was able to secure the contest for the Stadium, ensuring another sell-out at the hall. It was another thrilling contest, although Fallon's natural attacking style was shackled somewhat following a bad cut to his left eye sustained in the second round. Fallon still troubled Thom: he shook him with a right hook in the 10th round and

clearly won the 14th. However, such setbacks were to be expected as Thom was reluctant to take a step backward throughout the course of the contest. Like the first fight between them, this one went the distance, but this time it was Thom who prevailed, albeit by the narrowest of margins – Thom had regained his title.

WALLY THE REFEREE: On retirement, Thom became a world-class referee – this picture was taken on 14 August 1964

Eleven months later, Thom won the European title at the Stadium, defeating the incumbent Gilbert Lavoine of France. The fight had looked all over in the first round when Thom suffered a bad cut to his right eye, but Thom's skill and experience enabled him to

change tactics – rather than employ his natural attacking style, he let the champion do all the forcing and endeavoured to keep Lavoine at long range. The contest was a tense tactical battle, but from the ninth Thom was confident that he had sufficiently sapped the strength of the champion following a series of powerful body punches. Towards the end of the round he unleashed a two-handed attack that had the Frenchman on the canvas, but before Thom could follow-up, the bell signalled the end of the round. From the outset of the 10th round, Thom attacked once more, forcing the champion onto the ropes. Lavoine was now taking a barrage of punches, and with his defence dropping the referee was forced to stop the fight.

Just two months later, Thom secured the Lonsdale Belt by knocking out Lew Lazar in the sixth round at Harringay. This was the pinnacle of his career, as in June 1955 he lost his European title at the Stadium to Idrissa Dione of France. His final contest in the ring was at Harringay 12 months later, when he lost his British title to Peter Waterman of London. Defeat may have brought an end to Thom's illustrious career, but not to his links with boxing.

In retirement, Thom became a top-class referee, taking charge of British and world title fights at stadiums around the world. Thom died at the young age of 54 in 1980.

DIXIE DEAN (FAR LEFT, SHAKING HANDS WITH JOHN MOORES): Wally Thom and the Everton legend both came from the North End of Birkenhead, and Thom's first punch-ball came from Dean's shop

GILBERT LAVOINE

Lavoine was born at Laon (France) on February 1931. He is a railway worker and at one time looked liked developing into a first class footballer. Recently he received offers from several well known French teams but preferred to follow his career as a boxer. Lavoine is one of the hardest hitting boxers on the Continent and his record shows a large percentage of K.O. wins. He has conceded weight to top class middleweights, and one of his best performances was to box a draw against Claude Milazzo, one of the best middleweights in Europe. A fortnight ago Milazzo held the unbeaten German middleweight Gustav Scholz to a draw.

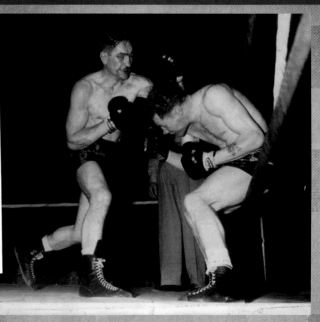

THOM V LAVOINE: The 1954 programme profiles Lavoine (above), and here he can be seen forcing Wally Thom onto the ropes in the third round. Thom won in the 10th

Pat McAteer – Birkenhead's Finest Boxer

In the 1950s, Pat McAteer was a name that got the pulses of Mersey fight fans throbbing. When in June 1955 he won the British and British Empire middleweight titles at the Liverpool Stadium, he became the first Merseyside boxer to reach such a milestone while remaining undefeated. It was his 37th contest in less than three years and all bar four had been at the Stadium, a record that endeared him to the knowledgeable Stadium boxing fans.

McAteer was part of the highly successful Johnny Campbell gymnasium. Throughout the 1950s and 1960s, some of Britain's finest boxers emerged from the Campbell stable, including other British champions such as Wally Thom and Johnny Cooke. Initially, Campbell only worked with amateurs, and his Provincial ABC was among the most successful in the country. However, when one of his boxers, Joe Bygraves, turned professional because of a dispute with the ABA, Campbell took out his professional manager's licence. Campbell quickly signed up Wally Thom as well as McAteer, who agreed professional terms in the autumn of 1952 giving Campbell one of the finest group of boxers of any manager in Britain.

Within 15 months of turning professional, McAteer had seen off every opponent put before him with relative ease. On Merseyside he was being talked about as a potential champion, but nationally he was still relatively unknown. However, continuing success during 1954 brought national and international recognition. During that year he had 17 contests, 15 at the Stadium, against some of the toughest middleweight opponents in Britain and Europe. In British championship terms, his victory over the Liverpool Dane Martin Hansen in September 1954 paved the way for a final eliminator against Les Allen of Bedford.

Best's offer of a £3,000 purse, a record for an eliminating contest, secured the bout for Liverpool and it eventually took place on 9 December 1954. Allen was certainly a stiff opponent: he had beaten good middleweights such as Billy Ellaway and Emile Delmine. He had a bobbing and weaving style as he looked to land his dangerous left and right hooks. McAteer, however, boxed coolly and methodically and never gave Allen a chance to catch him with a decent punch. At the end of 12 rounds, the referee had little hesitation in awarding the decision to the Birkenhead man. McAteer was now set to face the British and British Empire champion Johnny Sullivan of Preston.

Once again, Best secured the contest for Liverpool, and it was scheduled for June 1955. Although the younger of the two boxers, Sullivan had more professional experience than McAteer – he had also boxed in America and Canada. He had won the title two years before in 1954 at the Harringay Arena, knocking out Gordon Hazell of Bristol in the first round. Moreover, his record showed that more than half of his contests had been won by knock out, further demonstrating that he was a dangerous opponent for the challenger.

However, it was McAteer who was the master on the night. Sullivan tried everything to unsettle him – jabs, hooks, combination punches – but nothing worked on the ice-cool McAteer. By the ninth round, Sullivan was clearly a frustrated champion. He was well behind on points and was ▶

MCATEER V BILLY ELLAWAY: Picture from the *Liverpool Echo*, 3 August 1956

MCATEER: Pat McAteer drops Billy Ellaway at the Stadium, 1956 (top); Johnny Sullivan avoids a right cross from McAteer during their fight in June 1955 (above); training shot (left)

'Despite all of his wonderful achievements, the one McAteer fight that became most talked about on Merseyside in the 1950s was the local 'derby' with Billy Ellaway – a non-title fight at the Liverpool Stadium on 2 August 1956'

FOCUSED: McAteer in training

becoming increasingly desperate. At the beginning of the ninth round, he seemed to change tactics by encouraging McAteer to take the fight to him, but the challenger refused to deviate from his pre-fight plan. In need of points, it was Sullivan who was forced to come forward with two punches to the body that seemed low. The first was ignored by the referee but the second duly led to him being disqualified. McAteer had regained the British middleweight title for Merseyside, last won for the region by Ernie Roderick in 1945.

McAteer successfully defended his British and British Empire titles against Lew Lazar and Martin Hansen. He also defended his Empire title in South Africa, knocking out Jimmy Elliot in round six. Although he eventually lost his Empire title to Dick Tiger in 1958, he retired as undefeated British champion in the same year. However, despite all the wonderful achievements, the one McAteer fight that became most talked about

on Merseyside in the 1950s was the local 'derby' with Billy Ellaway.

The 'derby' was a non-title fight at the Liverpool Stadium that took place on 2 August 1956. Ellaway was the man with the big punch, the Alf Howard of his day – he could rescue a lost cause with a knock-out blow. Ellaway won 16 of his first 23 fights inside the distance. There was intense rivalry between the two sets of supporters, and the evening is also remembered for the fights that took place in the hall between rival fans. However, it is what goes on in the ring that counts, and the newly crowned champion was in no mood to become another victim of Ellaway's knock-out punch. At the end of 10 rounds, McAteer was the clear winner but it was now that the real controversy started.

At the final bell, both boxers crossed to the opposite corner to offer the traditional handshake to the opponent's ringside team.

The referee, Fred Blakeborough, seemed oblivious to this and walked over to McAteer's corner and raised the hand of Ellaway as the winner. There was immediate uproar in the crowd, with scuffles breaking out once more. Amidst all the trouble, Johnny Best had a quiet word with the referee who, upon realising his mistake, duly raised McAteer's arm. To be fair, the referee's card had been checked by ringside officials, who confirmed that the referee had McAteer down as the clear winner. It was a case of mistaken identity but it was no less embarrassing.

Pat McAteer was the first of a McAteer boxing dynasty that included cousins Neil, Les and Gordon. Of the three cousins it was Les who was the most successful, wining the middleweight title in 1969 at Nottingham against Wally Swift. Their boxing success reinforces the point that Birkenhead has provided Britain with some of the country's most outstanding boxers.

5 SEPTEMBER 1957: McAteer defeats Martin Hansen to win the Lonsdale Belt outright. Lft Colonel Graham, steward of the BBBofC (far left), congratulates him

The 1960s – Mounting Problems End in Another Period of Closure

The problems that had materialised and gathered pace in the 1950s became reinforced in the 1960s. Closures and temporary suspensions of boxing occurred throughout the decade. Following the death of Johnny Best Snr, and the subsequent change of ownership, a variety of promoters tried to revitalise boxing. Even high-profile promoters such as Mickey Duff could not re-kindle the Best magic of the 1930s.

Moreover, another post-war social change was having its affect upon Stadium attendances. In the post-war period, over-zealous slum clearance saw the population around the city centre drop significantly. Modern housing estates largely replaced the demolished houses, but these estates were several miles outside the city centre. Tony Vairo summed up the problem:

"With the city sprawling more and more, people are living further out and when they get home from work they don't want to come back in again. In the old days they used to stay in town."

One could add that changing employment patterns were also having their effect. The dock labour force was in terminal decline, and this also affected work associated with the docks, such as transport. As a consequence, there were fewer people working close to town. People were now travelling away from the city to places such as Halewood and Ellesmere Port to work in the new car plants.

Alongside these factors, another trend of Merseyside fighters boxing out of London emerged. These included some of Merseyside's finest boxers such as Harry

Scott, Alan Rudkin and Pat Dwyer. Scott only boxed at the Stadium 14 times out of 79 recorded fights, Pat Dwyer only appeared once, while Alan Rudkin made only five appearances out of a career total of 50 professional contests. Indeed, all of Rudkin's title fights took place outside the city. In the 1930s, the Liverpool Stadium under Johnny Best expected to win contracts to host British and world title fights that involved Liverpool boxers. Tarleton, Kane, Roderick and Rowan all won their first titles either at Anfield or the Stadium under promotions run by Best. Best may have lost out in the race to get to stage Kane's first world title attempt against Benny Lynch, and also lost out to Harringay to host the Armstrong/Roderick world title fight, but it was still accepted that Liverpool was a natural place to hold major title fights. In the post-war period, Wally Thom, Pat McAteer and Tommy Molloy either won or defended

their titles at the Stadium. However, from the 1950s onwards, Liverpool was not only losing out to London but was often losing out to the Ice Rink, Nottingham and Belle Vue, Manchester. This was a fundamental shift, and reflected the fact that the influence of the Liverpool Stadium was being marginalised.

Of course there were still fine boxers associated with the Stadium. Johnny Cooke defended his British welterweight title against Shaun Doyle in May 1967. He had won the title three months earlier at Belle Vue when he outpointed Brian McCaffrey in what is regarded as one of the finest fights ever to grace a British ring. The trend, however, was unmistakable: more and more championship boxing was being held outside the city as more of its finest fighters headed south where the big money was located. ▶

Mickey Duff
PROMOTIONS · LTD
by arrangement with
GUS DEMMY
(PROMOTIONS) LTD
PRESENT

Wally Swift

Assane Fakyh

Tony Smith

Larry Baker

THURSDAY, 11th AUGUST, 1960
LIVERPOOL STADIUM
Programme 1/-

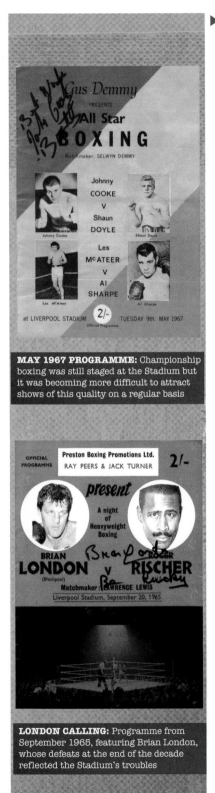

MAY 1967 PROGRAMME: Championship boxing was still staged at the Stadium but it was becoming more difficult to attract shows of this quality on a regular basis

LONDON CALLING: Programme from September 1965, featuring Brian London, whose defeats at the end of the decade reflected the Stadium's troubles

That Merseyside was still producing boxers of quality in the 1960s is undoubted, but even when such boxers came to the Stadium they were not guaranteed a sell-out at the box office. Take, for example, the Harry Scott/Les McAteer fight of September 1968, which was a final eliminator for the middleweight title. Both boxers were big draws around the country yet they failed to attract a sell-out attendance. Scott had fought the likes of Rubin Carter (twice) and Emile Griffith – he actually beat Carter on the second occasion – while just 10 months after the Scott fight, McAteer emulated his cousin Pat by winning the British title against Wally Swift.

Of course, not only Liverpool was suffering. Regional halls throughout the country were closing or failing to stage major promotions. But given Liverpool's historic significance in relation to British boxing as a whole, it was nothing short of a tragedy that the legacy left behind by Johnny Best was not built upon. Speaking in 1967, Johnny Wright, the assistant secretary at the Stadium since it had opened, said:

"Boxing was at its height in the Depression era when you had a terrific following. But those fans are getting on in years and there has been a break in the sequence and their interest has been lost. *The trouble is no substitute audience has been built up.*

"In the Depression era there were 3,400 registered boxers and even losers could be choosers. Now there are only 480 boxers with 300 of them having little or no work because there are fewer shows.

"The boxers and managers are killing the game. Boxers are charging tremendous prices and promoters, unless they charge sky-high prices, don't stand a chance of making a profit. If you get 3,000 at the Stadium now it's a miracle."

One could add that the lack of investment in the building, an inability to develop a strategy that could have incorporated the televising of boxing, and an inability to develop sufficient local talent all contributed to the Stadium passing through periods of closure and partial closure. The decade ended with the Stadium shutting its doors to

professional boxing once more – the last show was on 10 April 1969, when Brian London suffered a first-round knock out to Jimmy Fletcher. His victory over Zora Folley in 1967 was his last-ever success in a boxing ring. He had four further contests at the Stadium, against Roberto Davila, Jack Bodell, Henry Clark and the aforementioned Fletcher. With the exception of the Clark contest, which was drawn, London was knocked out on each occasion. His plight somehow reflected the troubled Stadium. The hall was looking tired, in need of repair, and it was finding it increasingly difficult to find suitable boxers that could pull in the crowds. Brian London had been a popular attraction at the Stadium in the late 1960s – he had been the cornerstone of Lawrie Lewis' promotions – but London's defeat was his last promotion at the hall. It would be more than four years before it would host professional boxing again.

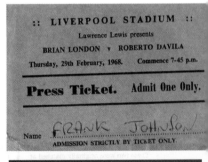

1968 TICKET: London, who had previously fought Muhammad Ali, was knocked out by Davila

BOXING LIVERPOOL STADIUM BOXING

THURSDAY 11th AUGUST

Doors open 6.0 p.m.
Commence 7.30 p.m.

MICKEY DUFF PROMOTIONS LTD. Proudly present
(By arrangement with Gus Demmy Promotions Ltd.)

AN INTRIGUING PROGRAMME WORTHY OF ANY ARENA IN GREAT BRITAIN

10 (3 min) Rounds
Welter weight Contest at 10st 9 lbs

WALLY SWIFT

Nottingham.   Welter-weight Champion of
Gt. Britain.   Conqueror of Virgil Akins,
Willie Toweel, etc.   versus

ASSANE FAKYH

Lebanon. Leading French Welter-wt. Swifts
first southpaw opponent prior to defending his
championship against Brian Curvis

10 (3 min) Rounds Return
Welter-weight Contest at 10st 9 lbs

LARRY BAKER

U.S.A. Remembered here for his sensational
K.O. win over Smith which he is confident
of repeating.   versus

TONY SMITH

Bootle.   Since losing to Baker has defeated
Southern Area Champ Albert Carroll & Irish
Champ Al Sharpe. Has asked for this return

---

8 (3 min) Rounds Fly-weight Contest at 8-3

TOMMY BACHE v EDDIE BARRACLOUGH

Liverpool's greatest Fly-weight since
Joe Curran. Undefeated to date
Just defeated Eddie O'Connor

Hull. Undoubtedly Bache's hardest test to date
Recently gave British champion
Frankie Jones a close fight

---

8 (3 min) Rounds Middle-weight Contest at 11-8

NEIL McATEER v DAVE GEORGE

Birkenhead. One of the hardest punchers
in Gt. Britain, just reversed his only defeat
to date by stopping Brian Coxhead

Leamington Spa. A strong and experienced
boxer.   A stiff test for McAteer
in his first 8 round contest

---

8 (3 min) Rounds
Welter-weight Contest at 10st 9 lbs

JIMMY McGRAIL

Liverpool. Britain's hardest punching Welterweight since Eric Boon. Still undefeated to
date and only one has gone the distance vs

PETER COBBLAH

Ghana. These two were originally matched at
Wembley. Can McGrail stop Cobblah where
Brian Curvis failed ?

8 (3 min) Rounds
Light-weight Contest at 9st 12 lbs

DAVE COVENTRY

Liverpool.   Considered by many as the outstanding prospect in Gt. Britain today. Tipped
as a cert for championship honours versus

PAT ARRON

Ghana. Recently fought a great contest at the
Royal Albert Hall against the
undefeated Johnny Kramer

☞ WATCH PRESS AND OTHER PUBLICITY FOR 2 MORE GREAT CONTESTS ☜

No increase in prices for this Super Show. 64 Rounds of TOP CLASS BOXING. Book now to avoid disappointment

63/-	42/-	25/-	12/6	7/6
Ringside Reserved	Corner Ringside Reserved	Ring Extension Reserved	West & Railway End Reserved	Standing

All Tickets Bookable in Advance from: Liverpool Stadium (Central 6316)
John Driscoll (Bootle 5617)   Ray Peers, Olivieris Cafe, opposite Hamilton Sq.
Station, Birkenhead (Birkenhead 5589) Duggie Pomford, 7 Bridgewater Close
Litherland, Liverpool (Waterloo 4684)   Dave Rent Jnr. (Aintree 6236)
Johnny Campbell (Birke...d 759)   And usual agents

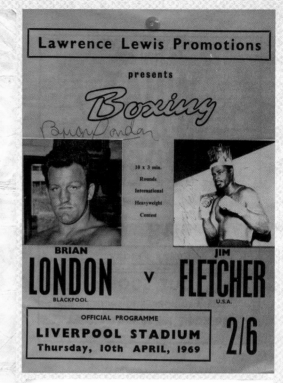

Lawrence Lewis Promotions

presents

Boxing

BrianDonlon

10 x 3 min.
Rounds
International
Heavyweight
Contest

BRIAN LONDON
BLACKPOOL

v

JIM FLETCHER
U.S.A.

OFFICIAL PROGRAMME

LIVERPOOL STADIUM
Thursday, 10th APRIL, 1969

2/6

Lawrence Lewis Promotions proudly presents a
10 (3 minute) Rounds
INTERNATIONAL HEAVYWEIGHT CONTEST

③   # BRIAN LONDON
BLACKPOOL—Former British and Empire Heavyweight Champion
versus

JIM (KING) FLETCHER
U.S.A. One of No. worlds most feared heavyweights

Appointed by the British Boxing Board of Control.

REFEREES: Mr. Billy Simpson (Blackpool), Mr. Ken Maynard (Stalybridge).   M.C.: Mr. Nat Basso (Manchester).
TIMEKEEPERS: Mr. Johnny Wright (Liverpool), Mr. John Burns (Southport). AREA STEWARD: Mr. Tom Bentley (Manchester).
INSPECTORS: Messrs. Joe Rashman, E. J. Marsden, Jack Hanlon and N. Crabtree.
MEDICAL OFFICERS: Doctor David Barnett.

All Officials MUST produce a ticket of admission

CLOSING ITS DOORS: Above, programme
and ticket from the last Stadium show – for
the time being – and left, a full Stadium bill

Alan Rudkin – Liverpool's Greatest Bantamweight

Alan Rudkin is Liverpool's greatest ever bantamweight. When one considers that the city has produced bantamweights of the class of Ike Bradley and Stan Rowan, it demonstrates just how good Rudkin really was. In a professional career that spanned 10 years and included 50 tough contests, Alan won five British title fights, claimed the European crown and contested for the world title on three occasions. The only time he was heavily beaten was in his final attempt to win the world title against Ruben Olivares, who stopped Rudkin in the second round.

Unlike other Liverpool boxers who became British champions, Rudkin did not box out of Liverpool but based himself in London. This, of course, reflected the changing nature of boxing, a change that increasingly required boxers of championship standard to be attached with a London promoter. This in turn reinforced the decline of the regional boxing halls, which were finding it increasingly difficult to pay the big purses needed to attract top boxers in this period.

Rudkin was born in Prestatyn, North Wales, in 1941. His mother was evacuated to North Wales with her young children during a time when Liverpool was at great risk from German bombing raids. She returned home two weeks after the birth of her third child, Alan.

As a young boy Alan developed a serious bone disease in his hip that required him to spend 18 months in Heswall Children's Hospital. Upon being discharged at the age of seven, Alan had to wear a metal brace on his weakened left leg.

Despite this condition, he joined the Florence Institute Boxing Club at the age of nine and was immediately recognised as a boxer with genuine talent. His natural style was always to go forward; he seemed to lose balance if forced to retreat. The reason for this did not come to light until he was 15: when he was measured for a suit, the tailor discovered that he had one leg shorter than the other. The disease of the hip had left a life-long legacy.

Alan remained at the Florence Institute until he was 13, but when the club trainer John Peers left for Australia, Alan moved to the nearby Golden Gloves ABC. It was here that Alan met what for him became the most important influence upon his career: Duggie Pomford, the trainer at the club.

Alan's amateur career began at flyweight. During his career he reached the ABA quarter-finals twice, losing to two Scots, Danny Lee and Walter McGowan in 1960 and 1961. In 1962, as a bantamweight, he reached the finals at Wembley, only to be outpointed by England international Peter Bennyworth. Rudkin also boxed for England on several occasions. Most famously he was part of the England team that beat the USA 10-0 at the Empire Pool in 1961. For the record, Rudkin beat Sherman Washington. He made his last appearance for England against Wales in 1962, beating Norman Coles inside two rounds. Immediately after this tournament Rudkin turned professional, signing for the London-based Scottish promoter Bobby Neil.

Despite being based in London, Alan made his professional debut at the Stadium against Dickie Hanna of Ireland. He made a winning start, knocking out Hanna in round two. By the end of 1964, Rudkin had won 18 of his ▶

'In a professional career that spanned 10 years and included 50 tough contests, Alan won five British title fights, claimed the European crown and contested for the world title on three occasions'

ALAN RUDKIN MBE
Liverpool
Former British, Empire & European
Bantamweight Champion
Outright Winner of the Lord Lonsdale Belt

ALBERT HALL ACTION: Missing with a right cross in his successful British title defence against Johnny Clark, 1970

SALUTE TO A CHAMPION: Alan, complete with Lonsdale Belt, surrounded by some of Liverpool's boxing legends

EUROPEAN RECOGNITION: Official diploma, presented to Alan in 1971

THE ROCKET AND RUD: Alan and his Lonsdale Belt meet three-times world snooker champion Ronnie O'Sullivan

▶ 19 contests, his powerful and forceful boxing quickly gaining him national attention. This brought him the prestigious award of the Best Young Boxer of the Year from the Boxing Writers' Club.

Just three months later, on 22 March 1965, he faced Johnny Caldwell at the Ice Rink, Nottingham for the British and British Empire bantamweight titles. Caldwell was no mean performer – he was a former world champion and had won the British title at both fly and bantamweight. Yet Rudkin dominated the contest, stopping the champion in the 10th round.

Alan's career was now in the ascendancy, and his victory over Caldwell earned him a world title shot against Masahiko ('Fighting') Harada in November of the same year. Prior to his title shot, Rudkin had three victories over Ben Ali, Ray Asis and Michel Lamora. He was, therefore, in great shape for the challenge, but in front of 15,000 Japanese fight fans, and some bizarre scoring by the referee and the judges, Rudkin was beaten on points. Perhaps Harada's post-fight comments give a truer reflection of the contest:

"This is the fastest-moving man I have ever met, and hitting him was like trying to hit a fish in deep water."

It would be over three years before Rudkin would get another crack at the world title. In the intervening period, however, he would lose and then regain his British and British Empire titles against Walter McGowan, his nemesis from his amateur days.

The first contest with McGowan had been scheduled for April 1966, but Rudkin required plastic surgery to his right eye following his victory in a warm-up fight against Raul Vega. The McGowan fight finally took place in September at the Empire Pool. McGowan entered the ring as the world's flyweight champion, having beaten Salvatore Burruni three months earlier at the same

venue. The McGowan fight was a tremendous 15-round battle, but once again Rudkin fell victim to a dubious decision as McGowan got the points verdict. The critics, however, were almost unanimous that the referee had got it wrong, a problem that affected Alan at several key points in his career.

It was nearly two years before a rematch with McGowan was arranged. During this period, Rudkin had a return contest with Ben Ali for the latter's European title in Barcelona. Alan lost once more on points and suffered further eye damage in the process. He had also been troubled by a persistent injury to the little finger on his left hand. An x-ray revealed a broken bone that required surgery. This kept him out of the ring for eight months, but on his return he knocked out Ron Jones in the second round and had a points victory over Thailand's Pornchai Poprai-ngam before meeting McGowan once more.

The McGowan/Rudkin contest drew a purse offer of £10,000 from promoter Harry Levene. The greatly anticipated event went ahead at the King's Hall, Belle Vue on 13 May 1968. Like the first, it was a scorching battle, with the fight in the balance right to the end. Rudkin dominated the first half of the contest ▶

'Harada's post-fight comments give a truer reflection of the contest: "This is the fastest-moving man I have ever met, and hitting him was like trying to hit a fish in deep water"'

BIG IN JAPAN: Alan in action during his first unsuccessful attempt to win the world title, against Masahiko Harada in 1965

▶ but McGowan came storming back in the 11th, 12th and 13th rounds. By now, however, McGowan was badly cut and was hindered in his attacking approach. This enabled Rudkin to take the initiative once again and take the closing rounds. Referee Harry Gibbs scored the fight 73 ¹/₂ points to 73 in favour of the challenger. Rudkin now had two notches on the Lonsdale Belt.

Either side of his next British title defence, Alan would have two further attempts at lifting the world title. The first in Melbourne, Australia on 8 March 1969 was against the aborigine Lionel Rose. Rose was the first aborigine to win a world title. Once again it was a storming 15-round battle, but Alan lost to what he considered were unjust decisions by the judges. His final attempt at becoming world champion came just nine months later – this time he faced the formidable Reuben Olivares of Mexico in California. Although he was only 21, Olivares had fought in 53 unbeaten contests prior to meeting Rudkin. Moreover, he had won all but two of these contests inside the distance. The signs were ominous for Rudkin and he was knocked out in the second round. It was the first and only time in his professional career that he was knocked out.

On home territory, Rudkin was more successful, securing the Lonsdale Belt outright by stopping Evan Armstrong in the 11th round at Belle Vue in June 1969. Following his defeat to Olivares, he successfully defended his title again at the Royal Albert Hall on 21 April 1970 when he stopped Johnny Clark in the 12th round. He also regained the Commonwealth title he had lost to Lionel Rose 12 months earlier.

Alan was now having difficulties with meeting the bantamweight limit, so with the Lonsdale Belt secure he made an attempt to win the British featherweight title. His opponent was Jimmy Revie, who was six years his junior and with a height and reach advantage. It proved just too much for Alan to overcome, although he only lost by half a point.

He returned to the bantamweight division and won the European title from Franco

Zurlo in February 1971. Alas, he surprisingly lost the title in his first defence six months later to Agustin Senin in the Bilbao Bullring. Rudkin was down three times during the contest but recovered to take the fight the full distance. Alan later admitted that he had underestimated the Spanish champion.

Rudkin was not finished yet. He made one more defence of his British and Commonwealth titles against Johnny Clark at the Royal Albert Hall on 25 January 1972. This time it was a much closer contest, with

Rudkin getting the decision by half a point. However, after the fight Alan had double vision in his left eye, a condition that required surgery. Initially, Alan aimed to go on but, although the op was successful, the doctors advised Rudkin to retire.

Like Roderick before him, Rudkin was one successful defence away from winning a second Lonsdale Belt and matching the great Nel Tarleton. This, however, does not undermine Rudkin's position as Liverpool's greatest ever bantamweight.

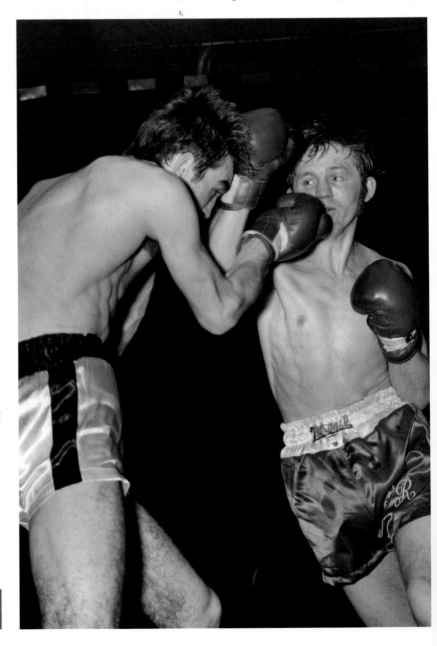

IN DOMINANT MOOD: Alan closing in on a 12th-round stoppage of Johnny Clark at the Royal Albert Hall, April 1970 (right)

Johnny Cooke – A Great Boxing Stylist

Boxing in schools may now be a subject of great controversy, but for Johnny Cooke in the 1940s it was the school boxing team, at Roberts Secondary Modern School on Pennington Street, Bootle, that introduced him to the sport. From the school boxing team, Johnny graduated to Ned Thomas' gym in Kirkdale, and from there he went to St Monica's ABC before joining the highly regarded Maple Leaf ABC. Cooke had a remarkable amateur career. In all, he had 368 contests, losing only 26. As an amateur, he met the 1956 Olympic gold medallist Dick McTaggart six times, losing to him on four occasions. He finally turned professional in 1960, the year of the Rome Olympics, after losing to McTaggart in the ABA quarter-finals – a result that effectively ended his chances of being picked for the Games.

At 25, many people thought he had left it too late to turn professional, but over the course of the next 11 years, during which he had 93 contests, Cooke was to prove the sceptics wrong. Upon turning professional, Cooke, unlike his contemporaries Harry Scott and Alan Rudkin, chose to remain on Merseyside and joined Johnny Campbell's gym on Whetstone Lane, Birkenhead. Campbell, of course, had built a big reputation after taking such boxers as Wally Thom, Pat McAteer and Joe Bygraves to European, British and British Empire titles.

Compared to modern-day boxers who expect to get the chance to fight for titles early in their careers, Cooke's professional career was something of a slow burn. It took him four years to get an opportunity to fight for the British title, by which time he had moved up from lightweight to welterweight. Powerful puncher he was not: there are not many knock outs on his record. His style was one for the purists; he was often compared to Nel Tarleton, one of the great stylists of boxing. He had a superb defence and an uncanny knack of slipping punches. It was a style that endeared him to the great Bill Shankly and Ian St John, who both closely followed Cooke's career.

In the first 18 months of his pro career, Johnny had 18 contests, losing on just one occasion to Maurice Cullen in Manchester. He was now ready to contest for his first professional title, the Central Area lightweight belt, against his cousin Dave Coventry at the Stadium on 30 January 1962. They had met once before, a year earlier when the referee could not separate them, but on this occasion Cooke emerged as the winner on points over 12 rounds.

Two years later, Cooke took on Jimmy McGrail at the Stadium in a final eliminator for the British welterweight title. It turned out to be Cooke's finest performance to date – his victory was so complete that it signalled the end of McGrail's career. More importantly, it set up a British and British Empire welterweight title fight against Brian Curvis of Swansea.

The contest with Curvis took place at the Coney Beach Arena, Porthcawl on 28 July 1964. However, it was not to be Cooke's night as he was stopped in the fifth round owing to a bad cut to his eye. A disappointed Cooke vowed that he would be back and, given a second chance, would ensure victory.

However, he would have to wait until February 1967 before he got another opportunity for the British title, against the undefeated Brain McCaffrey – Curvis had relinquished his titles in 1966. Although it was an all-Liverpool affair, the contest was held in Manchester. The fight has gone down in folklore among contemporary fight fans, with many regarding it as the finest contest they ever saw. According to the Birkenhead journalist Frank Johnson, the fight had everything: drama, speed, great skill and grit. Cooke prevailed, defeating his great rival on points over 15 rounds. It was to be the high point of McCaffrey's career, as later that year he retired from the ring. ▶

'His style was one for the purists; he was often compared to Nel Tarleton, one of the great stylists of boxing. He had a superb defence and an uncanny knack of slipping punches. It was a style that endeared him to the great Bill Shankly'

COVER STAR: The programme for Cooke's clash with Dave Coventry, 1962

TOP OF THE BILL: Cooke v Doyle meet for the British title at the Stadium, 1967

In contrast to McCaffrey, Cooke went on to have his most successful year in boxing despite being defeated by Carmelo Bossi of Italy for the European welterweight title. Either side of this defeat, however, he successfully defended his British title against Shaun Doyle of Barnsley and won the vacant British Empire title by defeating Lennox Beckles. Both contests took place at the Stadium.

In preparation for his second title defence against Ralph Charles at the Royal Albert Hall in February 1968, Cooke had a successful warm-up contest against Fred Powney at the Stadium. He was not so lucky against Charles, however, who took Cooke's titles on points. Following the defeat to Charles there was much talk of him getting a rematch, but this never materialised – Cooke always felt that he was frozen out of a return by the Board of Control.

However, his record following this defeat to Charles was disappointing: in 27 contests he won just eight, drew four and lost the rest. Age was clearly catching up with him, and following his drawn contest with Gielie Buitendag in South Africa in November 1971,

Cooke announced his retirement upon the advice of his manager.

Cooke's decision marked another milestone for Merseyside boxing, as Johnny Campbell also decided to call it a day. Looking back on his career a few months later, Cooke said:

"I realise that I turned professional too late, although my long and successful amateur career, spanning over 350 contests, has stood me in good stead. An earlier start in the paid ranks would have set me on the title trail at an earlier age and would have meant a longer reign at the top."

He also felt that the demise of the Liverpool Stadium affected his chances of winning a Lonsdale Belt outright:

"I feel sure that if it (the Stadium) had been kept going regularly, I could have held on to my title."

Such sentiments could be echoed by many of Liverpool's fine boxers. Despite these reflections, Cooke should be remembered as one of Merseyside's finest champions, a man that proved many of the sceptics wrong.

FINAL SHOT: Cooke and Shaun Doyle (left) following the former's win, 1967

Northern Counties Provincial
Associations of the
Amateur Boxing Association
CHAMPIONSHIP

This Diploma
awarded to

J Cooke (Maple Leaf A.B.C. Belle)

for winning the Lightweight

Northern Counties Provincial Associations of the Amateur Boxing Championship

at King's Hall, Belle Vue, Manchester

on the 7 March, 1958.

COOKE SUCCESS: Clockwise from top left – Cooke defeats Lennox Beckles to take the British Empire title, 1967; with Lonsdale Belt; a sporting gesture with fellow Liverpool fighter Brian McCaffrey after claiming the British crown, 1967; diploma from Cooke's amateur days – he fought in 368 contests; celebrating his British Empire victory, 1967

1970s – From Closure to a New Boom

The 1970s opened with no immediate prospect of professional boxing being staged at the Stadium. One problem that hindered attracting fight fans back to the hall was the condition of the interior of the building. Little in the way of maintenance or improvements had been done to the building since it had been opened in 1932. After 40 years of constant use, urgent repairs were essential but the management had been reluctant to invest in the building as it was under constant threat of demolition by the local authority.

There had been talk of developing the area for some years. Within the plan was a proposal to build an underground car park on the Stadium site. However, financial restraints meant that plans to redevelop the area were scrapped. With the building safe for the foreseeable future, the aim now was to get professional boxing going once more. The problem was finding someone who was prepared to promote professional boxing given the losses made by so many promoters since the mid-1950s.

Remarkably, in 1970 there was not even a boxing promoter on Merseyside. Indeed, there was only one full-time promoter in Britain at the time: Mike Barratt. Barratt, along with his matchmaker Mickey Duff, regularly filled the Albert Hall with imaginative programmes where up-and-coming fighters appeared on the same bill as leading national and international boxers. To broaden the base of boxing, Barratt was hoping to persuade the BBBofC to assist him in putting on shows in the regions at places such as Birmingham,

Leicester and Liverpool. Barratt, however, did not convince the Board.

Although there was no professional boxing at the Stadium in the early 1970s, there was a vibrant amateur scene on Merseyside that was holding sell-out shows at the hall. Among these amateurs were a number of young boxers that played a key part in the revival of the Stadium from the mid-1970s. These included the likes of John Conteh and Joey Singleton, both of whom were to win major title fights at the Stadium. As amateurs, both boxers were based at the now famous Kirkby ABC, which was run by Charlie Atkinson. Atkinson's two sons, Charlie and Mike, became important figures in the revival of the Stadium that began in 1973 and lasted for a decade.

Charlie Atkinson Jnr was managing both Joey Singleton and Tony Byrne when his brother Mike received his promoter's licence in 1973. Mike, who at 25 was Britain's youngest promoter, was attempting to

succeed where other leading promoters such as Mickey Duff, Gus Demmy, Jack Turner and Laurie Lewis had failed. His first show, held on 20 September 1973, was the first professional boxing promotion to be staged since the infamous night in 1969 that saw Brian London knocked out in the first round.

Atkinson returned to the Johnny Best formula of putting on shows that included several Merseyside boxers. His first show at the Stadium saw Joey Singleton outpoint Jess Harper of Manchester to win the newly constituted Central Area light-welterweight title. The hall was once again packed to near capacity, and there were great hopes for the future. When later that year John Conteh – who at the time was European, Empire and British light-heavyweight champion – fulfilled one of his ambitions of boxing as a professional at the Stadium, it looked as if the tide had turned. Conteh had been matched to face Reading's Les Stevens, but Stevens had to pull out, and he was replaced with Fred Lewis of America. Unfortunately, ▶

'After 40 years of constant use, urgent repairs were essential, but the management had been reluctant to invest in the building as it was under constant threat of demolition by the local authority'

AMATEUR STARS: John Conteh and Joey Singleton flanked by Tony Byrne (left) and George Turpin (right), 1971

WEIGH-IN: Singleton (left) v Harper was Mike Atkinson's first show at the Stadium in 1973; programme (right)

MIKE ATKINSON

PRESENTS

PROFESSIONAL BOXING

Matchmaker Tommy Miller

LIVERPOOL
STADIUM

****

THURSDAY SEPTEMBER 20th

Official Programme 10p

MISMATCH: John Conteh outclasses Fred Lewis at the Stadium, 1973

"A MESSAGE FORM THE PROMOTER"

Well this is it ! Professional Boxing is back in Liverpool Stadium and I hope for a long time to come. In presenting Boxing here again I am also seeking to give some of the good Local Fighters a chance to realise their undoubted potential and at the same time box before their own fans in the "electric" Atmosphere that the stadium can produce.

To succeed here and run regular shows I shall need support from the fans. the cost of living is going up and up and so is the cost of presenting boxing, but given the support for which I ask, you can rest assured that efforts will be made too get little fights for any deserving local fighter. Joey Singleton, George Turpin, Tony Byrne, Les McGowan and Tony Cunningham will be in there punching for Liverpool tonight so let them know your behind them.

I can say no more at this stage, just sit back and enjoy the boxing and thank you for coming !
MIKE ATKINSON.

THE FIGHTING ATKINSONS . . .
by SYDNEY DYE of the Liverpool Echo.

It's five long years since this famous fight arena housed it's last professional boxing show and after promoters from London, Preston, Manchester and Blackpool have all tried their hand, it is remarkable that the latest to take up the challenge is a comparative youngster from Kirkby.

He is Mike Atkinson, just 25 years of age but who comes from a famous fighting family.

His father, Charlie Atkinson, currently runs the Kirkby A.B.C., the Club which produced European light-heavyweight John Conteh, possibly Britain's best bet for world honours, and also A.B.A. champion Joey Singleton and many times England International Tony Byrne. He is also the man who steered that great middleweight Frank Hope to become the first Lpl fighter to win an A.B.A. title when he was with St. Teresa's way back in 1955.

Mike, himself, was a good-class amateur, though he quit at the early age of 19 to concentrate on business and now has an electrical contracting firm which has provided him with thhe necessary readies for tonight's show.

He was twice runner-up for a Junior A.B.A. title, and twice won national A.T.C. and Junior Imperial Services titles.

His brother, Charlie, jnr, was also a more than useful fighter in his amateur days when he boxed in the Divisional championship finals and later turned professional while working in Germany. An executive with a large chemical concern he is only 32 but has a wealth of experience to call on from his fighting days both at home and abroad. He now manages Singleton and Byrne, has just opened a superb gymnasium in Kirkby, a real showpiece and is still fit and capable enough to get in the ring with his fighters and show them what he wants.

Great fighters, then the Atkinsons . . . let us hope they win the battle to bring the crowds flocking back to the Stadium.

OPENING MESSAGE: Taken from the September 1973 programme – the first Stadium promotion by Mike Atkinson

---

the contest was a mismatch and the referee was forced to stop the bout in the third round. What was significant, however, was that once again a name was able to attract the crowds back to the hall. In the 1930s it was Tarleton, Roderick and Kane who drew the crowds in their thousands; in the 1950s it was McAteer, Bassey and Dick Tiger. Conteh had the same charismatic pull as the past greats, and the Liverpool public flocked to the hall to see him.

November of the following year saw Joey Singleton defeat Pat McCormack to win the British light-welterweight title. It was the first time the Stadium had staged a British title fight since May 1967, when Johnny Cooke had successfully defended his welterweight crown. The night got off to a bad start for Singleton, who was on the canvas in the first round. However, Singleton fought back to out-box the champion to win the 15-round contest on points. Within a year, Singleton had won the Lonsdale Belt outright by beating Alan Salter, at the Empire Pool and Des Morrison at the King's Hall, Belle Vue.

However, the mini-revival now came to an end, as there followed a two-year gap before the Stadium was to see professional boxing once more. During this period the Stadium actually lost its entertainments licence, forcing the management to carry out essential repairs to make the building safe for public use. The Atkinsons did not disappear at this point – they still kept trying to put on promotions in 1975, but were continually hit by the growing costs of staging top-level professional boxing. The problem for Atkinson was that there was not a lot of money to be made out of promoting top professional boxing. The British title fight between Singleton and McCormack had only realised a profit of £25, and this included the fee paid by the BBC to screen the event. However, in 1976 a partial solution to the problem was found in the guise of commercial sponsorship.

When professional boxing returned in September 1976, the scheduled top-liner was Phil Matthews of Rossendale. However, Charles Atkinson Jnr, who was now the joint promoter with his brother Mike, could not find a suitable opponent within their budget.

This problem deepened when Carl Watson agreed to take on Matthews, but his fee was three times the amount they had budgeted for. This predicament was solved when the car dealer Skellys agreed to sponsor the Matthews/Watson contest. Skellys had a history of sponsoring boxing in Glasgow, where they had supported the likes of John McCluskey and Walter McGowan. It was the first time, however, that a contest had been sponsored in this manner at the Stadium. They also installed bar facilities in the main hall to generate more revenue. This enabled the Atkinsons to price tickets at between £1 and £3.50 and still be in a position to pay the boxers their purses.

The Atkinsons had firmly established themselves as the main promoters on Merseyside. Under their guidance, the Stadium entered a period of revival that lasted until 1983. However, they failed to land the first-ever world title fight to be held at the Stadium on 5 March 1977. The honours for this went to Manny Goodall, the Blackpool promoter. The title fight he secured ▶

'The problem for Atkinson was that there was not a lot of money to be made out of promoting top professional boxing. The British title fight between Singleton and McCormack had only realised a profit of £25, and this included the fee paid by the BBC'

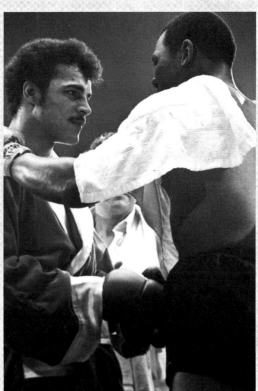

STADIUM SCENES: Clockwise from left
– Joey Singleton in the build-up to his
British title fight against Pat McCormack
at the Stadium in 1974; Singleton v
Harper, plus supporting bill, official
programme 1973; a victorious Conteh is
congratulated by Lewis, 1973

was between John Conteh and Len Hutchins. From the outset the contest grabbed the imagination of Mersey fight fans, and even though ticket prices ranged from £5.50 to £30, it was a complete sell-out.

In the Johnny Best era of the 1930s, Liverpool had of course hosted world title fights, but these had been at Anfield and on one occasion at Stanley Greyhound Track. It had been hoped that the hall would be opened in 1932 with a world title fight, but this did not materialise. When Best was able to match Tarleton with Miller for the world featherweight title in 1934, the boxing boom was at its height and the Stadium was considered too small. A similar situation occurred when Kane met Jurich in 1938, so on both occasions Anfield was the only viable venue. What was significant was that on each occasion it was a Merseyside boxer with a great reputation that caught the imagination of the Liverpool public.

The Conteh world title fight completed the stadium revival, and for the next five years the old Stadium witnessed some of its finest nights for a generation. A significant by-product of the contest was that the hall was given a complete makeover: hundreds of new seats were installed, toilet facilities were improved, and so were the changing rooms. As a result, the Stadium became a much pleasanter place to visit.

Such was the success of the fight that Goodall tried unsuccessfully to stage a British heavyweight title contest between Joe Bugner and Liverpool's Billy Aird. When Bugner retired he tried to match Aird with Richard Dunn of Bradford. Despite this failure to get another title fight, hopes were high that the fortunes of the hall had turned for good.

If Goodall had been successful, it would have been the first time the city had hosted an official British heavyweight title fight. Liverpool did stage two British heavyweight title bouts in 1914 and 1915, with Bombardier Wells beating Bandsman Rice on points on the first occasion, and knocking him out in the first round the second time they met. However, the contests were not recognised by the National Sporting Club, the body that issued Lonsdale Belts for title fights.

It is boxers that fill boxing stadiums, not promoters. Promoters play a key role in presenting attractive shows, but they can only do this when there are enough talented boxers around capable of grabbing the public's imagination. Following the Conteh fight, one boxer who did this more than most was Robbie Davies.

Davies was a former ABA light-middleweight champion who had represented England at international level, and was part of the Olympic boxing squad in 1976. He was a big hitter who would go after his opponent. His professional career was short but explosive. In the three years between 1977 and 1980 he had 15 contests, winning 11, nine via knock out. During 1977 he appeared on the bill four times at the Stadium, and each time the hall was at near-capacity. This led an excited Mike Atkinson to declare:

"The days are numbered when people are going to turn up on the night and take their pick of seats. It is going to be a case of fans buying their tickets in advance if this carries on."

The early 1980s seemed to confirm Atkinson's prognosis, as a new layer of exciting prospects emerged. These included Joey Frost, Brian Snagg, George Schofield, Tony Carroll, Robbie Robinson and Noel Quarless, all of whom were good crowd-pullers. However, boom was soon to turn to bust when the familiar problems of cancelled shows returned.

This problem coincided with Mike and Charles Atkinson losing the rights to promote boxing shows at the Stadium. In January 1983 the Stadium authorities handed control for boxing promotions to Manny Goodall, the man who had staged John Conteh's world title defence in 1977. Charles Atkinson complained that:

"Negotiations were conducted behind our backs, completely without our knowledge. We apologise to our regular fans, many of whom have had the same seats for the past 10 years...I can hardly believe all this talk of contracts. We never asked for or were offered a contract during our 10 years at the hall. It was all down to trust on both sides." ▶

TITLE ACTION: Conteh v Len Hutchins' world title clash in 1977 was another Stadium high-point; programme (opposite)

STADIUM FAVOURITE: Robbie Davies in action against Johnny Heard (1980) and (top) Joe Hannaford three years earlier

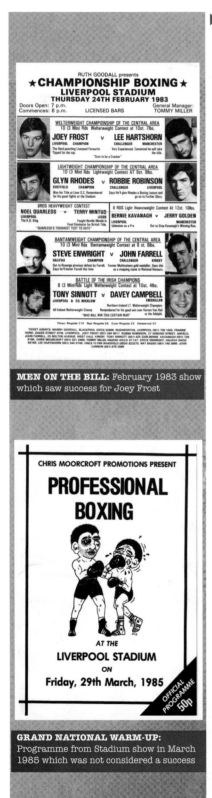

MEN ON THE BILL: February 1983 show which saw success for Joey Frost

GRAND NATIONAL WARM-UP: Programme from Stadium show in March 1985 which was not considered a success

Goodall responded, saying:

"The Stadium authorities approached me to see if I was interested because they were not happy with the situation. They felt the frequency was not so good. I expect to run up to eight shows during the contract starting on 24 February when Liverpool's Joey Frost will top the bill against a world-ranked opponent."

Amazingly, the Stadium authorities had awarded a contract to Goodall just days after he was refused a licence to promote in Liverpool by the Area Council BBBofC. But this did not faze Goodall:

"I have a contract for the use of the Stadium for boxing, and if the Area Council don't give me a licence then there will be no boxing at the hall – which is a situation nobody wants."

Goodall got his licence but his exclusive tenure was to prove a disaster despite having boxers such as Joey Frost, Sammy Brennan, Tony Carroll and Robbie Robinson under his banner. He certainly could not have had a better start, with a top-liner contest that saw Joey Frost successfully defend his Central Area welterweight title by stopping Lee Hartshorn in the fifth round.

However, his problems began with his next promotion held on the eve of the Grand National, which should have been the launch pad for more successful shows. This was a mandatory defence by Clinton McKenzie against Alan Lamb for the British light-welterweight title. Clinton held on to the title, beating Lamb on points. However, while there was little controversy in the ring, there was much outside it when it was revealed that more than 1,000 £5 tickets were forgeries, meaning that Goodall made a substantial loss on the promotion.

Police enquiries and a change to how tickets were sold led to the cancellation of the May promotion, meaning that there was a five-month gap between events – a gap that would make it almost impossible for Goodall to meet his contractual obligations of eight shows. When his September promotion was also hit, with the more traditional problems of top-liners pulling out leading to a poor attendance, Goodall was staring disaster in the face.

His last show, on 9 December 1983, which featured two local boxers – John Farrell taking on former ABA champion Ray Gilbody – was for the Central Area bantamweight title and was recognised as an eliminator for the British title. Goodall revealed that he had been given a commitment that the winner would get a British title chance at the Stadium. The outcome of the contest was as indecisive as Goodall's tenure at the Stadium, ending in draw.

It proved to be the last straw for Goodall who, blaming lack of support from the Liverpool public, did not renew his contract with Liverpool Stadium Limited. During his 13 months he had only managed four shows, all of which made losses. There was certainly no lack of boxing talent in the city – Gilbody went on to be a British champion – but somehow the promoters were not getting it right at the Stadium.

Next to try their hand at promoting professional boxing at the hall were Billy Aird, former challenger for the heavyweight title, and Jim Smith, chairman of South Liverpool FC. They came with big ideas and high hopes, but departed after just one promotion in June 1984 that resulted in a loss of between £4,000 and £6,000. A disappointed Aird blamed local fight fans:

"I remember the days when Liverpool fans were top of the league. But not any more. They are now bottom after last Friday's experience. Surely there must be at least 3,000 genuine fight fans in a city like Liverpool?"

To be fair, Aird and Smith had priced tickets at £2 for the unemployed while tickets for other parts of the hall were priced competitively. The bill featured two good local fighters, Joey Frost and Joey Joynson, but their programme failed to arouse local fight fans. Following Aird's comments, the *Liverpool Echo* received many letters from fight fans indicating that given quality shows, they would respond. One issue that came through was that the gap between promotions was too long, which resulted in fans getting out of the habit of going to boxing. Many of the letters urged Smith and Aird to continue, but when Smith pulled out owing to other commitments, the Stadium was once more left without a promoter. ▶

NOEL AT THE PIGGERIES: Noel Quarless putting on a sparring session for youngsters in Everton Valley

▶ A further nine months would pass before the hall hosted professional boxing. This time it was Chris Moorcroft who stepped in to run a show on the eve of the 1985 Grand National. He lined up Noel Quarless to take on Stewart Lithgo of Hartlepool. Moorcroft, who had successfully staged shows at Everton Park Sports Centre, had great hopes for local favourite Quarless. Indeed, after dispensing with Denroy Bryan in just 72 seconds in his previous outing, he was being talked about as a possible contender for the British heavyweight title. Quarless enhanced his chances that night by stopping his opponent in the fourth round.

Six months later, Moorcroft and Quarless were back. This time the contest was a final eliminator against Horace Notice of the Midlands. Alas, Quarless was no match for the future British heavyweight champion.

At the time, no one realised that this was the final night for professional boxing at the Stadium. Despite all its problems, amateur boxing had continued at the hall year after year. However, in February 1986 the ABA announced that the Merseyside stages of the championships would be moved to the Everton Park Sports Centre.

Clearly the hall was deteriorating rapidly. Eventually, the owners had a choice to make – either invest substantially or have the building demolished. Following a structural report that was issued on 4 February 1987,

it was found unsafe. A spokesperson for Liverpool Stadium Limited stated that:

"The building has been found to be unsafe following a structural survey and could only be put back into a safe and useable condition with a total rebuild."

The company was not prepared to take such a step, believing that there was "no longer any demand for its use". Within days of the report, the building was demolished. Prior to its demolition, the Merseyside Former Boxers' Association and *Echo* journalist Syd Dye organised a final photo call outside the building (see photograph and cutting below). More than 100 boxers and fight fans gathered outside, including six former British champions: Alan Rudkin, Stan Rowan, Joey Singleton, Johnny Cooke, Les McAteer and Johnny Sullivan. These champions stood side-by-side with ordinary fans. The Stadium was that type of place, a place that brought boxers, fight fans and boxing together.

Although not at the hall for the photo shoot, John Conteh summed up the feeling of most people connected with it over the years:

"To me the Stadium was like a perfectly fitting suit – a place built for boxing and what a magnificent atmosphere it produced.

"I never boxed in a better stadium. The ring was beautiful – big and spacious, and the

night I beat Lennie Hutchins in front of my own crowd was unbelievable...

"What does Liverpool do? Throw the towel in? Give up – or do we fight and make some good come of this?"

Johnny Best had similar thoughts in 1931 when Pudsey Street was demolished. At present, Merseyside boxing is resurgent, with many top amateurs turning professional. Derry Matthews was a recent world champion and is now set on winning the British featherweight title.

The boxers are there, the venues are in place, it is now the time for a top promoter to bring big-time boxing back to the city that has produced some of Britain's finest champions.

LAST NIGHT: On the eve of its demolition, more than 100 former boxers gathered outside the Stadium to commemorate one of Britain's finest boxing stadiums. After demolition, the site was used as a car park until 2006 – the site of the ring was marked by small garden in the shape of a boxing ring. It has now been redeveloped, encompassing a modern mix of shops, offices, restaurants and flats. Alas, there is no memorial stone

CALM BEFORE THE STORM: Ring view during the final days at the Stadium

John Conteh — One of Britain's Greatest Fighters

John Conteh's achievements in the boxing ring have often been overlooked by a press all too ready to sensationalise his lifestyle outside it. Admittedly, John's alcohol and drug abuse affected his career, but what no one can doubt is that he is one of the finest boxers ever to emerge from Britain. Moreover, John is the finest light-heavyweight boxer that Liverpool has ever had. His successful defence of his world title at the Liverpool Stadium in 1977 reinvigorated the old hall and brought back the fight fans in their thousands.

Conteh joined Kirkby ABC at the age of 11 and soon made rapid progress under the guidance of Charlie Atkinson and Tucker Hetherington. At junior level he reached the ABA semi-finals in 1968 and was ABA champion at senior level in 1970 and 1971. In 1970 he became the first English middleweight boxer in 36 years to win a Commonwealth Games gold medal when he defeated Titus Simba of Tanzania.

Prior to the 1970 finals, and unbeknown to the ABA at the time, Conteh had done some sparring in a professional gym with Harry Scott, the former Central Area middleweight champion. Some years later, Conteh told the *Echo*:

"Harry was a great teacher and showed me a lot. He was a strong fighter, and in a small ring he made me fast off the mark as I couldn't stand and trade punches."

John's preparations paid off at the ABA finals, but they also reflected that he was keen to learn new methods and take advice from others.

However, at the European Amateur Championships in 1971 he inexplicably lost in the first round to Richard Koleritscht of Austria — a result that pushed him towards the professional ranks. Conteh had hoped to represent Britain in the 1972 Munich Olympics, but comments in the dressing room by the ABA secretary after his defeat led him to believe that he would not be picked for the Games. Consequently, when he was approached by George Francis to sign professional terms for a reputed £10,000, Conteh jumped at the chance.

Like Rudkin, Conteh had chosen to box out of London, the place where a boxer of his calibre could command high purses. His choice of Francis was influenced by the way he had handled Bunny Sterling, who under his guidance had won the British middleweight title.

Conteh started his professional career as a heavyweight, and from the outset was tipped to become a British champion. While preparing for his 18th contest against Terry Daniels in Las Vegas, Conteh made a career-changing decision following some advice from Muhammad Ali (the Conteh/Daniels contest was on the same card as the Ali/Bugner fight). After finishing his training one day, Conteh stayed behind to watch Ali train. Ali broke off from his training and approached Conteh, saying:

"Hey boy, they tell me you're a heavyweight. Listen, let me give you some advice, you're a lightweight. You stick to that and you can be a champ one day. You're good, I've seen you. But don't go tangling with us heavyweights. This is the age of the super-heavyweight. Remember, you've gotta be a giant to survive." ▶

'Hey boy, they tell me you're a heavyweight. Listen, let me give you some advice, you're a lightweight. You stick to that and you can be a champ one day. You're good, I've seen you. But don't go tangling with us heavyweights. This is the age of the super-heavyweight. Remember, you've gotta be a giant to survive'

Muhammad Ali, 1973

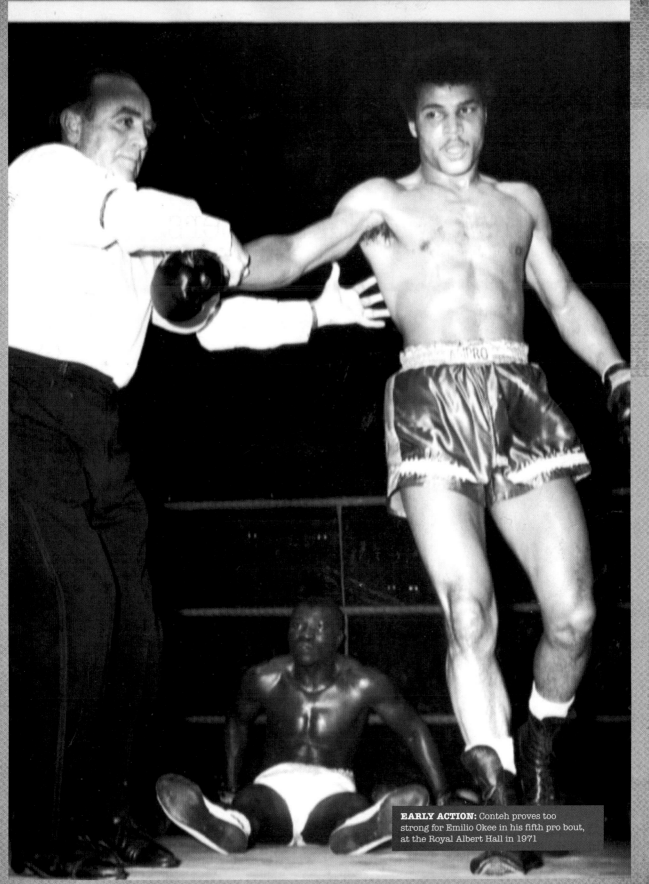

EARLY ACTION: Conteh proves too strong for Emilio Okee in his fifth pro bout, at the Royal Albert Hall in 1971

IN TRAINING: Preparing for the step up in class, 1973

Ali's words of advice were reinforced by Walter Young, who was assisting Ali:

"Son, Muhammad is right. You're too small to be a heavyweight, especially these days."

Despite only losing one of his first 17 fights and dispensing with Daniels in round seven, Conteh took the comments on board.

Remarkably, in his first contest as a light-heavyweight, on 13 March 1973 (and only his 19th fight overall) Conteh defeated Rudiger Schmidtke to win the European title. On the same bill that night, at the Empire Pool, Wembley was Chris Finnegan, who retained his British and British Commonwealth titles by beating Roy John. Immediately after Conteh's victory, Finnegan challenged him to a triple-crown showdown.

When Conteh met Finnegan just two months later at the same venue, it was to be a bitter affair that Conteh won on points. Incredibly, just three months after taking heed of Ali's advice, at the age of 21, Conteh was a triple champion. He would have two more successful title fights – the first for his Commonwealth title against Baby Boy Rolle

of the Bahamas, the second for his European title against Tom Bogs of Denmark – before meeting Finnegan in another triple-crown contest.

The second meeting with Finnegan took place on 21 May 1974 and was held at the Empire Pool once more. Like the first fight, it was a bitter affair, but this time controversy also marred the atmosphere between the two fighters. For the first few rounds it was an ultra-cautious contest, but it exploded towards the close of the fifth round when Conteh began to batter the challenger with his full range of punches. When the bell sounded to end the round, Conteh, who did not hear the gong, continued with his onslaught for a good five seconds before the referee was able to pull him away. It was a decisive turning point in the contest, as up to that moment Finnegan appeared to be holding his own, but the barrage of punches resulted in a cut to Finnegan's left eye.

Round six was an ugly affair. In effect, it was a brawl being fought at close quarters. Inevitably, there was a clash of heads after which blood began to spurt out from Finnegan's head. Conteh was now able to inflict further damage on a half-blinded Finnegan before the referee intervened to stop the contest. However, when the defeated Finnegan returned to his corner and was cleaned up, it was revealed that blood was not coming from his eye but from a bad cut above his ear. Quite clearly he could have continued, but in the heat of the contest, with Finnegan's face covered in blood, it had been impossible for the referee to get a clear view. The verdict had been given and had to stand, and Conteh was still a triple champion. Sadly, Conteh was booed as the Lonsdale Belt was put round his waist. Yes, it had been an unsatisfactory and an unconvincing performance, but the way was now clear for Conteh to meet Bob Foster for the world title.

Bob Foster had been world champion since he defeated Dick Tiger in May 1968. He had ▶

LONSDALE BELT: John Conteh showing off his domestic prize ahead of a court case related to a dispute with the BBBofC, 1975

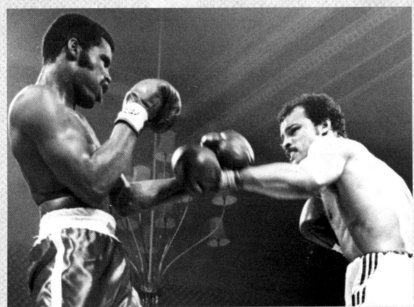

ACTION SHOTS: In rehearsal during filming of 1973 movie 'Man At The Top' (above); on the attack during his Liverpool bout against Ivy Brown, June 1979 (left)

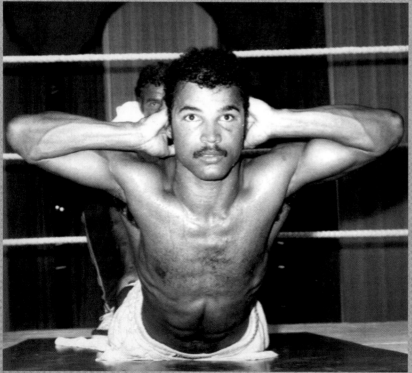

THE FINAL ACT: Conteh's final professional bout, at the Stadium in 1980 sees James Dixon suffer a knock-out blow (above); in training ahead of his successful world tilt against Argentine Jorge Ahumada at Wembley, 1974

made numerous successful defences, including one against Chris Finnegan in 1972, a contest the *Ring* magazine chose as its fight of the year. Following his last defence, a draw with Jorge Ahumada of Argentina, Foster was instructed by the world boxing authorities to make his next defence against Conteh. Clearly, an ageing Foster did not fancy a match with Conteh, and following several delays in exchanging contracts he was stripped of his title by the WBC. This set up a world title fight between Conteh and Ahumada, which took place at the Empire Pool, Wembley on 1 October 1974.

The build-up to the fight in the press was intense, particularly in Liverpool. Conteh was aiming to become the first Liverpool-born boxer to become a world champion. Three Liverpool-based boxers – Peter Kane, Hogan 'Kid' Bassey and Dick Tiger – had all won world titles. All three had developed into world champions from the Liverpool Stadium, and in Kane's case he had won the title in Liverpool. Prior to Conteh's world title attempt, there had been seven Liverpool-born fighters that had fought for world titles. These were: Ike Bradley, Charlie White, Ginger Foran, Nel Tarleton, Ernie Roderick, Joe Curran and Alan Rudkin.

That Conteh succeeded where the rest had failed is history now, but it was the manner of victory, and his subsequent defences, that puts him among the greats of British boxing. Ahumada was a quality boxer. He shook Conteh with a right in the seventh, but from the eighth onwards it was Conteh all the way. At the end of 15 rounds, Harry Gibbs, the referee, had no hesitation in raising Conteh's hand – he scored the fight 147-142, a decisive points victory. Conteh had become the first British boxer to win the world

light-heavyweight title since Freddie Mills in 1948.

Between the win over Ahumada and his first defence against Lonnie Bennett in March 1975, Conteh relinquished his British title as he was finding it impossible to accommodate the demands of the BBBofC to defend it. One more successful defence and he would have secured a Lonsdale Belt, but professional boxing is about money, and it was (and is) world titles where the money was for Conteh. The successful defence against Bennett, who was stopped on a cut eye in the fifth round, was to be a major turning point in Conteh's career. Alas, the turning point was not in the ring but outside it. Wrangles with his manager and legal suits against the Board of Control, linked to problems with his lifestyle, diverted John away from boxing.

Conteh's clash with Francis was essentially about money: he felt that the management team were taking too much of a cut from the purses he was winning. Conteh still wanted to keep Francis as his trainer, but take care of the business side himself. However, when Francis agreed a deal with promoter Harry

Levine for Conteh to defend his title against Alvaro Lopez, John sacked Francis. Following complaints from Francis and Levine, the BBBofC intervened and instructed Conteh to appear before a committee to explain himself. Conteh refused and took the matter to court – and won. The situation drained Conteh "physically, mentally and financially".

As a trainer, Francis had taken particular care of Conteh's slim "piano player" hands, but while they were estranged, Conteh arranged a lucrative non-title fight against Willie Taylor in America. Although he had a comfortable win it was a victory at great cost, as Conteh suffered a broken right hand. For the rest of his career, John would have problems with his right hand – it essentially made him a one-handed boxer as he became reluctant to use it to the same effect as previously.

Following the Taylor contest, Conteh was out of the ring for 14 months. Throughout this period there were constant rumblings that he would be stripped of his world title. Also, during this time there was a reconciliation between Conteh and Francis, who returned as ▶

JOB DONE: Following a 10-round points decision over Ivy Brown, 1979

END OF THE ROAD: John's final victory, over James Dixon, 1980

▶ his trainer. A title fight was lined up with Alvaro 'Yaqui' Lopez that eventually took place in Copenhagen in October 1976. The contest had originally been scheduled to take place in Uganda at the behest of Idi Amin, who had offered Conteh £250,000 to defend his world title. Amin had seen how Mobutu had benefited politically by staging the 'Rumble in the Jungle' between Ali and Foreman in 1974. However, the political situation between London and Kampala was worsening at this time, and it became impossible for the contest to take place as planned. When the contracts were eventually signed for Copenhagen, Conteh had to settle for £100,000, the biggest purse of his career. As for the contest, Conteh retained his title on a unanimous points decision, with the champion dominating the challenger with some tremendous left-hand work.

With two successful title defences under his belt, linked to his reconciliation with his former manager, Conteh had the world before him. His next title defence took place in Liverpool in the arena he liked best – the Liverpool Stadium. Originally, Conteh's opponent was to have been Miguel Culleo but when he pulled out Len Hutchins of America stepped in. The contest took place on 5 March 1977. With the fight being beamed live to America, Canada and most of Latin America, interest in the fight reached epic proportions. Venues such as Wembley and the Royal Albert Hall had staged such contests, but a worldwide broadcast was a first for Liverpool. It was estimated that the audience for the contest would exceed 40 million viewers. In Britain, however, there was no live coverage of the fight, which meant that demand for tickets was huge despite the prices ranging from £5.50 to £30.

The event was a great success. The old hall was reminiscent of its hey-day with the crowd creating a Kop-like atmosphere.

STILL HUNGRY: Preparing for another tilt at the light heavyweight crown against Matthew Saad Muhammad, 1980

Hutchins was considered a dangerous opponent – the *Liverpool Echo* of 2 March thought he would take the champion the distance. Conteh, however, was on top form, flooring Hutchins in the third round with a left hook. Hutchins got up but he could not continue, and the referee was forced to stop the contest. It was a ruthless performance from a great champion. In fact, the victory made Conteh the most successful post-war British champion, beating Ken Buchanan's record of two successful defences. Several British boxers have since surpassed Conteh's record of defences, but the statistic underlines how good a boxer he was.

Alas, this was as good as it got for Conteh – he lost his world title after he sensationally withdrew from a mandatory defence against Miguel Cuello. After Conteh failed to get the courts to accept that there were irregularities in the contract, the WBC brought in the American Jesse Burnett to face Cuello. For the record, Cuello knocked out Burnett in the ninth round. Cuello would only remain champion for eight months, however, losing his title in January 1978 to Mate Parlov of what was then Yugoslavia.

TITLE TUNE-UP : Conteh in action against Joe Cokes in Islington, 1978

After agreeing to drop any outstanding legal threats, Conteh was offered a chance to regain his title against Parlov. The contest was duly scheduled for Belgrade on 17 June 1978. Prior to meeting Parlov, Conteh had a warm-up contest, beating the American Joe Cokes over 10 rounds.

Like so much of John's career, controversy was not far away. When Parlov entered the ring, Conteh and Francis noticed that he had a resin-type substance coating his eyebrows. They appealed to the referee, who allowed Francis to try and remove the substance. However, before it could be removed the referee, conscious that the fight was scheduled to be shown on American TV, called the fighters together and ordered them to start the contest. Although John was slow in getting into his rhythm, he dominated the latter stages of the fight. But it was not enough on the night. The referee gave him the verdict, 147-141, but the two other judges thought otherwise and Conteh had failed to regain the title.

After two further unsuccessful attempts at regaining his title, both against Matthew Saad Muhammad, Conteh's career was over. There was a swansong contest against James Dixon of Texas at the Stadium, who he knocked out in the fifth round. Despite the knock out, John was not very convincing against a boxer who was not in his class. Afterwards there was talk of moving up to the new cruiserweight division, but John's heart had gone out of the game and he retired.

Without doubt John Conteh is one of Britain's greatest boxers. His achievements, however, did not quite reach what he was capable of. Perhaps better advice outside the ring would have enabled him to concentrate on matters inside it. In such a scenario he could have been one of the world's greatest ever boxers.

Joey Singleton – Won British Light-Welterweight Championship in Record Time

Joey Singleton was another product of Kirkby ABC, from where he was guided to an ABA light-welterweight crown in 1971. After winning the ABA title he was approached by several London managers, including John Conteh's manager George Francis, to sign professional terms. However, he did not like what he saw of the London scene and decided instead to sign for his long-time mentor Charlie Atkinson. Commenting upon his decision not to go to the capital, Joey said that a lot of Merseyside fighters "go down (to London) and don't make it. They get homesick and they don't seem to get looked after as well as they should. That's always frightened me about going to London."

Joey's professional career coincided with the revival of the Liverpool Stadium under the promotion of Atkinson's son Mike, and like so many local boxers before him, Singleton became a great favourite in his home city. Singleton turned professional at an opportune time, as the light-welterweight division had only recently been adopted by the Board of Control, leaving it wide open for a quality boxer to make rapid progress towards the British title.

Joey grasped this opportunity with both hands, and after beating Barton McAllister in his first professional contest, in March 1973 at Nottingham, he made speedy progress towards competing for the British title.

Indeed, just 18 months after turning professional, Joey found himself on the verge of boxing for the British title. He was matched to meet Jim Melrose in an eliminating contest for the title, at the Stadium in September 1974. Singleton took

his opportunity in dramatic style. Dramatic because Joey knocked out Melrose in the second round, which was something of a surprise as Singleton was a jab-and-move fighter, but on this occasion he produced a whiplash right hand that floored his opponent.

Joey was now in line to equal the record of Larry Paul and John McCluskey, both of whom won their British titles in their eighth fight. However, standing in his way was the champion Pat McCormack of Brixton, who had won the title by knocking out Des Morrison the previous March.

The fight with McCormack took place at the Stadium on 21 November 1974, and it turned out to be one of the finest fights staged at the Stadium during its revival period. Singleton entered the ring not to the time-honoured fanfare but to the stirring sound of 'You'll Never Walk Alone'. However, from the outset Joey nearly was walking alone, as in the first round he was caught with a flashing left hook that put him down for a count of eight. The second round got little better for the challenger, when another left hook rocked him back to the ropes. But Joey had strong survival instincts, and his jab-and-move style of boxing enabled him to keep McCormack at length until the end of the round. Remarkably, that was as good as it got for the champion, as for the rest of the contest, with the exception of the seventh round when Joey got caught again, Singleton outboxed McCormack to win the title by a margin of 147 1/2 points to 146. In the circumstances, it was a convincing victory and Joey had achieved his aim of equalling the record of flyweight John McCluskey and light-middleweight Larry Paul.

Over the course of the next 12 months, Joey successfully defended his title on two occasions to make the Lonsdale Belt his own property. His first defence was against Alan Salter of Peckham in September 1975 at the Empire Pool, Wembley, who he stopped in the ninth round. Just 42 days later, Singleton made his second defence, this time beating Jamaican-born Des Morrison on points. For his next title bout, in June 1976 at the Royal Albert Hall, Joey came up against the effervescent Dave 'Boy' Green. Green proved too good for Singleton on the night, stopping him in the sixth round.

Three months later, Singleton faced Charlie Nash in an eliminator for the British lightweight title. Once again he was stopped, this time in the ninth round. After two further losses to George Turpin and Colin Powers, Joey went into semi-retirement. When he returned to the ring 14 months later, he made a winning start against Tommy Glencross.

Although Joey went on to win two Central Area welterweight contests on his return, and boxed for the European welterweight title (losing to Joergen Hansen in Denmark in April 1980), the second half of his career did not reach the same heights as the earlier part. Joey eventually retired after losing to Frank Ropis in Australia in June 1982.

Singleton stands in the great tradition of Merseyside boxers, 11 of whom have won a Lonsdale Belt outright. Although he boxed under the shadow of John Conteh during his career, in hindsight both boxers should be looked upon as two of Kirkby and Merseyside's finest boxers.

1974 McCormack Build-up (*Liverpool Echo*):
'Regular running and gym work keep Joey fit throughout the year, but the pressure is really turned on when a fight is approaching. For five weeks beforehand it is hard grind. Joey is up at 5.30am, and off on a four-and-a-half mile run along the roads leading from his Kirkby home into the countryside. He has run some 150 miles in preparation for this fight, mostly in the dark before the world is stirring.
"I usually see the same milkman every morning when I'm out running. He shouts good morning to me."
Back home by six o'clock, Joey takes breakfast to his wife in bed and sees to the baby's bottle. At 7.30am he leaves for work, starting at eight and finishing at 4.30pm. From the factory it's straight to the gym for a two-and-a-half hour work-out under his trainer, Charlie Atkinson. Sparring, bagwork, circuit training, shadow boxing, physical exercise...
"My wife keeps the baby up late so I can play with her when I get in. Otherwise I would hardly see her from one day to the next."
After putting in a 14-hour day, Joey has less than two hours' relaxation before getting to bed for 9pm. Half-past five next morning it all starts again, and goes on seven days a week until just before the fight itself. "I get my birthday off and holy days, and that's it."'

1974 McCormack Build-up (*Liverpool Echo*):
'"I've known my manager, Charles Atkinson since I was seven or eight. I trust him. I would trust him with my life.
"When I won the ABA title in 1971 I was approached by several London managers, including George Francis, but I wasn't satisfied with what I saw. Then Charles approached me, and I had known him for 10 or 15 years, and I had no hesitation in turning professional with him.
"He has picked fights for me at the right time, when I'm ready for them. It's half the battle if you've got a good manager and a good staff looking after you."'

ADELPHI HOTEL: Amateur and professional boxing has often been held at the Adelphi. Local favourites Joe Lally, George Turpin, Pat Thompson and Paul Wright boxed there as pros. Boxing dinners hosted by private clubs have also been popular at the hotel. On this occasion Joey Singleton entertained members of the Anglo-American Sporting Club

Last Night at the Stadium

The last night of professional boxing at the Stadium, 3 October 1985, featured Noel Quarless and Horace Notice in a final eliminating contest for the British heavyweight title. In Liverpool at the time there were high hopes that Quarless could go on to win the heavyweight title. Indeed, Quarless had heightened expectations following his fourth-round demolition of Stewart Lithgo at the Stadium the previous March. Notice, despite only having his seventh professional contest against Quarless, was no pushover. He came into the professional ranks with a first-class amateur record and was a former ABA champion.

Quarless turned professional at 18 years of age, and his first contest was at the Stadium on 24 September 1981 against Phil Clark, who he knocked out in the first round. He shared the bill that night with crowd favourites Tony Sinnott, George Schofield and Brian Snagg.

His record prior to the Notice fight was somewhat mixed: he had competed in 19 contests, winning 12 and losing seven. However, before his convincing fourth-round victory over Stewart Lithgo, he had also beaten Denroy Bryan and Theo Josephs to end a run of three consecutive defeats. This return to form had many Liverpool fight fans believing that Quarless was a champion in the making.

For the contest with Notice there was a big crowd – a reflection that Quarless had built up a decent fan base. The fight started well for Quarless: for the first three rounds he landed some powerful body punches.

However, Notice appeared untroubled by Quarless' punches, and from the fourth round onwards he began to take control. He dominated the sixth round with a series of powerful jabs that clearly hurt Quarless. As they came out for the seventh, Notice was in the ascendancy and though Quarless caught him with a right to the head, Notice was able to respond with a flurry of punches that put Quarless not only on the canvas, but partially out of the ring. Many of Quarless' fans rushed forward to push him back inside the ropes, but they never had a chance as he was out for the count.

Following the contest, a disappointed Colin Moorcroft, Quarless' manager, put on a brave face and said that he would be back. Moorcroft also praised the support from the fans:

"They gave him fantastic support before, during and after the fight, and it was a marvellous turn-out of fans who showed there is still a demand at the Stadium."

Alas, Moorcroft's last words were never put to the test, as 14 months later the building was demolished.

Following his triumph, Notice had two more contests before winning the British title in only his 10th professional fight.

As for Quarless, his career continued to ebb and flow. He had two more eliminating contests, both of which he lost. Following a defeat to future world champion Lennox Lewis in 1990 at York Hall, he retired from boxing altogether.

The last night at the Stadium did not result in a victory for Liverpool's heavyweight hopeful. Despite a sombre ending, the arena is best remembered as one of the finest boxing halls Britain ever had. A place that made and broke champions, a place that will long be remembered by the hundreds of thousands of fight fans who had the privilege of seeing a fight there during its 53-year history.

'The last night at the Stadium did not result in a victory for Liverpool's heavyweight hopeful. Despite a sombre ending, the arena is best remembered as one of the finest boxing halls Britain ever had'

CLOCKWISE FROM TOP LEFT: Alan Rudkin and Syd Dye ringside on the eve of the demolition; Notice punches through the Quarless defence; Birkenhead journalist Frank Johnson; and the boxers involved in manager-promoter Chris Moorcroft's first show at Everton Park Sports Centre in 1984 – Quarless pictured fourth from left

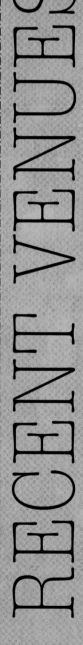

★

RECENT VENUES

Liverpool's **BOXING** Venues

★

AT THE OLYMPIA Runcorn's former super-middleweight champ Robin Reid

The Nark in the Park – First Ever World Title Fight Between Two Liverpool Boxers

In the post-Liverpool Stadium years, Merseyside has produced some of Britain's finest boxers. Two of the best were Shea Neary and Andy Holligan. The 'Nark in the Park' world light-welterweight title fight between Holligan and defending champion Neary was the first world title fight between two Liverpool boxers. That it took place in the unique atmosphere of a Liverpool boxing arena was down to the determination of the promoters Munro/Hyland. The contest that unfolded that night was also among the finest seen on Merseyside for many years.

Munro/Hyland faced a similar problem to the one Johnny Best faced in the autumn of 1931. They had secured the biggest-ever fight between two local fighters – the most important boxing contest in Liverpool since the Conteh/Hutchins world title fight at the Stadium – and, like Best, they wanted to hold the fight in the city. However, they faced the same problem as Best in that there was no venue big enough in the city to host such a fight. Unlike Best, who hired Anfield, the promoters decided to have a boxing arena built that could satisfy the expected demand for tickets.

Unbeknown to most fight fans, that night the chosen site for the arena was one of the city's most historic sporting places – namely Everton Football Club's first-ever football pitch. In the 1970s this section of Stanley Park underwent redevelopment with the area between the Arkles Lane gates and Priory Road being covered in tarmac. Several football pitches were marked out on the area that was also floodlit to enable people to play football on winter evenings. These football pitches were part of the Vernon Sangster Sports Centre that was built adjacent to the area.

However, the tarmac area was not maintained and deteriorated rapidly, leading to the abandonment of floodlit football. The area became a car park mostly used on match days. Moreover, as the park went into terminal decline during the 1980s, it was the sports centre that became the park's most used building. ▶

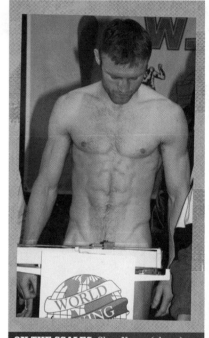

ON THE SCALES: Shea Neary (above) and Andy Holligan's (below) weigh in

ON THE UP: The marquee being erected for the 'Nark in the Park' fight

Stanley Park both divides and unites our two football clubs. This unity and division was symbolised on the night of the 'Nark in the Park', with Holligan wearing red gloves and Neary wearing blue. It was another great 'derby' in the long line since Everton played Bootle FC in the early 1880s.

Stanley Park is synonymous with Liverpool sport in general, and football in particular. When the Mayor opened the park in 1870, he described it as the 'People's Park' because it was the first Liverpool park to be aimed at attracting working-class people to a healthy open space. From its opening, two-thirds of the park was given over to green space to encourage sports and leisure of all kinds. In 1870 there was no organised football in Liverpool, but cricket, rounders (later to become English baseball) and rugby were very popular sports in the city. However, once football got a hold in 1878, the game grew so fast that Liverpool became one of the biggest centres for football in the country. St Domingo formed that year, changing their name to Everton in 1879. The club settled on land close to Anfield Road with the pitch located at the back of businessman John Houlding's house. In 1883 Everton moved, for one season, to an enclosed ground at Coney Green, off Priory Road, before a switch to Anfield for the 1884/85 season. Everton left Anfield at the end of the 1891/92 season, moving to Goodison Park.

How Everton moved to and then left Anfield has been told many times before, but what this early development of football in the park tells us is that both our Premier League clubs are located where they are because of the park; indeed, without Stanley Park the history of Liverpool football would have been radically different. Without doubt Stanley Park is the birthplace of Liverpool football.

FROM ABOVE: An aerial shot of Stanley Park and the two famous football grounds

Upon this site a 'super tent' was erected that held 5,500 spectators. It was therefore the largest venue used for boxing in the city since 1949, when Anfield had last been used for the Stan Rowan/Jackie Paterson British bantamweight title fight.

Unlike sports such as football, boxing has long been associated with theatrical entrances – a master of ceremonies introduces the contestants. To add to the drama, boxers often adopt an alias that relates to the style of boxing or their perceived boxing greatness. Muhammad Ali was 'The Greatest', while Julio Cesar Chavez was modestly known as 'J.C.'. Neary was nicknamed the 'Shamrock Express' – an alias that clearly fitted his forward style of boxing. Holligan was a high-pressure fighter, always trying to get close in and seeking a way on the inside of his opponent; unsurprisingly, he was announced as the 'Hunter'. The sense of theatre on the night was heightened with the promoters engaging lighting experts to use the latest laser technology that lit the path of the boxers from the back of the marquee to the ring. As the MC announced the 'Hunter', lights from above swirled and flashed, while Holligan's walk to ringside was accompanied by electronic music. Holligan's introduction to the arena was low key in comparison to Neary's, though.

Neary, in contrast, was standing behind a wall of green balloons as his name was announced, and these were burst by fireworks to reveal a six-foot shamrock which eventually dropped to the floor, enabling the whole arena to see the champion in a glow of green light. As he walked to the ringside he was showered with ticker-tape – the whole scene serving to heighten expectation amongst the crowd.

The Boxers – The Champion:

Jimmy 'Shea' Neary, whose nickname the 'Shamrock Express' highlighted his Irish roots, boxed under the name of 'Shea' in honour of his father, who died in 1989. He won the WBU world light-welterweight title at Everton Park Sports Centre in October 1996 when he outpointed American Darryl Tyson – it was his 17th contest since turning professional in 1992. He was a

hard-punching, two-fisted fighter whose body shots were capable of stopping any opponent.

As a teenager he joined the Imperial ABC where he came under the guidance of Tony Silvano. Aged 18, he joined the army where he continued his boxing. After he left the army he joined the famous Golden Gloves ABC before turning professional under the management of Brendan Devine. His professional career began in explosive fashion when he knocked out Simon Ford in the first round. In his subsequent 15 contests prior to his world title attempt with Tyson, Shea won 13 times inside the distance and remained unbeaten.

Tyson was seen as a tough opponent with just nine losses in 57 contests. But despite hurting his hand early in the fight, Neary was able to dominate Tyson and win the world title on a unanimous points decision. Shea dedicated his win to Charles Atkinson Snr, who had trained him since 1992 and was seriously ill in hospital at the time.

Neary's first defence against Jeremiah Malinga in March 1997 at the Everton Park Sports Centre resulted in Shea knocking out the challenger in the third round. It was 12 months before he made his next defence against Andy Holligan, in Stanley Park, and once again Neary was successful. Over the next 15 months Neary made three more successful defences of his title against Naas Scheepers of South Africa on 21 July 1998 in Widnes; Juan Carlos Caferino Villarreal of Argentina on 24 October 1998 at St George's Hall; and Mike Griffith of the USA, on 19 June 1999 in Dublin. The first two defences were secured on points, while the Griffith fight was stopped in the fourth round.

Shea's final defence came nine months after stopping Griffith, and it was against Mickey Ward of the USA in March 2000 at the London Olympia. The fight was on the undercard of the Prince Naseem Hamed world title defence against Vuyani Bungu. Although Neary regarded the Holligan fight as the hardest of his career because of local expectations, he regards the Ward fight as the toughest of his career. Neary hit Ward with some powerful blows, but Ward was not only capable of soaking up the ▶

On the site of Everton's first football pitch, workers erected the marquee that formed the boxing arena for the Neary/Holligan world title fight. With a capacity of 5,500, it was significantly bigger than the Liverpool Stadium, which was demolished in 1987. Presently, Liverpool Football Club has planning permission to build a new stadium on the site. However, financial problems relating to the global economy have delayed the start of the project. When the stadium is finally completed, Liverpool football will return to its birthplace. It would be fitting if the new stadium enabled boxing to have a mass audience once more in the city.

'Unlike Johnny Best, who hired Anfield, Munro/Hyland decided to have a boxing arena built that could satisfy the expected demand for tickets'

THE MARQUEE: Preparations under way ahead of the big fight in Stanley Park

punishment but could hit hard himself. Like the Holligan fight, it was clear that one of the boxers would have to give, and on this occasion it was Neary who was stopped in the eighth round. It was Neary's first defeat as a professional.

Shea had two more contests, the first against Alan Bosworth in July 2000, which he won on points. The second was for the Commonwealth title in Belfast four months later against Eamonn Magee. Shea fought a tactical fight with the aim of winning on points. Although many pundits thought Neary had done enough to take Magee's title over 12 rounds, it was Magee who got the decision.

Presently, Shea runs a professional boxing gym in conjunction with his former trainer and former lightweight boxer George Scholfield.

The Boxers – The Challenger:

Andy Holligan signed professional terms in 1987 with Barney Eastwood after winning the ABA title. For the next decade, Holligan would dominate the British light-welterweight division, taking on the great Julio Cesar Chavez for the WBC world title before losing in his final attempt to win a world title against Shea Neary in Stanley Park.

After 14 straight victories between 1987 and 1991, Holligan was matched against Manchester's Tony Ekubia for the British and Commonwealth light-welterweight titles at Everton Park Sports Centre on 20 June 1991. Ekubia had won the titles nine months earlier when he knocked out Alex Dickson in the 11th round. Although not vastly experienced, Ekubia was seven years older than Andy, and unlike him was experienced at championship level, having been a Commonwealth champion since 1989. However, in a stirring contest over 12 rounds Holligan emerged as the new British and Commonwealth champion.

Andy followed up this win with a successful defence of his Commonwealth title against Steve Larrimore, of the Bahamas, at Central Hall, Renshaw Street in November 1991.

Three months later, Holligan successfully defended both titles against Leicester's Tony McKenzie before meeting Tony Ekubia once more at Everton Park in September 1992. In the second defence of his British title, Andy demonstrated his dominance of the division by knocking out Ekubia in the seventh round to win the Lonsdale Belt outright.

Following his successful defence against Ekubia, Andy had three non-title bouts before taking on his biggest challenge, Mexico's Julio Cesar Chavez, for the WBC light-welterweight title in Chavez's home country on 18 December 1993. The Chavez fight was Holligan's first outside of the British Isles – a daunting task against one of the great world champions. Chavez was undefeated in 89 contests. The only one he had failed to win was against Pernell Whitaker for the WBC welterweight crown, which was drawn. He had, however, been a world champion since 1984, first as a super-featherweight, then lightweight, and since 1989 he had been the WBC light-welterweight champion having defeated Roger Mayweather. The meeting with Holligan was the 12th defence of his title. Moreover, Chavez had stopped or knocked out all bar two of his challengers.

As if this was not enough for Holligan, his preparation was hampered when he suffered a broken nose in a sparring session a few weeks before the contest. Some thought he was going to postpone the fight, but Holligan was not prepared to take the risk of losing out on such a big opportunity. However, in

the first round of the contest, Holligan received a direct hit to the nose and it broke once more. He battled on to the end of the fifth round but could not continue after a cut to his left eye exacerbated his problems. It was the first defeat of his professional career.

Just two months later, he was back in the ring against Italy's Massimo Bertozzi, at Earls Court. Bertozzi was not in the same class as Andy, and was duly knocked out in the fifth round. However, further disappointment was not far away. When he was matched to defend his British and Commonwealth titles against Ross Hale, of Bristol, he was seen as overwhelming favourite to retain his titles. But a lack of pre-fight preparation caught up with Holligan, who was stopped in the third round.

It was 13 months before Holligan would box again, but after three clear-cut victories over Tony Foster, Allan Hall and Karl Taylor, he was ready to challenge for the titles he had lost to Hale. Hale had lost his belt after three successful defences on a first-round knock out to Paul Ryan, of Hackney, in December 1995. Ryan was a dangerous opponent who had won all his 22 fights, 20 of them inside the distance. The contest with Ryan took place at York Hall, Bethnal Green on 13 July 1996. Being on home ground, Ryan had massive support, but Holligan soon silenced the crowd with a first-round knock out.

Holligan chose not to defend his titles as he wanted to concentrate on winning European and world titles. However, it was nine months ▶

> 'The Chavez fight was Holligan's first outside of the British Isles – a daunting task against one of the great world champions. Chavez was undefeated in 89 contests. The only one he failed to win was against Pernell Whitaker for the WBC welterweight crown, which was drawn'

ALL HANDS TO THE PUMP: The temporary arena being erected

FROM THE TIMES, 16 DECEMBER 1993: Andy Holligan with his Lonsdale Belt

before he had his next contest against Lithuanian Rimvidus Bilius, who he beat on points. Another year would pass before his next bout against Shea Neary – hardly ideal preparation for his second attempt to land a world title. As events unfolded, it was to be Andy's last appearance in the ring.

The Fight:

Although the contest only lasted 17-and-a-half minutes, it was packed full of power-punching from both boxers. Fellow scousers they may have been, but there is no greater rivalry in sport than a Liverpool derby. The derby atmosphere was further reinforced as the champion was a Blue and wore blue gloves, while Holligan, wearing red gloves, represented the other half of the city. The atmosphere in the arena was electric and both boxers did not disappoint as they produced some of the most compelling boxing seen in a Liverpool boxing ring.

Round 1: The opening round initially saw Holligan on top, with the challenger catching Neary with a right cross to the head. As the round progressed, Holligan was also able to land his fearsome left hook to the ribs of the champion. Neary, however, responded with several telling lefts and rights to head and body that brought the round level.

Round 2: From the outset, Neary dominated the round, landing a powerful uppercut followed by hooks to head and body that rocked the challenger. Holligan eventually got close in and was able to nullify Neary's attacks, but towards the end of the round the champion caught Holligan with a couple of his trademark body punches. If Holligan was hurt, he was hiding his pain well, as he returned to his corner still in control of himself.

Round 3: From the bell, Neary commanded the round once more, landing a right hook to Holligan's head. One particular left hook drew gasps from the supporters and rivals alike, such was its power. However, towards the end of the round Holligan regained his composure and landed a left hook that hurt Neary. For the last 30 seconds it was toe-to-toe boxing, with both boxers landing hurtful blows to head and body.

Round 4: Neary landed first again, but this was Holligan's best round. From Neary's initial attack, he put together several combinations that hurt the champion. However, as he attacked he was also getting caught. Neary came on strong towards the end of the round and landed some big body punches. As the round ended, Holligan's right eye had puffed up and was partially closed.

Round 5: Holligan once again had the better of the exchanges, but his eye began to close. It had been a draining contest, and it was now a case of which boxer had the greater resources of strength; both of them were soaking up enormous punishment. At the halfway point, Neary came back at Holligan, but the last 20 seconds of the round saw the challenger on top once more.

Round 6: The first five rounds had been a stirring contest, with punch and counter-punch swinging the advantage from champion to challenger and back again. Anticipation among the crowd was reaching fever pitch as the bell sounded for the sixth. The two local rivals did not disappoint as for two solid minutes they stood toe-to-toe, trading massive hooks and crosses, any one of which seemed likely to end the contest. Amidst this fusillade of punches, Neary caught Holligan with three punches in quick succession that rocked the challenger to the core. Somehow Holligan came back and trapped the champion in a neutral corner, and it now seemed advantage to Holligan. Many times in the past, however, Neary had shown great powers of recovery, turning adversity to his advantage. This proved to be another such occasion, Neary countering Holligan's efforts with a ferocious attack that forced Holligan to his knees. Holligan's grim smile betrayed the pain he was now suffering, but he got up at the count of nine only to be met once again by Neary who swarmed all over the challenger, landing a vicious uppercut followed by stinging left and right hooks. Holligan seemed incapable of defending himself at this point, and in this situation the

'Although the contest only lasted 17-and-a-half minutes, it was packed full of power-punching from both boxers. Fellow scousers they may have been, but there is no greater rivalry in sport than a Liverpool derby'

▶ referee was left with little choice but to stop the contest.

Post-Fight Comment:

It is not very often that a ringside judge shares his emotions about a fight, but Glenn Feldman broke all convention by spontaneously declaring: "That was the best fight I have ever seen."

The *Liverpool Echo* thought it was the greatest contest seen in a British ring for years. Clearly, the venue had helped to roll back the years: it brought out all the great traditions of Liverpool boxing, traditions that had been developed at Pudsey Street, Anfield and the Stadium. It demonstrated that given quality boxers and a good venue, Liverpool fight fans will respond in huge numbers.

Undercard:

All bar one of the contests on the undercard for the show featured a Merseyside boxer. Here is an overview of how they fared on the night and in their careers:

Heading the list was **Peter Culshaw**, who took on Foudil Madani of Algeria for the WBU super-flyweight international crown. It was an important contest for Culshaw, as in his previous bout six months earlier he had lost his Commonwealth flyweight title against the British champion Adey Lewis at Widnes. On this occasion, however, Culshaw returned to form with a convincing fourth round stoppage. The win set him up for a shot at the vacant WBU flyweight title against South

African Mzukisi Marali, at St George's Hall some six months later. Peter had enjoyed a stunning amateur career, becoming the youngest-ever boxer to win an ABA title at the age of 18 in 1991 when he stopped Scotland's Allan Mooney to win the light-flyweight title. He turned professional in 1993, and in a 27-fight career he won the WBU world title at flyweight and super-flyweight; he was also a Commonwealth champion at flyweight.

David Burke was an accomplished southpaw who was the only boxer to represent Britain at the Atlanta Olympic Games in 1996. He turned professional in 1997, having his first contest at Everton Park against Ervine Blake. His victory on points over Bamana Dibateza, at Stanley Park, was his fourth consecutive win. Following a series of impressive victories over the next four years, Burke took on Gary Hibbert in September 2002 at Everton Park Sports Centre for the Commonwealth title. He stopped Hibbert in the 10th round – a win that three months later earned him a shot at the WBU lightweight title held by fellow scouser Colin Dunne. Burke won the title from Dunne on a split decision. His next fight in June 2003 was for the vacant European lightweight title against Stefano Zoff, of Italy, but this time Burke lost on points. David would have four more contests before retiring from the ring in 2005. He retired without defending his world or Commonwealth titles.

Alex Moon was another local boxer who was victorious on the night, beating Deva Reymond of France, on points. The highlight of Alex's career was winning the

Commonwealth super-featherweight title in Glasgow against Charles Shepherd, in March 2001. He successfully defended his title the following month against Karim Nashar of Australia at the Liverpool Olympia. Moon made another successful defence of his title against Mick O'Malley, at Everton Park in April 2002, but three months later lost his title to Coventry's Dean Pithie. Following this defeat, Alex had two more contests before retiring in 2003. He also boxed for the British featherweight title, losing to the champion Jon Jo Irwin at the Telewest Arena, Newcastle in February 1999.

Welterweight **Paul Burns** was unbeaten in eight contests before his Stanley Park fight against French Algerian Mustapha Bouzid. However, Bouzid was a worthy winner on points, inflicting a first defeat upon Burns. From this point on, Burns' career rather fizzled out, losing three of his next five fights. He eventually gave up the game after beating Paul Denton on points in April 2001.

Another Liverpool welterweight **Lee Molyneux** dropped a four-round points decision to Manchester's Kevin McKillan. It was the first time Molyneux had boxed in his hometown. In a career total of 33 fights, Molyneux won just five contests before retiring in 2000.

Birkenhead featherweight **Jamie McKeever** made his pro debut on the Stanley Park bill. He made a promising start on the night, defeating Dave Hinds over four rounds. McKeever went on to win the British featherweight title in February 2003 when he stopped another local boxer, Tony Mulholland, in the sixth round at Everton Park. He lost his title at the first attempt just three months later at the same venue, being outpointed by Roy Rutherford of Coventry. He made an attempt to regain his title in February 2004 but dropped the 12-round contest on points to Dazzo Williams of Hereford. He won his next three contests after this defeat, but has lost his last four contests, the last being in June 2008 to Ryan Brawley of Scotland.

'The *Liverpool Echo* thought it was the greatest contest seen in a British ring for years. The venue had helped to roll back the years...it brought out all the great traditions of Liverpool boxing'

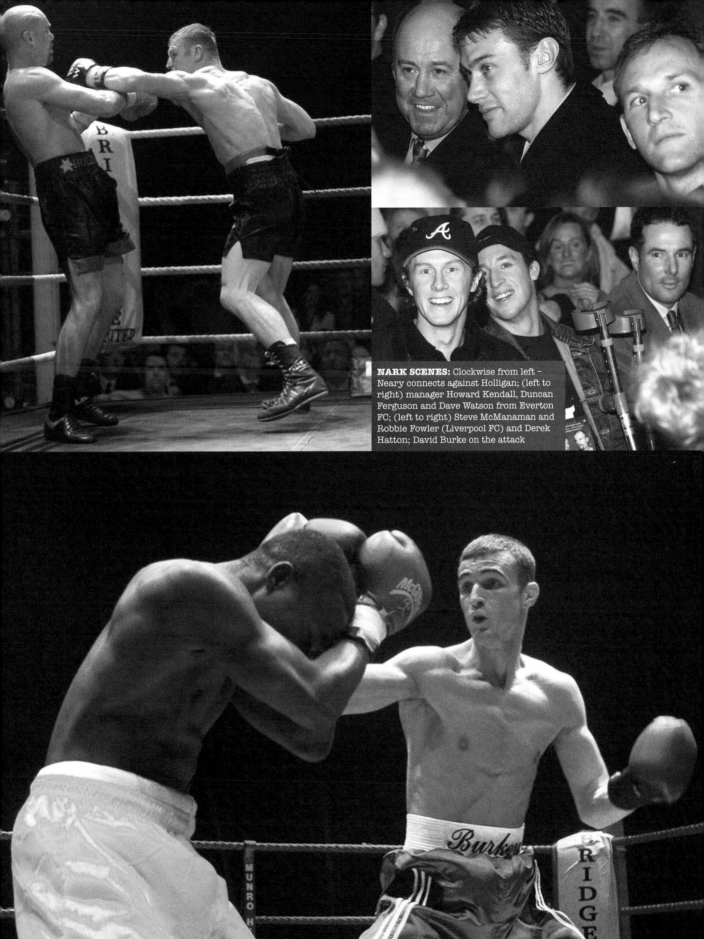

NARK SCENES: Clockwise from left – Neary connects against Holligan; (left to right) manager Howard Kendall, Duncan Ferguson and Dave Watson from Everton FC; (left to right) Steve McManaman and Robbie Fowler (Liverpool FC) and Derek Hatton; David Burke on the attack

Everton Park Sports Centre

Following the demise of the Stadium and its subsequent demolition in 1987, Liverpool has been without a dedicated boxing venue. In spite of this, the city has continued to host world, European, Commonwealth and British title fights at various locations around the city. The most significant venue in this period has been the Everton Park Sports Centre. Indeed, several of the city's world and British champions have either won or defended their titles there since it first hosted boxing in 1984.

Shea Neary was the first Liverpool boxer to win a world title there in 1996. He was quickly followed by Peter Culshaw, who successfully defended his world flyweight crown against South African Zolile Mbityi on 5 March 1999.

Small boxing halls have often been a breeding ground of future champions, and Everton Park is a prime example of this. A young Ricky Hatton, for example, defended his WBU intercontinental light-welterweight title there in December 1999 when he knocked out Mark Winters in the fourth round.

The centre continues to host important shows: promotions for the autumn of 2008 include two British title fights. In October, Dean Francis was due to defend his light-heavyweight title against Barry Morrison, while in November David Barnes was lined-up to defend his light-welterweight title against Colin Lynes. The October promotion includes several promising Liverpool boxers such as Paul Smith and Tony Bellew.

ON THE ATTACK: Paul Hodkinson, who never fought at Everton as a pro, in amateur action there in 1986

'Small boxing halls have often been a breeding ground of future champions, and Everton Park is a prime example of this'

Kirkby Sports Centre

Since its inauguration in 1961, Kirkby ABC has produced some of Britain's finest boxers, including John Conteh, Joey Singleton and Paul Hodkinson, who between them won world and British titles. Given the success of Kirkby ABC, it is hardly surprising that the town would be able to attract international boxing. The humble surroundings of Kirkby Sports Centre played host to several boxing shows in the 1980s that saw local favourite Paul 'Hoko' Hodkinson retain his European and British featherweight titles in 1988 and 1989. The centre, along with Kirkby Stadium, was demolished in 2007 to make way for a new sports complex nearby.

KIRKBY STARS: Joey Singleton (left) and Tony Byrne, ABA champions in 1971 (top of page); John Conteh makes an appearance at the Stadium – to watch his sister in athletics action during the mid-1970s

Paul 'Hoko' Hodkinson – Kirkby's Triple Champion

During a 27-fight career spanning eight years, Paul 'Hoko' Hodkinson won world, European and British featherweight titles. Remarkably, Hoko only boxed twice on Merseyside during his professional career, both times in his home town at the Kirkby Sports Centre.

Hodkinson made a tremendous start to his professional career, winning 10 of his first 11 contests – drawing the other. All his victories had come inside the distance, demonstrating Hoko's great ability to deliver powerful punches with both hands. His 12th fight was for the British featherweight title against Welshman Peter Harris, in Port Talbot on 18

May 1988. Harris was a tough customer and got the better of Hoko in the early part of the fight, but Paul fought back gamely to stop the champion in the final round. Thus, Hoko became the first Liverpool boxer since Nel Tarleton to win the featherweight title. The question now was whether he could emulate Tarleton and go on to win the Lonsdale Belt outright.

After winning the title, Paul expressed his desire to fight in his hometown for the defence of his title even though it meant boxing before a smaller crowd. He eventually got his wish seven months after beating Harris when he was matched against former

ABA champion Kevin Taylor, of Manchester. Prior to the contest, the press turned their thoughts back to the last time a Liverpool boxer fought a Manchester fighter for the featherweight title. This was the Tarleton v Johnny King fight at Anfield in 1936. Like Tarleton, Hoko did not disappoint the home crowd, retaining the title inside two rounds.

Taylor was seen as a tough opponent for Hoko but inside the first minute he was on the canvas following a right cross to Taylor's jaw. Paul later told the *Liverpool Echo*: "Even though I put him down I didn't think he was in any real trouble from the first punch. I've seen Kevin get up and win – even go the distance after being put down." But roared on by the capacity crowd, Hoko tore into Taylor, putting him on the canvas twice more before the bell ended the round. Worryingly, Paul received a cut to his eye following a clash of heads towards the end of the round. However, the second round saw the champion maintaining his onslaught, forcing the referee to intervene to stop the contest.

Following the fight, an excited promoter Barney Eastwood said that "it was worth the price of a ticket just to feel the atmosphere. We will definitely be coming back to Liverpool...I must say Kirkby Sports Centre reminded me of the King's Hall in Belfast."

Twelve months later, Eastwood was true to his word when he matched Hodkinson to defend his European title against France's Farid Benredjeb, in Kirkby on 13 December 1989. Paul had won the European crown the previous April, stopping another Frenchman, Raymond Armand, in Belfast. Before meeting Benredjeb, Hoko met Peter Harris once more in Port Talbot, against whom he defended his British and European titles. Once again Paul stopped the Welshman, this time in the ninth round, and as this was Hoko's second successful defence of his British title he won the Lonsdale Belt outright, thereby emulating the great Nel Tarleton. Hoko would subsequently give up his British title to concentrate on his world title ambitions.

Before he could do this, however, he had to defend his European title for the second time.

EARLY SUCCESS: Kirkby ABC prize presentation, 1985 sees a young Hoko (left) receive his trophy from Joey Singleton, with Charlie Atkinson Snr (right)

WORLD CHAMPION: A proud Hoko displays his WBC belt

His opponent was much tougher than Armand and had never been knocked down during his career. However, this was of no concern to Hoko, who set about the Frenchman in forthright style. Hoko in fact won the contest twice. In the eighth round, when the champion floored Benredjeb with a terrific right followed by a left hook, it appeared that the referee counted to 10 before Benredjeb got to his feet. But with Hoko jumping for joy the referee ordered the contestants to box on. The champion did not let the incident hinder his concentration though as he tore into Benredjeb once more, forcing the challenger's corner to throw in the towel.

The only downside of the night was the attendance, which was nowhere near full capacity. Clearly Eastwood had overpriced the tickets, which were £45 for ringside seats. Given the context of mass unemployment at the time and the fact that the fight was televised live, many fight fans decided to stay at home. It did mean, however, that any future title fights would not be staged at Kirkby.

Victory over Benredjeb now brought the chance of a world title fight closer. Three months after beating the Mexican Eduardo Montoya in March 1990, Hoko faced another tough Mexican, Marcos Villasana, in Manchester for the vacant WBC featherweight title. Despite dominating the first seven rounds of the fight, Hoko was eventually stopped in the eighth round after both his eyes closed.

Following this defeat, his first as a professional, Hoko was determined to get a return, as he felt that he was a better boxer than Villasana. After a gap of 17 months, Eastwood secured the rematch, which was held in Belfast. Hoko's preparations for the fight were meticulous. To avoid a repeat of his eye injuries, he worked on moving his head more and boxing behind his jab to protect himself. The strategy worked, as this time Paul received the unanimous decision of the judges to secure a points victory.

Over the next 15 months, Hoko made three successful defences of his world title, beating Steve Cruz (who had beaten Barry McGuigan for the WBA world title in 1986), Fabrice Benichou and Ricardo Cepeda. A fourth defence against another Mexican Gregorio Vargas, in April 1993 ended in

defeat when Hoko was stopped in the seventh round. There followed an attempt to take the WBO featherweight title from Steve Robinson in March 1994, but Paul was knocked out in the final round.

Despite this failed attempt Paul Hodkinson must be considered as one of Liverpool's finest boxers. During his career he was often

compared to Barry McGuigan, but Paul would rather be remembered as the third in a line of great Kirkby boxers, after Joey Singleton and John Conteh. All three boxers went to St Kevin's School, boxed for Kirkby ABC and brought major boxing honours to the town. A remarkable achievement and testimony to the great coaching young boxers receive at Kirkby ABC.

HOMETOWN HERO: Hoko sees off Farid Benredjeb to successfully defend his European title in Kirkby, 1989

CELEBRATIONS: Another successful outcome for Hoko

Liverpool Olympia

The Liverpool Olympia hosted boxing as far back as 1924 when the former British heavyweight champion Bombardier Billy Wells topped the bill. In a trademark performance, Wells knocked out his opponent Gunner Mick Bennett in the ninth round.

The theatre was built in 1905 for Moss Empires Limited as a purpose-built indoor circus and variety theatre. However, variety theatre soon came under pressure from cinema and, like many halls, was forced to either close or adapt. Hosting boxing in the early 1920s was an indication that the owners of the hall chose the latter.

In more modern times, the hall has hosted boxing at professional and amateur level. Peter Culshaw, for example, successfully defended his WBU flyweight title there in March 2000 against Oscar Andrade of Mexico. He also won the vacant WBF super-flyweight title at the same venue against South Africa's Ncedo Cecane in 2002.

More recently, in March 2007, 'The Fab Four' show reflected the growing strength of Liverpool boxing, all four boxers Derry Mathews, Paul Smith, Stephen Burke and Tony Quigley won on the night with Mathews retaining his WBU featherweight title. Although both Mathews and Smith have since lost their 100 per cent records they both remain in contention for British title fights at featherweight and middleweight respectively. The popular Mathews had been keen to make his first defence of his title in front of his home fans; his big following ensured a sell-out at the Olympia.

At amateur level, the Olympia hosted an international match between the four Home Nations and the Cuban team in April 2005. It was the first ever visit of the Cuban team to Britain. The only home-based boxer to win that night was David Price, who convincingly beat Lisovan Hernandez Vajarano 29-4. The hall was once again packed – testimony to the pulling power of Cuban amateur boxing, which is the best in the world. During their stay in Liverpool, the Cuban team trained at the Golden Gloves ABC.

VICTORY: Peter Culshaw holds the world title belt above his head (top) while Peter's arm is raised as he becomes the youngest boxer to win an ABA title

ON THE BILL: (Above and below) Two boxing promotions from the Olympia that demonstrate that Liverpool boxing is resurgent once more

CHAMPION: Peter Culshaw celebrates victory over Ncedo Cecane to win the vacant WBF super-flyweight title at the Olympia in 2002. (Inset) Culshaw checks out the venue ahead of his bout against Oscar Andrade in 2000

AMATEUR SCENE: International boxing at St George's Hall. The Hall has hosted several successful amateur tournaments and has helped secure Liverpool's position as the capital of amateur boxing in Britain. (Inset) ABA chairman Rod Robertson, left, and Cllr Joe Devaney at the launch of Liverpool's second Multi-Nations Boxing Festival

St George's Hall

The city's finest cultural building has played host to sport on many occasions. For example, in 1949 Joe and Fred Davis took part in an exhibition of snooker to promote J. Ashcroft & Co., the Liverpool-based manufacturer of billiard and snooker tables. The hall has also played host to world championship boxing at amateur and professional level on several occasions.

At professional level, in October 1998, Shea Neary successfully defended his WBU light-welterweight title there against Juan Carlos Ceferino, while Peter Culshaw defeated Mzukisi Marali to win the vacant WBU flyweight title on the same bill.

As part of its wider strategy to develop amateur boxing in the city, Liverpool hosted the Olympic boxing qualifiers, the first time they had been held in Britain for 52 years, at St George's Hall in 2000. In 2001 the hall also played host to the first home nations tournament to be held for a decade. The following year, the first ever England v USA amateur international held outside London was staged there.

More recently, in 2005 St George's Hall held the World Cadet Championships, the first world boxing championships ever to be held in Britain. The event was sponsored by the Liverpool Culture Company, an indication that sport was to form a core part of the cultural celebrations for 2008.

Lastly, in July 2007, Liverpool hosted the fourth Commonwealth Amateur Championships. Liverpool boxers David Price, Stephen Smith and Tom Stalker all won gold for England.

This long-term strategy of attracting world and international amateur boxing has paid off handsomely, with Liverpool set to host the European Senior Amateur Championships at the Echo Arena in November 2008.

LONG WEIGHT: Canada's Shane Hinton at St George's Hall for the inaugural Multi-Nations Boxing Tournament in May 1994. It was the first international event staged in Britain for 46 years

REID ABOUT: Local amateur stars David Mulholland (left) and Stephen Burke (right) promote a Multi-Nations Boxing Festival alongside Runcorn's super-middleweight star Robin Reid

Echo Arena

Since the closure of the Stadium, Liverpool has been without a permanent venue capable of putting on large and prestigious boxing shows. Liverpool has lost out to cities such as Manchester and Newcastle, who have built large indoor arenas capable of holding up to 21,000 spectators. However, with the opening of the Echo Arena in January 2008, Liverpool now has the facilities to stage top-level boxing shows at amateur and professional level.

The Echo Arena is a multi-purpose venue designed to host music, family entertainment and sports events, with a 10,000-plus seating capacity. Its location on the Kings Dock also provides visitors to the city access to the Albert Dock area where people can enjoy the diverse entertainment and cultural outlets offered by Liverpool.

Nowadays, major sporting events such as boxing have become increasingly dependent upon big-business sponsorship and TV coverage linked to venues capable of attracting large audiences. This is the only way boxing promoters can pay the ever-expanding purses that the best boxers command. Clearly, the Echo Arena has the capacity to satisfy all of these requirements and should develop into a venue capable of hosting some of the country's most important boxing shows.

In the past, all of Liverpool's greatest boxers have expressed how important the home crowd was to their success. Nel Tarleton, for example, acknowledged this when he was cheered home by the Kop to become the first Liverpool boxer to win a Lonsdale Belt in 1931. In more recent times, Johnny Cooke believed that he could have made the Lonsdale Belt his own had the Liverpool Stadium been able to hold more British championship contests in the late 1960s. Moreover, John Conteh regarded his win over Len Hutchins in 1977 in front of a home crowd as one of the finest nights of his career.

Presently, Liverpool has a fine generation of boxers emerging in both the amateur and professional codes. At amateur level, Liverpool was the first city to employ a boxing development officer – an initiative that has paid enormous dividends. David Price is the most obvious example of the success of the policy, having recently returned from Beijing with an Olympic bronze medal. At professional level, Paul Smith and Tony Bellew, both former ABA champions, are two great prospects with championship potential. Moreover, Derry Mathews, the former WBU world featherweight champion, has set his sights on the British featherweight title.

It was Liverpool's commitment to amateur boxing that paved the way for the city to host the 40th European Amateur Boxing Championships. The city saw off strong competition for the honour, and a major part of the bid to host the event centred on the Echo Arena, which was still at the planning stage at the time of application. It will be the first time the championships, first held in 1924, have been hosted by the Amateur Boxing Association of England (ABAE).

The championships provide Liverpool and its amateur boxers with a great opportunity to show the world that the city can put on first-class boxing shows. The championships should provide a springboard for the city to attract other prestigious boxing shows, including top-level professional boxing.

The reality is that the days of weekly boxing shows served up at Pudsey Street and the Stadium will never return. But what those two great stadiums demonstrated is that a healthy boxing scene enables a city to attract the top boxing shows. Johnny Best demonstrated this in the 1930s, and so did Hyland/Munro in 1998 – they showed that fight fans will turn up in their thousands given a good boxing show and an arena to match. Moreover, it is the big boxing tournaments that provide the fan base for the smaller boxing venues, which in reality are the nurseries of the sport. It was this philosophy that Johnny Best adopted, a philosophy that led to Liverpool having some of the country's finest boxers.

READY FOR ACTION: David Price outside the Arena where he's set to compete in the European Amateur Boxing Championships

HOST WITH THE MOST: The fabulous Echo Arena will host boxing for the first time in November

The Echo Arena will host the 2008 European Amateur Boxing Championships from 6-15 November. It will be the first time the championships have been held in England. The event will provide the city with an ideal opportunity to show the world that it is capable of hosting world-class indoor sports events. The championships are the culmination of the city's contribution to sport during its year as the European Capital of Culture. During the year, the Liverpool city region hosted the Grand National, The Open, the World Firefighter Games, a basketball international between England and Israel and the final stages of the Tour of Britain cycle race. Several of these events could not have been held in the city but for the building of the Echo Arena.

Tickets for the championships can be bought from the Echo Arena box office. Season tickets cost £80 (£40 concessions), day tickets £15 (£10 concessions). Box office telephone number: 0844 8000 400.

David Price is one of several Merseyside boxers with a realistic chance of winning a medal. Only a handful of Liverpool boxers have been successful in the event, including Harry Scott in 1959 and Stephen Smith in 2006. Hosting the championships will cement Liverpool's position as the number one amateur boxing city in Britain. The finals will draw the biggest boxing crowds to Liverpool since the 1940s, when boxing was hosted at Anfield.

Mersey Boxing Hall of Fame

The Merseyside and Wirral Former Boxers' Associations, formed in 1973 and 1974 respectively, have joined forces with the aim of establishing a Mersey Boxing Hall of Fame. A project that was funded by the Heritage Lottery Fund in 2006 enabled the associations to record the lives of 60 former boxers and digitise over 1,000 images. Over the years the associations have also collected a diverse range of boxing memorabilia including boxing belts, trophies, programmes and tickets. Some of the material presented in this book has come from this collection.

Unable to secure immediate premises for the Boxing Hall of Fame, the associations have agreed to loan a substantial part of their collection to National Galleries Liverpool with a view to them exhibiting the material in the new Liverpool Museum which is due to open in 2010. The material included in the exhibition will be on display for a minimum of two years during which time it is hoped that the associations will be able to secure a permanent home for its extensive boxing memorabilia and artefacts.

The star attraction of the exhibition will be the foundation stone of the Liverpool Stadium. The stone, which was saved by the Thompson family at the time of the demolition of the Stadium, has been loaned to Liverpool Museums for the duration of the exhibition by the Thompson family.

Interest in the cultural heritage of sport has never been greater. The innovative Played in Britain series presented by English Heritage has been a great success. Recently, Everton Football Club in conjunction with the Liverpool Record Office secured the David France Collection (now known as 'The Everton Collection') for the city. Moreover, Liverpool Football Club's museum is one of the most popular sports museums in the world attracting visitors from all parts of the globe.

The Merseyside and Wirral Former Boxers' Associations regard the establishment of a Mersey Boxing Hall of Fame as essential if the region's boxing heritage is to be preserved. It would provide the public with open access to a fine collection that would tell the story of boxing on Merseyside.

It is hoped that this book will raise cultural awareness and demonstrate the important role boxing has played in the development of sport on Merseyside.

THEY BOXED AT THE STADIUM: Bob Jameson's 1976 collage of famous Liverpool boxers, opposite page (with thanks to Janet Jameson)

COMMUNITY SPIRIT: Merseyside's former boxers' associations play an important role in keeping former boxers together. The associations hold monthly meetings on both sides of the water and organise regular events. Guest of honour at this social (below) was Liverpool's finest bantamweight Alan Rudkin

'Associations regard the establishment of a Mersey Boxing Hall of Fame as essential if the region's boxing heritage is to be preserved'

They Boxed at The Stadium

Other publications produced by Sport Media, Trinity Mirror North West:

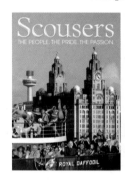  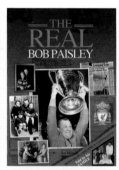 

All of these titles, and more, are available to order by calling 0845 143 0001,
or you can buy online at www.merseyshop.com